WOMEN AND WORK IN
EIGHTEENTH-CENTURY FRANCE

WOMEN AND WORK IN
EIGHTEENTH-CENTURY FRANCE

—— EDITED BY ——

Daryl M. Hafter AND *Nina Kushner*

LOUISIANA STATE UNIVERSITY PRESS

BATON ROUGE

Published by Louisiana State University Press
Copyright © 2015 by Louisiana State University Press
All rights reserved
Manufactured in the United States of America
FIRST PRINTING
LSU PRESS PAPERBACK ORIGINAL

DESIGNER: *Mandy McDonald Scallan*
TYPEFACE: *Whtiman*

Library of Congress Cataloging-in-Publication Data

Women and work in eighteenth-century France / edited by Daryl M. Hafter and Nina Kushner.
    pages cm
  Includes index.
  ISBN 978-0-8071-5831-9 (pbk. : alk. paper) — ISBN 978-0-8071-5832-6 (pdf) — ISBN 978-0-8071-5833-3 (epub) — ISBN 978-0-8071-5834-0 (mobi) 1. Women—Employment—France—History—18th century. 2. Women—France—Economic conditions—18th century. I. Hafter, Daryl M., 1935– II. Kushner, Nina.
  HD6145.W66 2015
  331.40944'09033—dc23

                                                                    2014018901

For our children,
Leah & Miles
and
Naomi & Matthew

CONTENTS

PREFACE

From its very inception, the history of women and work was tied to the drive by women for greater self-determination. Early investigations were not solely abstract queries but personal endeavors. It is hard, then, to resist imagining Alice Clark reading histories of active, tough seventeenth-century women as well as Shakespearean heroines and then trying to take in the changing gender constructs of her own era, the 1910s. It is also hard to forget what life was like in the academy for many of the women who pioneered women's history in the 1970s, when their field was not considered valid, their very right to be in the profession was openly challenged by their colleagues and students, and their ability to get work done was hampered by the entrenchment of the second shift.

While the period from the 1970s until today has seen the emergence of a number of new historical paradigms through which we can investigate the lives of women in the past, it has also seen a betterment of the conditions of women workers, particularly women academics. Sexual harassment law has since been written, and in its wake is coming a slower cultural shift that denies the acceptability of such behavior in the workplace. The right of women to careers outside of traditional female domains has gained currency. In academia, women are constituting an increasing percentage of the professoriate. Many universities provide substantial family and parental leave. Some have daycare centers. But not all is so rosy. At the time of this writing, the U.S. Congress had just failed to pass the Equal Pay Act, opponents citing its potential drain on the profitability of businesses, dependent, we assume, on cheap female labor. Women are still making only 77 cents for every dollar a man makes. And while women constitute 36 percent of the professoriate, they make up only 23 percent of its most senior members—full professors.[1] Some are slowed down by extra service burdens. Many are penalized, even though not deliberately, for having families.[2]

History is not supposed to be personal, but it often is—or perhaps, we might argue, it always is. The questions we ask, the answers we seek, and the methods by which we seek them are inevitably reflections of the times in which we live. And they are, sometimes, a product of the lives we lead. If "the personal is political," as 1970s feminists taught, then the personal is surely academic. Women's history came out of the women's movement and the effort to determine "what happened and how it could be fixed" such that women could experience equality. When that generation of women sat down to write history, were their children underfoot or did they have helpful partners, easy access to affordable childcare, and the social support that made it acceptable to spend time writing rather than caring for those children?

Beyond intellectual paradigm shifts, changes in social environment shape the questions we ask. The shift in methodology that this volume addresses, from the family economy to a more integrated approach, parallels a shift in the experience of both women academics and historians of women more generally. As one contributor mentioned in a roundtable at the 2005 meeting of the Western Society for French History that launched this project, "I don't look for women in the sources. I look for people and I see what happens." This is a general trend in the field, and perhaps a luxury. Women's history has evolved to the point where women are not necessarily isolated as historical subjects by authors, who, similarly, did not necessarily experience extreme isolation as subjects. Yet, there is much to learn about women in the past, and it is to that effort that we endeavor to contribute.

One of the most pleasant moments on completing a book-length project is the opportunity to express our deeply held feelings of appreciation for so many people. We would like to begin with the Western Society for French History, at whose annual meetings many of the papers in this volume, and its central concept, were debated. In particular, we would like to thank Dena Goodman, who encouraged us to form that first roundtable and whose feedback over the years has been invaluable. We also would like to thank Clare Crowston, both for her comments at the Western and for her close and careful reading of this text for Louisiana State University Press. Her comments made the volume much stronger. We thank our editor at LSU, Alisa Plant, who believed in this project from its inception and patiently waited for us to finish it. We also must thank our contributors, without whom there would be no book. Their insights and excitement made this project not only possible, but joyous. We thank our colleagues for their generosity in sharing information and citations. Most of all, we thank our families for providing balance to our lives while the project took its course—to Leah, Miles, Naomi, and Matthew, our children. Special appreciation goes to our partners, Joon and Monroe, who read our drafts, helped to edit all the chapters, and provided technical assistance.

NOTES

1. Mary Ann Mason, "The Pyramid Problem," *Chronicle of Higher Education*, 9 March 2011.

2. Ibid.; Mary Ann Mason, "The Baby Penalty," *Chronicle of Higher Education*, 5 August 2013.

WOMEN AND WORK IN
EIGHTEENTH-CENTURY FRANCE

INTRODUCTION

Nina Kushner and Daryl M. Hafter

THIS collection of essays explores the diversity of women's work in the long eighteenth century, paying particular attention to questions of women's economic agency. The authors investigate how marital status, legal constraint, custom, class, gender, and changes in market organization shaped women's economic opportunities, and how women, in turn, negotiated these parameters. We will find that women at all levels of the social hierarchy contributed to and helped shape the economy. These essays concern enterprising women in every sense of the word: enterprising as engaged in commerce (as producers and vendors of goods and services, and managers of business ventures) and enterprising as resourceful and imaginative agents taking advantage of and creating opportunities for themselves. Regardless of what women earned and in what sorts of economies—formal, informal, family, criminal—this particular lens brings to the fore questions of women's economic agency, work identity, as well as the gendering of work and the workings of gender. Considered together, these essays give us a much fuller picture of women's economic activities in the eighteenth century than has been offered.

Our goal, however, goes beyond presenting new case studies that testify to the experience and significance of women's work. It is also to stage a particular historiographical intervention. In recent decades, a number of scholars have moved away from the traditional practice of understanding women's work specifically within the context of the family or the "family economy." Historians are also finding more examples of successful women—those who supported themselves financially or who had substantial careers—at a moment when opportunity was supposedly contracting.[1] Collectively, we have not yet taken the opportunity to consider the meaning of these developments, either in terms of the methods we as historians use to study women workers, or in terms of the narrative of women's history. It is to these two efforts that our volume hopes to contribute.

In doing so, we focus on the eighteenth century and its business, both in manufacturing and other employment. As we will see below, one tendency in the history of women and work has been to show women "standing still." The eighteenth century was an era of rapid economic transformation that included the explosion of the transatlantic economy, an emerging consumer revolution, an "industrious revolution," and the acceleration of proto-industrial and capitalist organization. Women were instrumental in and profoundly affected by all of these developments. Yet at the same time they experienced a deterioration in their public position. Hence the eighteenth century is rich territory in which to explore the set of interrelated questions that interest us about women's economic agency and work experience, their importance to the economy, and how we should understand these developments. We begin with an overview of women at work in eighteenth-century France.

WOMEN AT WORK IN EIGHTEENTH-CENTURY FRANCE

A true vision of economic activity in the eighteenth century shows female presence everywhere—always active, always busy, always earning. They were embedded in manufacturing, so omnipresent that few remarked on the fact. These unnoticed actors performed the menial tasks needed in every industry: preparing raw materials, carrying firewood, readying products for the finishing processes, and keeping up the workshop. Who but the painter reminds us of the girl sitting in a corner with a broom? In the textile trades, whether silk, linen, or cotton manufacturing, the tasks of auxiliary female workers were integral to production. In food preparation and sales, papermaking, watch-polishing, artificial pearl manufacturing, and myriad other trades their work was crucial, if uncelebrated by any other treatment than Diderot's *Encyclopédie*. But women were not always invisible, nor did the meanest work always fall to them. Mistress craftswomen and master's widows ran their own workshops, taking on the training of apprentices as well as the manufacture of goods, the management of their businesses, and sometimes that of a guild. The seamstresses in Paris and the linen drapers in Rouen exemplify women in charge of their own guilds.[2]

In commerce women were equally present. They ran businesses with partners, their husbands, and sometimes alone. They dominated market stalls, sold goods in the streets and from door to door, and ran small shops. *Marchandes de modes* (fashion merchants) became popular arbiters of changing fashion. Their shops were gathering places for the *bon ton*.[3] Traditionally, wives managed their husband's businesses, ordering supplies, selling finished products, and keeping the books. Not all of these businesses were small; some were international. (They were the successors of Renaissance merchants and the antecedents of Bonnie G.

Smith's "women of the Nord.")[4] Women even managed estates, which, while not considered businesses, often functioned like them, generating profit for their owners. Women sold services. Some, like nursing and midwifery, acting and singing, or cooking and cleaning, were legal. Others, like having sex for money, were not, but prostitution nevertheless formed the basis of a considerable underground economy staffed and managed largely by women.

We do not mean to suggest that women's work existed without problems or detriments. Social practice determined that most women's wages were one-third to one-half of men's wages for comparable work. Legal restrictions hindered female activity; women were devoid of a legal personality in all but a few instances and might need a male relative to represent them in a business, for an inheritance, or as guardians of their children. Widows were legally minors until the age of thirty and could be hampered by family members. And indeed, widows were often among the poor, struggling to support children or in poorhouse shelters. As Olwen Hufton shows in *The Poor of Eighteenth-Century France, 1750–1789,* poverty and destitution were the fate of many women.[5] Women also had special vulnerabilities. Sexual harassment and assault were constant issues in the workplace. It is also true that most guilds legally excluded women from skilled trades at least until 1777, as Turgot and the eighteenth-century social reformers asserted. Because of this, women working illegally at tasks exclusively claimed by guilds were frequently apprehended by the police and fined.

Some professions were, by definition, on the wrong side of the law. Women who were elite prostitutes might have the protection of wealth and a patron's influence, but common prostitutes were incarcerated in the Hôpital or other prisons under harsh conditions.[6] Artisans, especially spinners, used their access to materials to steal thread and other items, participating in black market networks. They sold their stolen goods to woolen, cotton, and silk masters who were eager to economize on materials. Even when a guild or manufacturer permitted women without licenses to do unskilled work, they were frequently taught those more complex tasks that were the legal purview of guildsmen. Servants in artisan households surely undertook such activity. These illegal practices, as well, demonstrate the profound integration of women in eighteenth-century economic life.

However, the government's positive attitude toward women's legitimate work was routine and expected. Tax assessors acknowledged a wife's independent business with a formula such as, "Abraham Normand, carriage purveyor, his wife Marie Almon, blanchisseuse, pays the tax." It is important to emphasize that when her business differed from that of her husband's, it was the woman herself who was responsible for buying her goods or making her products, and managing their sale. These businesswomen might well have had husbands, and they could benefit or suffer from their husband's success or failure, but they were in charge of their own affairs. Officials often sponsored craft instruction and distributed free instruments to encourage earning that would keep women from becoming prostitutes or wards of the state. Royal decrees and religious sanctions allowed women stalls without charge in the Paris market until the Revolution, as Rene Marion discovered.[7] Local officials elsewhere sometimes scolded guilds for hindering poor women from earning small sums in casual, unskilled work. The most enthusiastic government evaluation of female employment, however, came in the last third of the eighteenth century. Women's work was considered a national resource, especially by the 1770s, when new inventions for spinning and other textile preparation were being widely used in the countryside to counter British competition.[8]

Furthermore, in the eighteenth century women found more opportunities for earning. The consumer revolution expanded the manufacture and sale of household and personal goods. With the new emphasis on acquiring fashionable items, clothing, jewelry, and furniture were bought and discarded at an unheard-of rate. In dress and hats, Paris became the epicenter for style, employing hundreds of women in designing and making new creations for the French. Exports too increased, not only to other European nations, but also to the markets in Atlantic colonies. In the 1770s, French vessels were legally allowed to supply goods to the Spanish colonies and the new United States, trade they had earlier carried on clandestinely. The entire system of this world economy affected women's work, from gathering the raw materials, making the products, packaging them, getting contracts, and acquiring capital to buy and ship them. Even such political events as the French Revolution implicated women's work, as Haim Burstin and Dominique Godineau revealed.[9]

Despite the restrictions they faced, women were everywhere involved in economic life. In part, this was because *everyone* worked in the early modern period. Without power-driven machines, without long-distance message conveyers, every pair of hands found tasks. A natural occurrence in families, an imperative for single individuals, work filled the day—and sometimes the night as well.

THE FAMILY ECONOMY MODEL AND SCHOLARSHIP
ON WOMEN AND WORK

This expansive vision of women throughout the economy has been colored by the lens that we have applied to the subject of women and work. Almost a century ago, that lens was considerably larger when Alice Clark asked how capitalism affected women's lives.[10] Clark was inspired by Olive Schreiner's powerful argument in *Women and Labour* that modernity had robbed women of their "honored and socially useful toil" and by a dominant historiography claiming the exact opposite, that women literally had no history: as wives and mothers—"the eternal feminine"—women had experiences that remained unchanging through time.[11] By identifying women's roles in multiple forms of premodern economic organization, Clark's work broke new ground and was able to capture the relationship between domestic work and that which was done by women beyond the home. But of equal importance to the field—and to this project—was her methodology and the wide nature of her inquiry. Clark was interested in how women's position in society, and indeed how women themselves, had changed from the Elizabethan period to the Restoration, a period she connected with the rise of capitalism. Influenced by Marxism and anticipating important critiques of it, Clark sought the answer in studying women's "productive capacity," which included all that women did, save "the spiritual creation of the home and the physical creation of the child."[12] It was the role of women in economic structures, she argued, that determined their lived experience. She showed that changes in economic organization affected opportunity, status, and constructions of gender and identity negatively, leaving women of all social classes worse off for economic modernization. Writing a decade later, Ivy Pinchbeck shifted Clark's framing from "capitalism" to "industrialization" and moved her periodization forward from the seventeenth to the eighteenth and nineteenth centuries. Pinchbeck also disagreed with Clark, seeing in the wage-earning potential of industrial work a certain freedom for women. But whether good or bad, the impact of economic modernization on women became one of the central questions in women's history.[13]

In French history, the question would not be taken seriously until the 1970s, when trends in social history intersected with the women's movement.[14] As Joan Scott and Louise Tilly explained in the introduction to the second edition of their book, *Women, Work, and Family* (1987), "much of the theorizing stressed the relationship between work for wages and improvements in women's status of the early 1970s."[15] Scott and Tilly found in their study that the wage labor that came to dominate in industrialization did not advantage women. In making this argument, Scott and Tilly created a formidable intellectual framework with which historians of women and work are still engaging.

The family economy was first widely publicized as a model for understanding women's past economic roles in 1975, through the work of Olwen Hufton. Hufton's approach was further developed by Scott and Tilly. In the first edition of *Women, Work, and Family,* they drew a portrait of the preindustrial household that was a center of domestic manufacturing, with work determined by gender and age.[16] In later editions they explored the function of the family economy when production took place outside the home and wage labor substituted for home crafts. The increased flexibility of designating wives and daughters as wage earners sometimes permitted the husband to maintain his position as a skilled handworker in the face of industrial competition. The last phase of the family economy carried into the nineteenth century, when the family became a unit of consumption. In short, the family shifted from a productive unit to a wage-earning group, and finally it became a consumer unit. By family economy model, then, we are referring to three items: (1) the model in which a family worked together in the preindustrial period as a productive or wage-earning unit; (2) the assumption that within this unit women generally performed labor that was less skilled and often tangential, readily adapting their work as family needs changed; and (3) the argument that women's labor should be understood within the context of the family.

Within a decade, historians (including Scott and Tilly in the introduction to the second edition of their book) began to expand, nuance, and challenge these findings.[17] The use of industrialization as the great divide in economic life flattened and homogenized the history of women's work on the far side of the caesura. It also posited, in Hufton's words, "a *bon vieux temps* when women enjoyed a harmonious, if hard-working, domestic role and social responsibility before they were downgraded into social parasites or factory fodder under the corrupting hand of capitalism." Yet, as Hufton argued, "So far the location of this *bon vieux temps* has proved remarkably elusive."[18]

Monographs, articles, and dissertations that examined women's work—most were primarily concerned with one or two industries within a limited geographic region—showed a much more varied history. Scholars of the late Middle Ages and early modern period found evidence of a decline in women's position not with industrialization, but much earlier, as early as the fourteenth century, and certainly during the sixteenth. Some of these studies elongated the period of proto-industrialization to half a millennium, arguing that it was economic reorganization as opposed to industrialization that was the major force in shaping women's work.[19] Judith Bennett, for example, in showing how small-scale women brewers lost in competition against men with enough capital to form large enterprises, signaled that it was lack of capital that hindered women's control of enterprises, not their lack of skill.[20]

Still other historians attributed the decline neither to industrialization nor to economic reorganization, but to different developments. These included large demographic shifts, the position of guilds, and the strengthening of the patriarchal structure of society.[21] Lastly, scholars such as Daryl M. Hafter, Gay Gullickson, Nicole Pellegrin, and Tessie Liu clearly demonstrated that proto-industrial and industrial techniques of production coexisted.[22] Women were still embroidering, weaving, and making lingerie and parts of shoes by hand well into the nineteenth century.

As scholarship immeasurably complicated the periodization of the family economy, so too did it complicate its structure. As soon as scholars dug into the archives, they found a wide variety of family arrangements beyond that which supposed all members worked together as an economic unit in the production of a single item. In many families, husbands and wives worked in different industries, a view developed by Olwen Hufton.[23] What perhaps was less anticipated, however, was the strength of women in these relationships. Clare Crowston, Nancy Locklin, Daryl Hafter, and others found instances in which the family was structured around the wife's career, rather than that of the husband. Hafter and Crowston similarly explored women's roles as full-fledged members of guilds, while Locklin has shown the reality of women's relative independence in Brittany, as merchants, handcraft workers, and property owners.[24] These authors make an argument that many women had a strong and stable work identity, thereby demonstrating that women's work was not always ancillary, shifting, and dependent. They also bring to light evidence of women who were not involved in a family economy at all, being single, widowed, or simply working alone or with other women.[25]

But perhaps most telling are the number of studies, beginning in the late 1980s, on women and work that do not even bring the family economy into consideration. Sara Maza and Cissie Fairchilds, for example, documented the experiences of female servants and the structure of their industry in the eighteenth and nineteenth centuries without paying much attention to servants' families.[26] By positioning women's work within a particular field rather than within the context of family life, these studies destabilize the family economy model. In this way they challenge one of its assumptions, that women who were economically successful were by definition exceptions, as opposed to just being rare. The nonfamily approach has come to dominate much of the scholarship that has emerged in the last decades concerning women who earned money engaging in occupations that would not qualify as "work" by the traditional definition that equated it with material production. It is hard to know whether the choice not to identify what these subjects did as work is a full embrace of an older ethos or a full rejection of it. Have we moved so far in our understanding of women's value that it is no longer necessary to identify what they did as work to give it meaning, as Alice Clark tried almost a century ago? Yet, as Bonnie G. Smith intimates in the afterword to this volume, the full expansion of what constituted "women's work" has not yet been integrated into women's labor history.

Whatever the opinion of particular authors on the definition of work, collectively this scholarship has demonstrated a wider range of women's occupations, and in doing so has brought to light the need to rely on multiple frameworks of analysis, of which the family, however important, is only one. We learned of women tax collectors, managers, shopkeepers, food sellers, innkeepers, landladies, small-goods vendors, teachers, decorators, dancing mistresses, actresses, scholars, translators, billiard hall proprietors—the list could go on for lines. In Barbara Hanawalt's volume, for example, scholars documented the presence of midwives, wet nurses, market women, and artisans.

In documenting women's occupations, many historians also focused on the social hostility and the legal hindrance women faced, and how they navigated such obstacles. Bias against women was a continual fact, as Sheilagh Ogilvie, Merry Wiesner, and Jean Quataert remind us, where the law and society sharply curtailed women's freedom of how and where to work.[27] The question of how women manipulated and negotiated the legal, social, and cultural constraints placed on their work (and their lives) is a central problematic of women's history. It is one at odds with earlier considerations of women's work that rendered women passive, working as stop-gap fillers in production processes, and no matter how brave and resourceful, without ambition of their own.[28] Studies by Clare Crowston, Lauren Clay, and Daryl Hafter, among others, show women to have been aggressive in protecting their right to work: the act of spreading rumors took its place alongside widespread industrial theft, joining men in riots, and using the law to gain one's end. Julie Hardwick's careful study of law and gender politics reveals the dynamics of family interaction, with its unexpected outcomes.[29]

The family economy model launched an entire field of study. It created a space in which scholars were justified in taking on the subject of women and work. It stimulated those scholars to think about women's work, paid and unpaid, in the wider contexts of social, political, and gender relations. The result is a wide body of work that has so nuanced the model that the family is now one of several factors scholars consider in trying to understand and make sense of women's experiences. Others include legal frameworks, constructions of gender, and social and cultural norms. Each of these norms both shaped and informed family life but was not limited in their expression to it. While no one can deny the importance of marriage and family to eighteenth-century people, especially women, thinking about women in the context of the family helps to illuminate the ways in which their work might change over the life course. Looking at several factors simultaneously, however, gives us a broader understanding of the women's experiences. Moreover, doing so highlights in particular their agency, the ways in which they negotiated and manipulated the constraints to which they were subject.

THEMES

The ten essays in this volume concern women across the economic spectrum, from prostitutes to aristocrats, who participated in a range of economic activities. Collectively, they engage five themes.

They show first and foremost that women could be economically successful in the eighteenth century. Here we define "success" as the ability to support oneself financially. For some, like Marie-Magdelaine Royer, a woman who ran her husband's transatlantic business and the subject of Jennifer L. Palmer's essay, that success was contingent on the work and rights acquired by another family member, in this case Royer's husband. But in other studies we see women successful in their own right. Nancy Locklin found high incidences of women having their own professions in Brittany. Cynthia M. Truant discovered that women artists in the guild and Royal Academy might acquire these positions without family connections, and that they might be able to support themselves through their art. The ways in which these women were able to translate their financial success into other forms of freedoms, relevant in the Old Regime, varied. For example, kept women, the subject of Nina Kushner's essay, functioned as heads of household.

This wealth of evidence brings us to our second theme. Women participated in a broad array of economic activities beyond the traditional female occupations. Some were involved in emerging economic spheres, part of the modernizing, globalizing economy that developed over the long eighteenth century. James B. Collins shows that women were offering novel goods and services in the provinces. Jennifer Palmer describes them running the metropole-end of transatlantic businesses. Daryl Hafter sees women as technically accomplished agents in the workforce of preindustrialization, the textile urban-rural *fabrique*. Nina Kushner identifies women who used free market principles to establish themselves as elite prostitutes. Judith A. DeGroat demonstrates how women worked not only in production, but also in consumption in the long eighteenth century and afterward to maintain their homes. These essays certainly do not constitute a full survey of women and work in the eighteenth century. Nevertheless, the evidence they contain is sufficient to disrupt any call to exclude women from the public space of economic life.

In fact, many of the women studied here had strong work identities. James Collins's findings, that women were increasingly listed on tax roles under their own professions, suggest that female work identity and official recognition of it may have been increasing. This is important. Work identity—the degree to which the personal, public, and official identity of a person is bound up in his or her work—is seen as a measure of status. We know now that individuals engaged in a craft, whatever the skill level, without work identity tended to be low status and poorly paid. A strong female work identity suggests that successful women were not simply making money and going (or staying) home. They had social recognition.

When we consider the diversity of female work activity, we come to our third theme—that women were important to economic growth and modernization in the eighteenth century. By economic modernization we are referring to shifts in methods of production and property relations, the expansion of the French economy both within France and overseas. As French industrialists separated various manufacturing processes into skilled urban work and unskilled countryside production, the country's textile work came to resemble the structure that Jan de Vries classified as steps toward modernization. The invention of new devices took entrepreneurs further in the eventual possibility of segmenting work even more, and adapting it to unskilled women and children with ever lower pay.[30] Daryl Hafter shows how women were crucial members of the preindustrial workforce and adapters of early industrial technology. James Collins and Jennifer Palmer show the importance of women not just to industrialization but to modernization, a concept articulated by Collins. He further establishes that women as producers, not just as consumers, drove French economic growth. Nina Kushner's essay on elite prostitution indicates how madams and mistresses developed a lucrative market in luxury goods and human services. What this suggests is that guilds and traditional work organizations should not be the only measure by which we determine the position of women as workers in the eighteenth century. We must also consider emerging economic domains, and this brings to mind the role of women in both the industrious and consumer revolutions.

Our fourth theme returns to a traditional topic, the place of women within the family economy. This is one of the best-studied aspects of women's economic activity. Jacob D. Melish, Jennifer Palmer, and Jane McLeod show us how women could continue to exercise a great deal of agency as wives, and how they manipulated the family economy to their own advantage. In these instances, family position enabled market access for these women and facilitated the development of their work identities. In the case of McLeod's printers, only through their husbands' rights were these widows allowed to be printers. Yet we see that while legally empowered by their families, they did not always privilege family interests over their own. Jacob Melish's research shows how wives, because of their control of accounts and earnings, worked at the heart of Old Regime small businesses. Judith DeGroat contrasts the need for women's wage work to support a family with increasing hostility to such endeavors. Rafe Blaufarb shows how female lords protected family property through the courts.

Other essays in this volume show women who achieved success without reference to their husbands. Nancy Locklin gives us examples of women who had their own businesses. Nina Kushner shows how successful elite prostitutes became independent heads of household and often left their families. Several of these essays do not mention families at all. For Daryl Hafter and James Collins, the records that captured the work of their subjects did so without consistent reference to husbands or fathers. The state was interested in these women as generators of national wealth, not, in this instance, primarily as wives and daughters.

The power of patriarchy leads us to our last theme, that of women's legal capacity, meaning the rights of women as established by law. Legal capacity is a topic of central importance in women's history, as it sets the parameters of possible action for women. Equally important, gender is actively constructed in the interpretation of the application of law. For example, Jennifer Palmer shows that while Marie-Magdelaine Royer's husband had invested her with his power of attorney so that she could see to his affairs, doing so was greatly complicated by her gender. Nancy Locklin documents how the particular inheritance patterns of Brittany, codified in law, allowed women opportunities to accrue sufficient property to support themselves. Jane McLeod examines the ways that printers and printers' widows alternatively tried to enforce the law and petition to be exempted from it—shifting strategies as legal capacities also shifted—to retain printer's licenses. Rafe Blaufarb argues that because female lords ran their estates through agents in the same way male lords did, they had the same functional legal capacity. In contrast, the wives studied by Jacob Melish and the professional mistresses studied by Nina Kushner had ambiguous legal rights to their work. While legal instruments existed to give women public authority over their commercial activities—the category of *marchandes publiques* and *séparation des biens* (legal separation of marital property)—most women could not afford the legal costs of securing them. The wives were able to manage their husbands' earnings because it was the custom to do so. In addition, it was custom that shaped the work practices of elite prostitutes, leaving both groups—wives and prostitutes—more vulnerable to exploitation.

These themes raise a number of questions that we hope will stimulate future research. For us, perhaps, the most important concerns these success stories in which women were able to support themselves, to develop professional work identities, or both. We tend to think of these as the function of "loopholes of patriarchy," in the words of Blaufarb, as structural anomalies where women cleverly exploited exceptional circumstances. The essays in this volume attest to the ingenuity of women in negotiating Old Regime economic structures to find places for themselves. We need more research before we can determine if the examples of successful women in both the old and modernizing economies are merely bright lights in a moment of declining fortune or emblematic of the ways in which women prospered in the eighteenth century. Given the trend of recent scholarship on women and work, as we broadly define it, we suspect the latter to be true. Hence, we extend Blaufarb's challenge to the economic realm, and ask whether we should continue to think of these success stories as atypical. How many exceptions do we need before we stop seeing these stories as anomalous, but rather as structurally normative? And once we integrate both these success stories and an understanding of the centrality of women to the French economy, what will the narrative of the history of French women in the eighteenth century look like? If we can manage to orient readers' view of the long eighteenth century to this wider understanding of women, work, and agency, our volume will have done its task.

NOTES

1. See, as examples, Clare Haru Crowston, *Fabricating Women: The Seamstresses of Old Regime France, 1675–1791* (Durham: Duke Univ. Press, 2001); Nancy Locklin, *Women's Work and Identity in Eighteenth-Century Brittany* (Aldershot, Eng.: Ashgate, 2007); Daryl M. Hafter, "Female Masters in the Ribbonmaking Guild of Eighteenth-Century Rouen," *French Historical Studies* 20, no. 1 (winter 1997): 1–14; Nina Kushner, *Erotic Exchanges: The World of Elite Prostitution in Eighteenth-Century Paris*

(Ithaca: Cornell Univ. Press, 2013); Lauren Clay, *Stagestruck: The Business of Theater in Eighteenth-Century France and Its Colonies* (Ithaca: Cornell Univ. Press, 2013).

2. Crowston, *Fabricating Women;* Hafter, "Female Masters in the Ribbonmaking Guild of Eighteenth-Century Rouen."

3. See, for example, the work by Jennifer M. Jones, *Sexing La Mode: Gender, Fashion and Commercial Culture in Old Regime France* (Oxford: Berg, 2004).

4. Bonnie G. Smith, *Ladies of the Leisure Class: The Bourgeoises of Northern France in the Nineteenth Century* (Princeton: Princeton Univ. Press, 1981).

5. Olwen Hufton, *The Poor of Eighteenth-Century France, 1750–1789* (Oxford: Clarendon Press, 1974).

6. Erica-Marie Benabou, *La prostitution et la police des moeurs au XVIIIᵉ siècle* (Paris: Librairie académique Perrin, 1987).

7. Rene Marion, "The *Dames de la halle:* Community and Authority in Early Modern Paris" (Ph.D. diss., Johns Hopkins University, 1995).

8. The well-illustrated, collected volume of essays by Emonde Charles-Roux et al., *Les Femmes et le travail: Du moyen-âge à nous jours* (Paris: Éditions de la Courtille, 1975), was one of the earliest books devoted to the continuity of women's work. See also François Guélaud-Leridon, *Le Travail des femmes en France* (Paris: Presses universitaires de France, 1964). For other early work that dealt with the question of women and economic modernization, see Louis Dubois-Butard, *Les Femmes dans la maîtrise d'Amiens au XVIIIᵉ siècle* (Amiens: Archives départementales de la Somme, 1975); Joan Wallach Scott and Louise Tilly, *Women, Work, and Family* (New York: Holt, Rinehart, and Winston, 1978); and Natalie Zemon Davis, "Women in the *arts mécaniques* in Sixteenth-Century Lyon," in *Lyon et l'Europe, hommes et sociétes: Mélanges d'histoire offerts à Richard Gascon,* ed. Jean-Pierre Gutton (Lyon: Presses universitaires de Lyon, 1980), 1:139–167.

9. Haim Burstin, *Le Faubourg Saint-Marcel à l'époque révolutionnaire: Structure économique et composition sociale* (Paris: Société des Études Robespierristes, 1983), and Dominique Godineau, *Citoyennes tricoteuses: Les femmes du people à Paris pendant la Révolution française* (Aix-en-Provence: Éditions Alinea, 1988), 65–105.

10. Alice Clark, *Working Life of Women in the Seventeenth Century* (London: Routledge, 1919).

11. Ibid., 8; Olive Schreiner, *Women and Labour* (1911; reprint, Project Gutenberg EBook, 2008), 25.

12. Clark, *Working Life of Women,* 4. Under Michelle Perrot's direction, such questions were squarely posed in her *Une Histoire des femmes: Est-elle possible?* (A History of Women: Is It Possible?) (Paris: Éditions Rivages, 1984). By 1997, a conference in Normandy answered with a volume entitled *L'Histoire sans les femmes: Est-elle possible?* (A History without Women: Is It Possible?) (Paris: Perrin, 1998). To establish platforms for feminist writing, the press Éditions des Femmes was founded in 1972 and the periodical *Clio-Histoire, Femmes et Sociétés* in 1995.

13. Ivy Pinchbeck, *Women Workers and the Industrial Revolution* (1930; reprint, Virago Press, 1981). For a more recent assessment of Pinchbeck's work, see Bridget Hill, *Women, Work, and Sexual Politics in Eighteenth-Century England* (Oxford: Basil Blackwell, 1989), and Pamela Sharpe, *Adapting to Capitalism: Working Women in the English Economy, 1700–1850* (New York: St. Martin's Press, 1996).

14. One earlier work was Françoise Guélaud-Leridon, *Le travail des femmes en France* (Paris: Presses universitaires de France, 1964). For early work which dealt with the question of women and economic modernization, see Dubois-Butard, *Les femmes dans la maîtrise d'Amiens au XVIIIᵉ*

siècle; Scott and Tilly, *Women, Work, and Family;* Davis, "Women in the *arts mécaniques* in Sixteenth-Century Lyon," 1:139–167.

15. Scott and Tilly, *Women, Work, and Family,* 2nd ed., 1.

16. Olwen Hufton, "Women and the Family Economy in Eighteenth-Century France," *French Historical Studies* 9, no. 1 (spring 1975): 1–22; Scott and Tilly, *Women, Work, and Family.*

17. In reviewing the scholarship published since the first edition of *Women, Work, and Family,* Tilly and Scott wrote that their work "is rather like a map of relatively uncharted territory. It lays out some major conceptual routes to be taken through a vast and complicated countryside. . . . That after all is the purpose of a book of this kind: to raise and resolve a set of questions about the history of women's work and at the same time to open a field of inquiry that continues to address new social and political issues on contemporary feminist agendas" (Tilly and Scott, *Women, Work, and Family,* 2nd ed. [New York: Routledge, 1989], 9).

18. Olwen Hufton, "Survey Articles in Women's History: Early Modern Europe," *Past and Present,* no. 101 (November 1983), 126.

19. Martha Howell found evidence of proto-industrialization in northern European cities in the fourteenth century, and Gay Gullickson's study of the weavers of Auffay, in Normandy, shows it continued deep into the nineteenth. Howell, *Women, Production, and Patriarchy in Medieval Cities* (Chicago: Univ. of Chicago Press, 1986); Gay L. Gullickson, "The Sexual Division of Labor in Cottage Industry and Agriculture in the Pays de Caux: Affay, 1750–1850," *French Historical Studies* 12, no. 2 (autumn 1981): 177–199, and her book *Spinners and Wavers of Auffay: Rural Industry and the Sexual Division of Labor in a French Village, 1750–1850* (New York: Cambridge Univ. Press, 1986).

20. Merchant capitalism fostered the division of tasks, turning artisans into proletarian workers, as Jan de Vries and A. M. van der Woude pointed out. Jan de Vries and A. M. van der Woude, *The First Modern Economy: Success, Failure and Perseverance of the Dutch Economy, 1500–1815* (Cambridge: Cambridge Univ. Press, 1997); Judith M. Bennett, *Ale, Beer, and Brewsters in England: Women's Work in a Changing World, 1300–1600* (New York: Oxford Univ. Press, 1996).

21. See, for example, Martha C. Howell, "Women, the Family Economy, and the Structures of Market Production in the Cities of Northern Europe during the Late Middle Ages," in *Women and Work in Preindustrial Europe,* ed. Barbara Hanawalt (Bloomington: Indiana Univ. Press, 1986), 198–222; Natalie Zemon Davis, "Women in the Crafts in Sixteenth-Century Lyon," *Feminist Studies* 8, no. 1 (spring 1982): 46–80. See also Sarah Hanley, "Engendering the State: Family Formation and State Building in Early Modern France," *French Historical Studies* 16 (spring 1989): 4–27.

22. See Nicole Pellegrin, *Les Vêtements de la Liberté, Abécédaire des pratiques vestimentaires en France, 1780–1800* (Aix-en-Provence: Alinéa, 1989), and Tessie P. Liu, *The Weaver's Knot: The Contradictions of Class Struggle and Family Solidarity in Western France, 1750–1914* (Ithaca: Cornell Univ. Press, 1994).

23. Hufton, "Women and the Family Economy"; Hufton, *The Poor in Eighteenth-Century France.*

24. Judith M. Bennett and Amy M. Froide, eds., *Singlewomen in the European Past, 1250–1800* (Philadelphia: Univ. of Pennsylvania Press, 1999); Crowston, *Fabricating Women;* Daryl M. Hafter, *Women at Work in Preindustrial France* (University Park: Pennsylvania State Univ. Press, 2007); Locklin, *Women's Work.*

25. Bennett and Froide, *Singlewomen;* Janine M. Lanza, *From Wives to Widows in Early Modern Paris: Gender, Economy, and Law* (Aldershot, Eng.: Ashgate, 2007).

26. Sarah Maza, *Servants and Masters in Eighteenth-Century France: The Uses of Loyalty* (Princeton: Princeton Univ. Press, 1983); Cissie Fairchilds, *Domestic Enemies: Servants and Their Masters in Old Regime France* (Baltimore: Johns Hopkins Univ. Press, 1984).

27. Sheilagh Ogilvie, *A Bitter Living: Women, Markets, and Social Capital in Early Modern Germany* (Oxford: Oxford Univ. Press, 2003); Merry E. Wiesner-Hanks, "Guilds, Male Bonding, and Women's Work in Early Modern Germany," *Gender and History* 1 (1989): 125–137; Jean H. Quataert, "The Shaping of Women's Work in Manufacturing: Guilds, Households, and the State in Central Europe, 1648–1870," *American Historical Review* 90, no. 5 (December 1985): 1122–1148.

28. Barbara A. Hanawalt, ed., *Women and Work in Preindustrial Europe* (Bloomington: Indiana Univ. Press, 1986); Daryl M. Hafter, ed., *European Women and Preindustrial Craft* (Bloomington: Indiana Univ. Press, 1995).

29. Julie Hardwick, *The Practice of Patriarchy: Gender and the Politics of Household Authority in Early Modern France* (University Park: Pennsylvania State Univ. Press, 1998).

30. De Vries and Van der Woude, *The First Modern Economy*.

THE PHENOMENON OF FEMALE LORDSHIP

The Example of the Comtesse de Sade

Rafe Blaufarb

THE scholarship on women in Old Regime, Revolutionary, and Napoleonic France has concentrated on issues of status and rights, exclusions and incapacities. These have been approached from a variety of angles. Given the Revolution's experiment with citizenship, it is not surprising that women's access to public authority and political power—both formal and informal—has been a principal concern.[1] The question of nationality and its relation to sex and marital status has also begun to attract attention.[2] Another cluster of studies centers on the family. A range of questions about marriage—its cultural meanings, the decision to enter into it, the decision to truncate or abrogate it—has been the subject of study.[3] Relations between spouses, in idea and practice, have also been a focus of research.[4] Finally, the issue of inheritance (highlighting concepts of parental authority, relations between younger and older siblings, and relations between brothers and sisters) has not been neglected.[5]

All of these lines of inquiry intersect with the question of women's property rights. The scholarship on French women before the Revolution offers a fairly consistent response to this question. The critical factor determining a woman's property rights, the consensus holds, was her legal incapacity. Barbara Diefendorf has summarized this view: "A married woman was under the authority of her husband. He was, in the words of one of Grenoble's seventeenth-century barristers, 'her head, her eye, her guardian, and her master.' Any legal actions she undertook without his explicit consent were null and void. The husband administered his wife's properties and in some areas could even dispose of them without her consent."[6]

Diefendorf, like most historians currently working in this field, is fully aware that such a blanket assertion of women's disempowerment requires qualification.[7] In fact, the scholarship of the past decade has emphasized the possibilities for independent action that women found within the overarching framework of patriarchy. Several historians have highlighted the economic autonomy of female guilds and of women possessing the status of *femmes marchandes publiques*.[8] In the absence of husbands, widows could enjoy status similar to that of male artisans—even in the male guilds to which their deceased spouses had belonged.[9] Women across the social spectrum could even engage their husbands' credit without their consent, thanks to a legal loophole in the Custom of Paris.[10] Other scholars have noted that even within the family the "practice of patriarchy" was not a top-down imposition, but rather a collective endeavor in which women enjoyed some freedom of maneuver.[11] The overall picture that has emerged from these various findings is so generally shared within the field that it may be considered a new orthodoxy, albeit a highly nuanced one. Within a deeply patriarchal society that deprived them of full property rights, women nonetheless enjoyed "a significantly greater measure of responsibility, autonomy, and equality within the family than has generally been assumed."[12]

At the heart of this view is the notion that the law profoundly circumscribed the legal rights exercised by wives. To the extent that such women enjoyed opportunities in early modern Europe, they largely had to do so by exploiting gaps in the otherwise solid mesh of a deeply patriarchal society that deprived them of rights, of official possibilities for independent status and power. This view is widespread and informs much of the research being carried out. But is it really the case that when women exercised power, they mostly had to do so informally? Did the law really bar them from wielding public authority openly? To put my question into sharper focus, have we overlooked significant formal legal opportunities for exercising agency by early modern French women because we assumed they did not exist?

There were provinces of Old Regime France where married women had direct legal rights to, and full disposition of, independent property. In the areas governed by written law—specifically, within the jurisdictions of the sovereign courts of Aix, Montpellier, Toulouse, and Grenoble, although not within those of Bordeaux and Lyon—the default matrimonial regime observed a strict separation between the property of husbands and wives. Against the seventeenth-century Dauphinois barrister cited above by Diefendorf, one might oppose maître Billecoq, an early nineteenth-century lawyer, also from Dauphiné. During the Old Regime, he explained, "Roman laws were in vigor in Dauphiné; but they contained no disposition relative to the community of goods between spouses, a type of conjugal society unknown to the authors of that immortal legislation."[13] In the Roman-law provinces of the south, the rule of separate property applied not only to dotal property, which was essentially immobilized, but also to the freely disposable *biens adventifs* (property acquired by wives in the course of their marriage) and *biens paraphernaux* or paraphernalia (non-dotal property owned by a woman at the time of her marriage). By clearly recognizing and focusing on the formal right to independent property possessed by married women in the Midi, we aim to challenge the current consensus about the extent of formal female legal incapacity, particularly in relation to property rights, in Old Regime France.

The pages that follow explore this issue through a case study of one female lordship—the Sade family's seigneurie of Eyguières in Provence. I chose this particular female-held seigneurie partly because of the pull of the Sade name. But I could have chosen other, better examples from other seigneuries I have studied. Such a choice would have been the seigneurie of Cuges, whose lord, the dame de Girenton, engaged her community in legal battle continuously from the 1770s to the 1820s, when she finally triumphed. Although she was married to an Aixois parlementaire of noble ancestry and a lord of his own seigneurie, Girenton owned Cuges as separate property, and her husband did not play a discernible role in its affairs.[14] Or, I could have discussed the seigneurie of Peynier, in the pays d'Aix, where Madame la Présidente de Thomassin ran things for sixteen years in the 1770s and 1780s while her husband was on the other side of the Atlantic, serving as governor of the Windward Isles. In addition to outwitting her community by selling it her feudal cense just before it was swept up by the National Assembly's general abolition of feudalism, Madame de Thomassin managed at least one slave, whom her grateful husband sent her as a present from America.[15] These women deserve their own studies. Here, however, I will focus on the comtesse de Sade and her community of Eyguières.

Before beginning the case study, I must first say a few words about the incidence of female lordship both in Provence and in France as a whole, as well as about the nature of seigneurial property. Thanks to the existence of two comprehensive lists of Provençal lords, one from 1668 and the other from 1778, we can demonstrate not only that female lordship was common in the province, but also that its incidence remained constant over time. In 1668, approximately 7 percent of Provençal seigneuries (41 out of 580) counted a woman as legal lord and owner.[16] In the 1778 survey this figure had grown to 8 percent (71 out of 900).[17] The list of the female-owned seigneuries naturally changed over time, with thirty-three of the forty-one figuring on the 1668 list passing into male hands 110 years later. As a result of this mobility, at least 11 percent (104 of 900) of Provençal seigneuries were owned by a woman at some point in the reigns of Louis XIV, XV, and XVI. Given the 110-year gap between the two lists and the additional lacunae for the period 1778–1789, these figures probably understate the scale of the phenomenon.

Moreover, the lists only note female lords who owned seigneuries in their own right, as separate *adventif* or *paraphernal* property. They include neither widows acting as lords for their minor sons nor wives exercising seigneurial authority on behalf of absent husbands. Both cases were frequent, although the absence of province-wide lists of these types of female lords makes it impossible to offer figures or percentages. My work on litigation over seigneurial tax exemption has revealed a number of examples. Male-owned seigneuries in which women temporarily exercised lordship on behalf of minor children or absent husbands during the eighteenth century included Allan, Cabannes, Cabris, Cannet , Clari, Fos-Amphoux, Grasse, La Cadière, La Valette, Mons, Puget, Sallonet, Sausses, Simiane, Ubraye, and Viens.[18] These seigneuries all appear in the correspondence of the provincial administration from 1750 to 1787 because they were involved in lawsuits over fiscal privilege significant enough to merit the attention of the province.

This points to another way in which female lordship was typical: female lords exercised the business of lordship in the same way as their male counterparts, by lobbying provincial authorities and litigating against their communities.[19] The lawsuits of male and female lords are indistinguishable from one another in frequency, content, form, and outcome. The gender of the lord was not a factor in these legal actions, which is not surprising given that they were argued entirely in writing by the same group of lawyers. Lords, whether male or female, were almost never called upon to testify in person. Female lordship in Provence would be utterly unremarkable—had it not gone unremarked until now.

But what about the rest of France? Was female lordship a purely Provençal phenomenon? Anecdotal evidence, such as the jurist Ferrière's complaint that the historical evolution of fiefs into patrimonial property had allowed "daughters" to become lords, suggests that it was more widespread.[20] Such comments, however, are not conclusive. Nor do they provide any sense of the magnitude of the phenomenon. Fortunately we have a readily available document that can shed a brighter light on these questions, at least for the end of the Old Regime. This is Armand Brette's published collection of *procès-verbaux* of the *bailliage* assemblies of the nobility that met in the spring of 1789 to prepare for the meeting of the Estates-General. Although Brette died before completing his monumental work, the four volumes that were published contain approximately half the noble procès-verbaux, distributed throughout all regions of France.[21]

The electoral regulations permitted women who owned seigneuries to take part in the assemblies' proceedings, and many did, both in person and by proxy. Not all of the procès-verbaux, however, distinguish married female lords who held their fiefs as separate property, widows, *tutrices* (guardians), and other women who were administering fiefs temporarily on someone else's behalf. Fortunately, several procès-verbaux note the precise status of the seigneurial women who attended, allowing us to calculate the percentage of independent, married female lords in those bailliages. In Amiens 28 out of 230 (12 percent) of the district's lords fit this category, in Boulonnais 14 out of 87 (16 percent), in Langres 10 out of 66 (15 percent), in Etampes 7 out of 59 (12 percent), in Melun 12 out of 73 (16 percent), in Vendôme 11 out of 76 (14 percent), in the Bourbonnais 35 out of 350 (10 percent), in the Nivernois and Doniois 44 out of 212 (21 percent), in the Haute Marche 9 out of 95 (9 percent), in the Limousin 24 out of 183 (13 percent), in Albret 7 out of 72 (10 percent), in Saumur 11 out of 136 (8 percent), and in Loudon 15 out of 63 (24 percent). Ranging between 9 percent and 24 percent, these figures are comparable to those we find in Provence. Female lordship was a common phenomenon across France.

The significance of this for the question of women's official capacity for public authority in Old Regime France becomes clear when we consider the nature of seigneuries. First, seigneuries were treated as private property in early modern France and, like all other property, could be bought, sold, subdivided, inherited, used as collateral for loans, be foreclosed upon, etc. With some exceptions that do not undermine our present argument, property in seigneuries was governed by the same laws as property in other goods. Second, seigneuries, although regarded first and foremost as property, were property of a special kind. They were property in public authority, ownership of the right to exercise a sovereign function.[22] This sovereign function—long-denounced by absolutist theorists as an intolerable usurpation of regalian right—was the power and responsibility to exercise justice over all people living within one's jurisdiction. In the case of the Sades' seigneurie of Eyguières, the rights of justice were complete—in the words of the time, encompassing *justice haute, moyenne, et basse*—and were symbolized by the gallows looming before their château. A seigneurie was thus an especially potent form of property, one partaking of royal sovereignty itself. By owning this kind of property, therefore, a woman could officially, openly, and legally acquire a prominent public position and exercise the weighty functions attached to it.

One might object that the situation of female lords did not differ fundamentally from that of mistresses in female trade guilds—that female lordship was not qualitatively different from other forms of authority exercised by women in Old Regime France. After all, like female lords, guild mistresses also owned a type of property, an office, that conveyed the right to exercise public authority, in their case related to the regulation of their particular craft or trade in a given locale. This is an important point. Nonetheless, there were significant differences between the public authority of mistresses and that of female lords. Whereas the jurisdiction of mistresses pertained to the internal regulation of the guild and the defense of its privileges, that of female lords encompassed all aspects of civil and criminal law within their seigneuries. More extensive than that of guild mistresses, the seigneurial jurisdiction wielded by female lords extended beyond the workshop to fall upon a much broader swathe of society. While there are exceptions, guild mistresses exercised authority primarily over other women. In contrast, female lords exercised their rights of justice over men and women alike. Finally, female lords held their public authority as true property, in the form of a seigneurie, whereas guild mistresses held theirs in the more precarious form of an office.[23] Whereas guilds could be suppressed by royal fiat and sometimes were, seigneuries were more stable. With the possible exception of allodial land (at most, 5 percent of the total), the seigneurie was the most secure form of property in Old Regime France. Thus, compared to that of guild mistresses, the public authority *owned* by female lords was more extensive (indeed, it was regalian), more socially inclusive, and based on a significantly firmer title.

But could women own and actually administer seigneuries in their own right? They certainly could in the Midi. In Provence, the tendency toward separate marital property was particularly strong; indeed, it was the norm. By the eighteenth century, provincial jurisprudence had firmly established that in marriages concluded without a marriage contract, the wife retained full, independent control of the property she had brought into the union, as well as property she might subsequently acquire.[24] To signify their independence, Provençal women who had married without a contract—including those who owned seigneuries—systematically noted in their legal acts that they were "free in their actions," "free in the disposition of their properties," and "free in their biens adventifs."[25] Since these women had no marriage contracts, moreover, they necessarily had no dowries (which could only be established by contractual stipulation) and thus were not limited in their property rights by dotal constraints. Technically, the property they owned was not even paraphernal (non-dotal), since this type of property was defined in opposition to dotal property, which, in their case, did not and could not exist. The preeminent legal historian of Provençal matrimonial regimes, the

jurist Jean-Philippe Agresti, has concluded that the closest modern approxima-
tion to this system of truly separate property is "the present-day *concubinat.*"[26]
He has estimated that at least 50 percent of Provençal marriages were concluded
without contract and, thus, observed this type of marital property regime. Such
unions, moreover, were practiced evenly across the entire social spectrum.[27] It
would not be until 1985 that French women recovered such extensive property
rights within marriage.

Our story begins in 1714. In July of that year the royal government ordered
the community of Eyguières to pay off its debts by transferring its communal
properties to its creditors.[28] The community owned a number of these properties,
of which the most valuable were three bread ovens. The first had been owned
by the community since time immemorial. The second had been erected by the
community on the town ramparts in 1552, and the third was built in 1655. The
community generally farmed out these ovens to private entrepreneurs at public
auction and used the proceeds to pay a portion of the community's annual tax
contingent. To make the acquisition of the *ferme des fours* more attractive to the
bidders and drive up its price, the community often stipulated that the ovens
would be *banal*—that is, that the townsfolk would be prohibited from baking
their bread anywhere else. The same financial logic dictated that when the ovens
were turned over to the community's creditors in 1716 they were declared banal.
After some contention, they were valued together at 17,500 livres. Although the
comte de Sade, lord of the community, was not one of the original creditors, he
gradually bought out creditors' shares in the ovens. By 1739 he owned all three.

The community quickly came to regret the alienation of its ovens. By the
1740s they were bringing the comte de Sade 3,000 livres in annual revenue, an
impressive 15 percent return on his investment, and imposed a correspondingly
heavy burden on the hard-pressed inhabitants.[29] But the community was powerless to do anything. However, in 1764 a royal declaration offered new hope.
This was the Declaration of 3 February 1764, on the "rachat des tasques et bannalités constituées à prix d'argent" (buying-back of payments in kind and baking
monopolies).[30] It permitted communities to recover all "redevances en fruits,
grains & tous autres droits, tasques, cens, bannalités, que les Communautés jus-
tifieront avoir été acquises autrefois, soit par leurs Seigneurs, soit par d'autres
particuliers, moyennant des sommes d'argent, ou pour la libération d'anciens
arrérages dus" (payments in kind and all other rights, charges, feudal dues, and
baking monopolies that the communities prove to have been previously acquired
either by their lords or by other individuals in exchange for sums of money or

for the dismissal of old debts) simply by reimbursing the sum they had originally received. Excepted from these generous provisions, however, were banalities of feudal origin. Invigorated by the Declaration, the community of Eyguières instituted legal proceedings against its seigneur. This was now the comtesse de Sade, a lord who would prove herself "less tolerant toward the community than her deceased husband" during the years she governed the seigneurie as tutrice for her young son, Jean-Baptiste-Joseph-David, until he himself took the reins in 1770.[31]

The community initiated legal action in August 1764. For the next seventeen years the case meandered through the judiciary labyrinth of the Old Regime: from the court of the *senechaussée* of Arles to the Parlement of Aix to the Royal Council and finally, in 1780, back to the Parlement of Aix. There, on 20 July 1781, that court rejected the community's proofs and denied its request to buy back its banalities. The community immediately appealed this decision to the Royal Council, with the backing of the provincial assembly and the counter-intervention of the provincial nobility. The Eyguières-Sade affair had become a direct clash between the Second and Third Estates of Provence, an affair described by the Third Estate administrators of the province in 1787 as "no less important" than the successful efforts then under way to restore the long-defunct Estates of Provence.[32]

The community had made its opening move in August 1764 with a *requête* (petition) to the Royal Council asking for permission to buy back its former banalities. This initiated a complex legal conflict that was still not entirely resolved in 1789.[33] First, the Royal Council rejected the community's requête on the grounds that the proposed *rachat* (repurchase) was a routine matter that should be handled by the ordinary, local tribunals. So in December 1764 the community's lawyers instituted rachat proceedings against the comtesse de Sade in the senechaussée of Arles. After several years of maneuvering, the two parties agreed to arbitration, a typical stage in Old Regime legal conflict. The arbitrators issued their decision in 1768. Both parties found the decision unsatisfactory and, by mutual accord, reopened their *procès* (case) before the Parlement of Aix. On 21 July 1776, the Parlement issued its ruling, an *arrêt* (ruling) requiring the community to prove that the banalities in question were not of feudal origin.[34] The Third Estate municipal elites who administered the province considered this presumption of feudal origin contrary to the Declaration of 1764 and "truly destructive" of "the laws, maxims, and titles of the *pays*." Accordingly, they intervened on behalf of Eyguières in its appeal to the Royal Council.[35] The Corps de la Noblesse responded by intervening on behalf of Jean-Baptiste-Joseph-David comte de Sade.

On 12 September 1780, the Royal Council sent the affair back to the Parlement of Aix on procedural grounds. On 20 July 1781, the Parlement rejected the proofs furnished by the community, and denied its request to buy back its banalities. The community immediately appealed this decision to the Royal Council, again with the backing of the province and the counter-intervention of the Corps de la Noblesse.

Lawyers for the community and the province attacked the seigneur's claim that the banality was feudal and hence exempt from buy-back.[36] Both the seigneur's legal argumentation and the Parlement's 1781 ruling had erred in asserting that, without titles to the contrary, banalities were to be presumed feudal. This assertion, they claimed, willfully inverted a fundamental maxim of Provençal jurisprudence.[37] According to Jean-Joseph Julien, author of the latest and most comprehensive repertoire of Provençal law, seigneurs "do not have banal ovens and mills through the droit de leur fief and their lordly personal status. . . . Only in certain provinces of France does this right exist as a feudal right. . . . Everywhere else, . . . the banality, which is an extraordinary right contrary to natural and public liberty, can only be claimed by seigneurs through an explicit seigneurial title."[38] If doubts arose about the origin of a given banality, it was thus up to the seigneur—not the community—to prove feudal origin. But the Sades had based their case on the false doctrine of feudal presumption and the Parlement, agreeing, had strayed from the path of constitutionality. This departure from legal principle was why the community had lost its case.[39]

But even allowing the feudal presumption, continued the appellants, the Parlement still should have authorized the buy-back. This is because the community had provided irrefutable evidence that the banalities could not have been feudal in origin. This evidence was (1) a municipal deliberation of 1550 which first established the banality, (2) the fact that the banal ovens had never been subject to various domainial exactions (to which only feudal property was subject), and (3) the original act from 1221 creating the seigneurie of Eyguières, a document that mentioned neither banality nor oven. Although the Parlement had violated Provençal law when it had ordered the community to prove nonfeudal origin, the community had nonetheless satisfied this rigorous requirement.

Having addressed the issues of presumption and proof, the lawyers of Eyguières and the province then made a far-reaching claim: however much the banality was feudal in origin, the buy-back would still be legitimate. This is because, even if it had been originally part of the fief, the banality had subsequently left it. Whether directly or indirectly, whether by purchase or gift, it had at some point passed from the seigneur to the community and joined the mass of communal goods. This alone sufficed to extinguish it because, according to the Roman maxim "nulli res sua servit," no one can be in servitude to oneself.[40] Although a community could maintain a feudal banality it had acquired, it was necessarily no longer feudal in character. It had become a "municipal charge meant to lighten the fiscal burden on landed property." Thus what the comte de Sade had purchased between 1716 and 1739 was a municipal tax, not a feudal banality. Nonfeudal and *acquise à prix d'argent* (acquired by purchase), it was thus rachetable according to the Declaration of 1764.

The comte de Sade and the provincial nobility responded that their adversaries were misinterpreting the Declaration. They noted that when the Parlement of Aix had registered it, the court had deliberately changed the phrase "acquises à prix d'argent" to "établies à prix d'argent" (established by purchase).[41] In doing so, it had wisely removed a dangerous ambiguity in the original wording of the law that the community of Eyguières was now trying to exploit. For centuries, fiefs (as well as particular feudal rights) had been bought and sold. Rare was the seigneurie which had never changed hands for cash. If the province prevailed in asserting that all banalities and other feudal dues "acquises à prix d'argent" were rachetables, meaning that they could be repurchased, the social and economic consequences would be devastating. Only those few fiefs which had remained in a single family since their creation would be free from the oppression of their communities. "Do you not see," pleaded the Sade lawyers, "that this would destroy all fiefs and withdraw them from commerce? Could such a law, which would throw the kingdom into disorder and attack property rights, have ever entered into the mind of the Sovereign?"[42] In his justification of the Parlement's decision, its *procureur-général*, Le Blanc de Castillon, echoed these fears.[43] The province's intervention, he claimed, aimed not only at "favoring the unsettled and litigious spirit of certain communities and fomenting division between lords and tenants." It was also part of a sinister plan to "confuse all ranks" and thereby "abolish the distinction between the different orders in which resides the force, security, and peace of the kingdom." If the province were allowed to continue its attack on legitimate seigneurial rights, "there would be no end to litigation, no more stability of jurisprudence, judgments would lose their authority, there would be no tranquility between lords and their subjects, no more peace between the Second and Third Estates."

In substituting the word "*établies*" for "*acquises*," therefore, the Parlement had not usurped legislative authority, but had merely eliminated an ambiguity that could be used by the seditious to subvert a solemn royal declaration.[44] The king had meant to exempt banalities of feudal origin from buy-back; by changing one word, the Parlement had ensured that this would be so. But what of the province's argument that feudal banalities necessarily changed their nature upon leaving the hands of the seigneur? This argument overturned the fundamental principles of feudal property law, claimed the Sade lawyers. If adopted, it would effectively abolish feudalism in France. A basic characteristic of feudal property was its division into two domains. The first was the *domaine utile,* which consisted in the right to exploit a physical property, such as a field, or an incorporal one, such as a banality. The second was the *domaine directe,* which can be understood as a kind of theoretical overlordship over the domaine utile. The Sade lawyers noted that, under this system of divided property, when a seigneur sold a land, banality, or any other feudal right, only the domaine utile changed hands.[45] The seigneur retained the "domaine directe," which allowed the exercise of various feudal prerogatives—such as the *droit de lods*—over the alienated "domaine utile." "When a seigneur transports banal ovens to a community, . . . these ovens and the attached banality belong to the community; but they remain inviolably attached to the seigneurie by dues and the 'mouvance' [another term for the domaine directe] which the seigneur has retained, and which perpetually represent the domaine utile transported to the community." The community and the province were making the outrageous argument that a seigneur who alienated the domaine utile of a property thereby extinguished the directe as well. If this doctrine were allowed to stand, they warned, "all seigneurial rights would be destroyed because they are only due to the lord by reason of the lands or rights which he has transported, in reserving for himself the mouvance, censes, and other services." If the province prevailed, feudalism would cease to exist.[46]

During 1786 and 1787, as the Royal Council considered these arguments, its members found themselves subject to heavy lobbying by the Sades. To this end, the comte de Sade and his wife the comtesse (née Marie-Françoise-Amélie de Bimard) had taken up residence in Paris.[47] Although both pressured the councilors, Madame de Sade seems to have played the principal role. It was her name and address (not her husband's) which the Council noted on the cover of the case dossier.[48] She repeatedly wrote to M. Harivel (the all-important premier *commis des finances* who managed the *comité*'s docket), as well as to the councilors, Laurent de Villedeuil, and to the *contrôlleur-général.*[49] Her intervention may have been decisive. At the start of its deliberations, three of the five committee members (de Fourqueux, de Monthyon, and the *rapporteur* de Sartine) were in favor of reversing the Parlement's 1781 arrêt, as was the intendant of Provence, whose opinion usually determined the Council's verdict in such matters.[50] But under intense pressure Sartine changed his mind and sided with his colleagues de Vidaud de la Tour and de Bacquencourt to reject the community's appeal at the end of October 1787.[51] It is perhaps significant that Villedeuil first announced the decision not to the comte de Sade or the deputies of the Corps de la Noblesse, but to Madame de Sade.[52] According to a lawyer who worked with the intendant of Provence on this affair, "the intrigues of the comtesse de Sade, who had some credit at Court," were largely responsible for the final outcome.[53] But while recognizing the impact of this formidable woman, it is important not to overstate her importance. Ultimately, the case was won by an elite group of lawyers who served as the public face and voice of the seigneurie.

The Council's decision of 30 October 1787 was still not the end of the story. In a rather desperate move, the province petitioned the Council for authorization to appeal its own judgment. It justified its plea in fiscal terms—a line of reasoning calculated to strike a chord with the hard-pressed royal government. If the ruling were allowed to stand, it would result in the "absolute rejection of all buy-back demands" in the future.[54] Since it concerned communal properties "destined to support the public charges," it in fact concerned the "property of the State itself." The decision had to be reversed "so that the communities could easily pay their taxes."[55] We will never know how the government would have responded to these entreaties because the political crisis of 1788–1789 intervened. In effect, the Sades had won their case. But they would have been better off had they lost. By having their banality declared feudal, they unwittingly ensured that it would be caught up in the great wave of revolutionary feudal abolition. Had they lost and the banality been declared nonfeudal, it would have survived the maelstrom well into the nineteenth century as Sade private property.[56]

CONCLUSION

The Eyguières-Sade affair is rich in conclusions about seigneurialism and female legal capacity in Old Regime France. Here I will confine my final remarks to the importance of women and gender to the feudal institution. This may seem like an abrupt, even unwarranted non sequitur, a vast jump from the detailed legal narrative that forms the bulk of the present essay. After all, very little in the litigation described above had anything to do specifically with gender, but it did have a lot to do with a woman. That is exactly the significant point. The female experience of lordship was very similar to the male experience of lordship. If one were to focus only on those areas of lordship in which gender difference mattered, the resulting account would be extremely narrow, barren, and incomplete. To get at the experience of female lordship, we first have to get at the experience of lordship itself.[57] And we find that it was similar for men and women.

There is no doubt that, today, we find the concept of female lordship more remarkable than did people in the eighteenth century. But if female lordship was as commonplace as I suspect, then early modern society was perfectly accustomed to seeing numerous elite women in possession of public dignities and exercising sovereign powers, notably the right of justice. This would not be the case again in France until after World War II. While I do not follow Joan Landes's argument about Rousseau's deleterious impact on women after 1789, the prevalence of female lordship in the Old Regime does suggest that the women (together with the men, of course) who owned this type of property-in-public-power lost the possibility of owning and exercising a quasi-sovereign function in 1789. But this was because of the abolition of feudalism, not because of the Enlightenment's purported obsession with classical republican notions of manhood and citizenship.

As Suzanne Desan and others have noted, matrimonial property and inheritance regimes were gendered and thus influenced the possession of seigneuries by women.[58] In regard to the transmission of seigneurial property by inheritance, sex may well have played a decisive role. But once a seigneurie was in the hands of a dame, at least in a Roman-law province, the defense and exercise of its prerogatives were largely unaffected by sex. As the Eyguières-Sade trial illustrates, the sex of the lord did not matter to the courts. When a lord engaged in litigation, matters were handled by professional jurists. Lords were rarely, if ever, called upon to plead or testify in person before a court. Whether men or women, they were represented by lawyers, professionals who appeared for and spoke on behalf of their clients. The same is true of the day-to-day exercise of seigneurie. Seigneurs in Provence visited their fiefs infrequently. The economic exploitation of their properties and the administration of seigneurial justice were again handled by professionals—*hommes d'affaires, fermiers,* and the minor venal magistrates who staffed their courts. Provençal lords, whatever their sex, spent their time in urban settings, generally the towns of Aix and Avignon. Whether in litigation or routine estate management, the face of seigneurial power was a salaried professional, not the lord or dame.

For male and female lords, the seigneurial *état* was more significant in many contexts than the sex of its seigneur. This may also have been true of other social categories during the Old Regime. Whatever the case, sex was just one criterion of distinction among many, and its relevance varied across the landscape of social practice. It existed in a complex, fluid relationship with other modes of social distinction. Perhaps one of the more significant effects of the Revolution for women was that when it abolished the formal hierarchies of estates, orders, and corps, it unintentionally increased the importance of gender by radically simplifying the social order and eliminating rival forms of social distinction, leaving gender one of the few measures of difference left standing.[59]

NOTES

1. This concern is found throughout the literature, but is treated systematically in Anne Verjus, *Le cens de la famille: Les femmes et le vote, 1789–1848* (Paris: Belin, 2002). Of interest as well are the essays in Sara E. Melzer and Leslie W. Rabine, eds., *Rebel Daughters: Women and the French Revolution* (New York: Oxford Univ. Press, 1992).

2. Jennifer Ngaire Heuer, *The Family and the Nation: Gender and Citizenship in Revolutionary France, 1789–1830* (Ithaca: Cornell Univ. Press, 2005).

3. Suzanne Desan, "Making and Breaking Marriage: An Overview of Old Regime Marriage as a Social Practice," in *Family, Gender, and Law in Early Modern France,* ed. Suzanne Desan and Jeffrey Merrick (University Park: Pennsylvania State Univ. Press, 2009), 1–25; Dena Goodman, "Marriage Choice and Marital Success: Reasoning about Marriage, Love, and Happiness," in *Family, Gender, and Law,* 26–61; Goodman, *Becoming a Woman in the Age of Letters* (Ithaca: Cornell Univ. Press, 2009), 274–306; Julie Hardwick, "Women 'Working' the Law: Gender, Authority, and Legal Process in Early Modern France," *Journal of Women's History* 9, no. 3 (autumn 1997): 28–49.

4. Margaret Darrow, *Revolution in the House: Family, Class, and Inheritance in Southern France, 1775–1825* (Princeton: Princeton Univ. Press, 1989); Julie Hardwick, *The Practice of Patriarchy: Gender and the Politics of Household Authority in Early Modern France* (University Park: Pennsylvania State Univ. Press, 1998); Julie Hardwick, *Family Business: Litigation and the Political Economies of Daily Life in Early Modern France* (Oxford: Oxford Univ. Press, 2009).

5. Darrow, *Revolution in the House;* Suzanne Desan, *The Family on Trial in Revolutionary France* (Berkeley: Univ. of California Press, 2004), 141–176.

6. Barbara B. Diefendorf, "Women and Property in *Ancien Régime* France: Theory and Practice in Dauphiné and Paris," in *Early Modern Conceptions of Property,* ed. John Brewer and Susan Staves (London: Routledge, 1996), 175.

7. She is particularly sensitive to the differences between the various provincial legal systems, particularly those of the southern written-law regions that granted some separate property rights to married women. See especially page 189, note 22.

8. Clare Haru Crowston, *Fabricating Women: The Seamstresses of Old Regime France, 1675–1791* (Durham: Duke Univ. Press, 2001); Daryl M. Hafter, *Women at Work in Preindustrial France* (Univer-

sity Park: Pennsylvania State Univ. Press, 2007).

9. Sandra Cavallo and Lyndan Warner, eds., *Widowhood in Medieval and Early Modern Europe* (Essex: Harlow, 1999); Janine M. Lanza, *From Wives to Widows in Early Modern Paris: Gender, Economy, and Law* (Aldershot, Eng.: Ashgate, 2007); Nicole Pellegrin and Colette H. Winn, eds., *Veufs, veuves et veuvage dans la France d'Ancien Régime: Actes du colloque de Poitiers, 11–12 juin 1998* (Paris: Champion, 2003).

10. Clare Haru Crowston, "Family Affairs: Wives, Credit, Consumption, and the Law in Old Regime France," in *Family, Gender, and Law*, 62–100.

11. Hardwick, *The Practice of Patriarchy*. For a different perspective, see Sarah Hanley, "Engendering the State: Family Formation and State Building in Early Modern France," *French Historical Studies* 16, no. 1 (spring 1989): 4–27.

12. Diefendorf, "Women and Property," 184. See also Desan, *The Family on Trial*, 2.

13. Archives départementales de l'Isère, 29 J 87, Billecoq, ancien avocat à la cour royale, "Consulation," Paris, 12 July 1821.

14. Archives départementales des Bouches-du-Rhone (henceforth AD B-d-R); Archives Communales (henceforth AC), 113.

15. AD B-d-R; AC 147.

16. Bibliothèque Méjanes, MS 1143 (630), "Etat du florinage contenant le revenu noble de touts les fiefs et arriere fiefs de la province avec les noms des possesseurs, fait par M. le Premier President d'Oppede en 1668."

17. AD B-d-R, C 1383 and 1384, "Afflorinement" (1778). The dramatic growth in the number of Provençal seigneuries reflects the tendency to divide large holdings into smaller co-seigneuries. See Monique Cubells, "La propriété féodale en Basse-Provence dans la deuxième moitié du XVIIIᵉ siècle: Nobles et bourgeois," in *La noblesse provençale du milieu du XVIIᵉ siècle à la Révolution*, ed. Monique Cubells (Aix-en-Provence: Presses universitaires d'Aix-Marseille, 2002), 171–203.

18. AD B-d-R, C 1352–1372.

19. Rafe Blaufarb, "Conflict and Compromise: *Communauté* and *Seigneurie* in Early Modern Provence," *Journal of Modern History* 82, no. 3 (September 2010): 519–545.

20. Claude-Joseph Ferrière, *Dictionnaire de dróit et de pratique* (Paris, Bauche, 1771), 1:919.

21. Armand Brette, *Recueil de documents relatifs à la convocation des états-généraux de 1789*, 4 vols. (Paris: Imprimerie nationale, 1894–1915).

22. Charles Loyseau, *Traité des Seigneuries*, 3rd ed. (Paris: Veuve A. L'Angelier, 1613).

23. The distinction between the precarious nature of the office and the truly patrimonial nature of the seigneurie is a central them in Loyseau, *Cinq livres du droict des offices, avec le livre des seigneuries, et celuy des ordres* (Paris: Veuve A. L'Angelier, 1613).

24. Jean-Philippe Agresti, *Les régimes matrimoniaux en Provence à la fin de l'ancien régime: Contribution à l'étude du droit et de la pratique notariale en pays de droit écrit* (Aix-en-Provence: Presses universitaires d'Aix-Marseille, 2009).

25. Dauphinois notarial acts passed by women who had married without marriage contracts used exactly the same terminology. In a typical act, Demoiselle Anne Robert, wife of Pierre Allouard Biron, was described as "disposing of her free goods, given that she had not passed any civil marriage contract." Archives départementales de l'Isère, 3 E 3213, Notary Pierre-Adrien Accarier of Grenoble, Act of 31 March 1792.

26. Agresti, *Les régimes matrimoniaux*, 120.

27. For a systematic social analysis, see ibid., 135, 141–42.

28. The following summary of the origins of the trial is based on a synthesis of various mémoires in the Archives Nationales (henceforth AN), H1 1273.

29. Figures from AN, H1 1273, no.7, untitled and undated requête.

30. *Déclaration du Roi, Qui regle entre le Parlement & la Cour des Comptes, Aydes & Finances de Provence, la connoissance des demandes en rachat des tasques & bannalités constituées à prix d'argent* (Versailles, 3 February 1764).

31. Abbé L. Paulet, *Eyguières, son histoire féodale, communale, et réligieuse* (1901; reprint, Paris: Le livre d'histoire, 2011). The comtesse de Sade, dame d'Egyuières, was Margueritte-Therèse le Gouche de Saint-Etienne. She assumed direction of the seigneurie in early 1761 and retained control until 1770, when her son, Jean-Baptiste-Joseph-David, turned twenty-one and became lord in his own right. I thank Sébastien Avy, an Aixois *érudit* and expert in the Provençal nobility, for furnishing me with this reference.

32. AD B-d-R, C 1371, "Procureurs du pays to the Archbishop of Aix" (Aix, 3 August 1787).

33. The following paragraph is based on a synthesis of mémoires in AN, H1 1273.

34. The Parlement based itself on the feudal jurist Louis Ventre de la Touloubre, who wrote that "it is presumed that [the banality derives from the act of *inféodation*] if no constitutive title is found." *Jurisprudence observée en Provence sur les matières féodales et les droits seigneuriaux divisée en deux parties* (Avignon: Chez la Veuve Girard, 1756), 2:154; see also AN, H1 1273, no. 111, Le Blanc de Castillon, "Motifs de l'arrêt du Parlement d'Aix rendu en faveur du comte de Sade, seigneur d'Eyguières" (Aix, 1 May 1786).

35. *Abregé du Cayer des délibérations de l'Assemblée Générale des Communautés du pays de Provence, convoquée à Lambesc au premier Décembre 1776* (Aix, 1777), 166. Another observer described the Parlement's ruling as the "overthrow of the national law [*droit national*] of Provence." AN, H1 1273, no. 7, untitled and undated requête.

36. These arguments are distilled from the numerous mémoires submitted by the community and the province found in AN, H1 1273. The most important are no. 2, "Requête d'intervention pour les procureurs des gens des trois états du pays de Provence" (9 July 1782); no. 15, *Mémoire signifiée pour les maires, consuls, habitans, et communauté de la ville d'Eyguières . . .* (Aix, 1780); no. 29, "Réponse aux motifs de l'arrêt du Parlement" (n.d.); no. 43, *Réponse au précis communiqué le 17 juillet 1781 pour M. le comte de Sade, seigneur d'Eyguières, contre la communauté dudit lieu* (Aix, 1781); no. 94, "Mémoire pour les procureurs du pays dans l'affaire de la communauté d'Eyguières contre le seigneur" (n.d.); and no. 97, "Observations pour la communauté d'Eyguières" (n.d.).

37. AN, H1 1273, no. 83, "Lettre de Dubreuil, assesseur d'Aix, à Harivel à la Cour" (Aix, 10 September 1786). Dubreuil charged that the Parlement of Aix was "biased in favor of the seigneurs" and that it did not even bother to "hide its desire to see [buy-backs] entirely suppressed." For his part, the comte de Sade charged that the *assesseur* was "suspect" because "he was born on my land." "I have cause to regard him as my veritable adversary." AN, H1 1273, no. 107, "comte de Sade to Monsieur [probably the *contrôlleur-général*]" (Paris, 24 September 1787).

38. Jean-Joseph Jullien, *Nouveau commentaire sur les statuts de Provence* (Aix: Esprit David, 1778), 2:412.

39. Bibliothèque Méjanes, MS 1025 (834), Avis de l'intendant, 111.

40. AN, H1 1273, no. 29, "Réponse aux motifs"; see also Jullien, *Nouveau commentaire sur les status de Provence,* 2:256.

41. The following discussion of the Sades' legal arguments is based on analysis of the numerous

mémoires in AN, H1 1273. The most important are no.10, *Mémoire signifié pour le comte de Sade . . .* (Aix, 1780 [but submitted to the Royal Council in 1782]); no. 13, "Observations pour M. le comte de Sade" (n.d.); and the unnumbered *Mémoire servant de réponse pour M. le comte de Sade* (Aix, 1781).

42. AN, H1 1273, no. 113, "Mémoire pour M. le comte de Sade" (n.d.).

43. AN, H1 1273, no. 111, Le Blanc de Castillon, "Motifs de l'arrêt."

44. The arguments in this intensive debate over the meaning of the words "acquises" and "établies" is summarized in AN, H1 1273, no. 80, "Reflexions sur le mot 'acquise' et le mot 'établie'" (n.d.).

45. AN, H1 1273, no. 113, "Mémoire pour M. le comte de Sade" (n.d.).

46. For this backstory, see Rafe Blaufarb, *The Politics of Fiscal Privilege in Provence: The Procès des Tailles, 1530s–1830s* (Washington, D.C.: Catholic Univ. of America Press, 2012).

47. They married in 1770, at about the same time Jean-Baptiste-Joseph-David took over the seigneurie from his mother. Paulet, *Eyguières,* 36.

48. AN, H1 1273, unnumbered, "Residu, la communauté d'Eyguières en Provence" (n.d.). While in Paris she stayed at 17 rue Jacob.

49. AN, H1 1273, nos. 15 (bis), 27, and 28.

50. Bibliothèque Méjanes, MS 1025 (835), 107–119. The opinion, sent by the intendant to Calonne, is dated 31 October 1785.

51. AN, H1 1273, no. 75, "Affaire de la communauté d'Eyguières en Provence contre M. le comte de Sade" (1787). The Council's arrêt was dated 30 October 1787.

52. I have been unable to find the letter, dated 29 July 1787, but it is mentioned in another letter written by the comte de Sade to the contrôlleur-général in September 1787. AN, H1 1273, no. 105.

53. Bibliothèque Méjanes, MS 1025 (834), 119.

54. AN, H1 1273, no. 29, "Réponse."

55. AN, H1 1273, no. 73, "Memoire pour la communauté d'Eyguières en Provence" (n.d., but in a dossier marked 1789).

56. To follow this ironic postscript, one must turn to the municipal deliberations of the community (and then commune) of Eyguières, 1788–1790. These are uncataloged and can only be consulted on appointment in the municipal library.

57. Since the publication of Jonathan Dewald's excellent study of the barony of Pont-Saint-Pierre in Normandy, almost no work has been done in English on seigneurialism. A great deal, however, has been written recently about seigneurial justice. See, in particular, François Brizay, Antoine Follain, and Véronique Sarrazin, eds., *Les justices de village: Administration et justice locale de la fin du Moyen Age à la Révolution* (Rennes: Presses universitaires de Rennes, 2002); Anthony Crubaugh, *Balancing the Scales of Justice: Local Courts and Rural Society in Southwest France, 1750–1800* (University Park: Pennsylvania State Univ. Press, 2001); and Jeremy Hayhoe, *Enlightened Feudalism: Seigneurial Justice and Village Society in Eighteenth-Century Northern Burgundy* (Rochester: Univ. of Rochester Press, 2008).

58. Desan, *The Family on Trial.*

59. A similar conclusion was expressed in Hafter, *Women at Work,* 235–36. "As the horizontal divisions between estates and privilege fell away, the vertical division of sex separation emerged to take its place as the prime organizing principle of society."

WOMEN AND WORK IDENTITY

Nancy Locklin

L OUIS LE MACE and his wife, Louise Calvarin, wanted to protect their daughter. According to the laws of Brittany, a province in northwest France, all their goods would be divided equally among their families once they both had died. This was an automatic process, and heirs were often eager to claim a share in whatever there was to be had. Thus, on the 3rd of August in 1734, Louis and his wife formally declared that all of the goods and furniture in the front room on the second floor of their home belonged solely to their oldest daughter, Louise.[1] She was a trained and certified mistress tailor in the guild of Quimper, and she had earned everything in her possession over the course of several years. The other heirs of Le Mace and Calvarin could not touch a thing in that room.

The traditionally accepted family economy model has little room for someone like Louise Le Mace, mistress tailor. The model, which prevailed for decades, is based on the assumption that the male head of household has a profession and that his wife and children essentially work for him. Sons would eventually take over the trade from their fathers, and daughters would be married off to serve as assistants to their husbands. Eventually, a woman might be widowed and was expected to see her sons take over for her deceased husband. Women rarely developed a sense of "work identity," according to the theory, because their work changed regularly to serve the needs of the household. Women helped men, whether those men were fathers, husbands, or sons, and had no reason to see their own work as a meaningful part of their lives. Generally speaking, this model probably does describe life for a lot of artisan and merchant families in the premodern world. But models are designed to simplify, and human society is always more complex than the models we use to understand it. Over time models are frequently taken to represent the whole of reality, and the true range of possibilities is then lost.

In the case of women and their work, the acceptance of the family economy model in history led to a mistaken belief that women's work was usually supplemental to someone else's. This belief is still common despite numerous studies outlining the complicated nature of family life in the past. Relevant scholarship addresses a wide range of issues related to the model. Clare Haru Crowston's *Fabricating Women: The Seamstresses of Old Regime France, 1675–1791,* for example, details the shift from informal work to recognized guild status for women in the sewing trades of Paris and elsewhere.[2] Daryl M. Hafter's *Women at Work in Pre-industrial France* outlines the disconnect between ideas about a woman's proper place in society and the realities that demanded that women step away from those ideas whenever necessary.[3] Janine M. Lanza describes in *From Wives to Widows in Early Modern Paris* how far removed our assumptions and stereotypes about widows are from true life for such women in the past.[4] Finally, James R. Farr puts the new, complex model into the context of labor and occupations for both men and women at every level of society in *The Work of France.*[5] It should be clear by now that the old family economy model does not fully reflect the lives of women, yet the misperceptions persist in mainstream histories.

Louise Le Mace was a fully professional woman in her own right. The municipal laws of the city of Quimper required anyone working at a trade to belong to the appropriate guild. The guilds, for their part, accepted as members only those who had completed a formal apprenticeship and had demonstrated the necessary skills to meet the guild's standards. Most European guilds were male-dominated, to be sure. The tailor's guild in Quimper was unique, perhaps, because it accepted both men and women on the same basis. Women were members in full standing if they had met all the entrance requirements and were up to date on their dues. Louise was a member of the tailor's guild according to both her parents' statements in 1734 and according to the guild's tax rolls for 1748.[6] This means that Louise had been admitted on a professional basis and not through the work of her father or a husband. Her father was a shoemaker, so she was not even working in her father's trade. Furthermore, the guild in Quimper accepted members at different levels in accordance with their training and skill. Louise could have simply qualified as a seamstress, worked for someone else, and paid a lower rate in the guild. As a "tailor," however, Louise had to have achieved the highest level of skill possible. Finally, she was listed in the tax roll for 1748 strictly as a member of the guild. She was listed alone at her parents' former address in the tax roll of 1755, and with two apprentices in 1763.[7] There is no evidence that she ever married. Thus, the professional identity of Louise Le Mace might be the only historical record she left.

The family economy model should have plenty of room for stories such as these. Louise Le Mace did still live with her parents, at least up to 1748, but had a professional life completely distinct from theirs. Other families and households show an even greater range of possibilities that do not fit into the traditional model. Some wives had occupations and even guild memberships that were separate from those of their husbands. Some people lived and worked with siblings or sought out roommates to share the costs of living. Some women lived alone and survived off of paid work or inherited property. The variety of household arrangements found in eighteenth-century sources, such as tax rolls, notarized contracts, and police investigations, shows that the family economy model could not adequately account for the way many people lived. By extension, the family economy model cannot fully describe the variety of work that people did, and what that work meant to them.

The sources cannot tell us how Louise Le Mace felt about her work. Did she really have what modern scholars would recognize as a "work identity"? Did she define herself by her work? It is difficult to say. At the same time, it seems likely that her work was crucially important to her. Louise must have completed an apprenticeship in order to join the guild, so someone, most likely her parents, had seen fit to invest in her professional future. Louise herself had taken the effort to achieve the title of "tailor" in her guild, instead of opting for the simpler role of "seamstress." She had already been working "for several years" in 1734, according to her parents, and was still identified as a tailor in 1763, meaning she had maintained the professional identity for most of her life. Even the fact that she paid her taxes through the guild in 1748 rather than as a member of her father's household indicates that her status as an artisan figured prominently in her life. It would have been far cheaper to have been listed as a daughter with no declared occupation, but she chose to pay alongside the other members of the guild.

The goal of this chapter is to expand the family economy model in order to create a more nuanced picture of women's lives, their relationship to the household, and their place in the economy of the eighteenth century. The province of Brittany will serve well as a case study because it encompassed several cities and small towns, benefited from a variety of markets and industries, and operated under a clear set of customary law codes. Thus, it provides examples of life in a broad range of settings. The first part of the chapter will address the variety of household arrangements found in both urban and rural areas. The second section will explore the way in which a woman's age and stage of life contributed to her work and identity. A third section will explain the legal rights accorded to women in the province of Brittany, as well as their access to resources, and a fourth will address formal trade affiliations. Once all of these factors have been taken into account, a richer history of women's work identities will emerge.

HOUSEHOLD ARRANGEMENTS

The family economy model, in which all members of a household assist in the work of the male head of household, was based on the assumption that all or most people in a society are attached to a traditional, male-headed household. So, the first step will be to examine what proportion of the population lived in that sort of arrangement, and, more importantly, how many people did not. The *capitation* tax rolls are an excellent source for establishing these numbers. This universal head tax was imposed across France between 1695 and 1789, and most entries in the rolls specify the composition of each household. This makes it possible for us to track the names of the heads of household and the number of people living with them, as well as, in most cases, their marital status, occupation, and level of wealth. This last characteristic can be estimated for each household based on the tax assessed. In homes with no clear "head of household," such as those occupied by two or more unrelated roommates, each person was named separately and the occupation of each was identified. The capitation tax roll was also imposed equally from small villages to large urban centers, with only members of the clergy being exempt from paying it.

There are some difficulties in relying so heavily on these tax rolls, of course. First of all, some documents have been lost, so it is not possible to study the tax rolls for each city for every year. Second, recording practices differed from one town to the next. Some clerks liked to include as much detail as possible for every household being taxed, while others were content to record one name and the amount paid for each home. In some cities, guilds preferred to pay as a group and distribute the tax burden internally among their members. That was the case for Quimper in 1748, when Louise Le Mace paid with the tailor's guild. A third problem is specific to the task of tracing women's work in the eighteenth century. A married woman might not be identified by her own name, but simply counted as someone living in her husband's house. If she had a separate occupation from her husband's, it would only be noted if the clerk saw fit to include the information. If her husband died, she might be recorded the following year under her own name or simply as "the widow of . . ." A woman recorded under her own name one year could be either single or widowed, and if she then married she could disappear from the sources altogether. And so, we can only make generalizations about household arrangements based on these sources, and we will need to turn to other sources in order to make sense of what women were actually doing throughout these life changes.

When imagining life in the premodern period, we might assume that female-headed households were an anomaly. It is true that most people got married and that few people, male or female, ended up living alone. Nevertheless, common sense tells us that life in any era can be unpredictable and that some people will always have to fend for themselves. In the towns and cities of Brittany during the eighteenth century, women headed between 14 and 30 percent of taxed households. The figures varied over the course of the century and depended largely on local opportunities for women to support themselves. It depended as well on factors that might reduce the population of men. Port cities, for example, tended to have a higher percentage of female-headed households because many of the men were occupied at sea. This meant two things: there were more opportunities for women to work independently at jobs that might have been filled by men in landlocked cities, and men were more likely in this setting to be absent for years or to lose their lives. This was the case at Brest, where women headed 33 percent of the households and the majority of those female heads of household were widowed.

The largest commercial urban centers in Brittany were Rennes and Nantes, each supporting a population of fifty thousand to eighty thousand people at mid-century. The tax rolls for both of these cities show an average of 15 percent of households being headed by women. Less than half of these female heads of household were widows, meaning that a slight majority was made up of unmarried women living alone or with roommates. This makes some sense. Urban centers were often a magnet for unattached people who flocked from the countryside seeking work. It would be logical for women in this situation to migrate into Nantes and Rennes from rural areas, and that is what they did. In fact, the percentage of female-headed households does not nearly reflect the number of women who would have come to the city. Many female migrants ended up as servants, and would have been counted as members of other people's households.

The only real surprise in the statistics for Brittany is that some of the highest percentages for female heads of household were found in the rolls for small towns and villages. The sources for Dinan, a weaving town with a population of five thousand, and Montcontour, a village of fifteen hundred, reveal that an average of 28 percent of households were headed by women in both places. As in the large cities, less than half of these women were widows. This seems surprising, given that small towns presumably had fewer opportunities for women to work independently and that most people in a "traditional" setting would have gotten married. And yet, women headed roughly one-fourth of households. One possible explanation may be that Breton law gave men and women equal inheritance rights, so it is possible that many women were able to survive on inherited property. Either way, the example offers evidence that we cannot assume that all people were members of a male-headed household.

STAGES OF LIFE

The old family economy model assumed that a woman's stages of life have a far greater impact on her work than a man's do on his. A typical male's life stages would have included several levels of training beginning in his childhood and leading up to a profession during his adulthood. Standard changes in life such as marriage, child rearing, and widowhood would not have dramatically altered the kind of work most men did. It would have been very different for a woman raised in a male-headed household that conformed to the family economy model. Such a woman would have had very little formal training since she was unlikely to adopt the trade of her father, and might have had to learn a new trade in order to assist her husband. Childbearing and child rearing placed great limits on the kinds of tasks a woman could perform, so those events would have changed her work once again. Finally, widowhood might require that a woman learn yet another trade in order to make ends meet, whether or not she could count on the support of her children. The changes that accompanied every stage in a woman's life certainly explain why it seemed rare for women to develop a work identity. When women's work was so erratic, how could women have felt much attachment to what they did?

While there is no doubt that many women's lives followed the pattern outlined above, the reality was much more complicated. Many girls did receive training in a trade as children. This was true even for women who intended to serve as assistants or partners to their husbands. A butcher's daughter, for example, was very likely to marry a butcher in most places. It would have made sense for her to learn the trade in order to help run the family business, and then guide her own children into the trade when it came time. When families maintained trades for several generations, why would we assume that the work meant less to the women in those families?

Unfortunately, we can only speculate about the work identity of a woman who stayed with a family business and handed it off to her children. It may be easier to establish a sense of work identity for women who maintained a trade of their own over several years and through life's many changes. Louise Le Mace, for example, needed to have been trained as a tailor in order to be accepted into the guild. Sources reveal that she was working at her trade for at least the time period between 1734, when her parents filed their declaration about her property, and 1763, the last tax roll listing her as a tailor. She was successful enough to have listed two apprentices in her household in 1763, indicating that other families recognized her professional status enough to place their daughters with her for training.

It is true that Louise Le Mace remained unmarried, but the tailor's guild in Quimper accepted women as members regardless of their marital status. The same was true of the tailor's guild in the city of Rennes. Women who had been admitted as mistresses in the trade on their own merits kept their individual status in the guild when they married, as long as they married men who were not tailors. If they married tailors, then the women were counted along with their husbands. Here we see an example of how complex the situation was: the male head of household was the recognized representative of the family even if his wife was a trained and skilled tailor on her own. This does seem to support the prominence of the patriarchal household as the norm. However, it is also true that a female tailor who chose to marry a butcher or carpenter could keep her work distinct from that of her husband. The numbers bear out the existence of such households. Nearly 40 percent of the married women named in the tax roll for Quimper in 1763 were identified as clothing retailers, and only 13 percent of those wives were married to men in the same or similar trades.[8] In Rennes, for the year 1753, 17 percent of the married women named in the tax rolls were in clothing retail, and none of them were married to men in the same trade.[9] Recall that most married women were not named in tax rolls, so these numbers do not reflect women who worked with their husbands in conformance with the traditional model. Nevertheless, for the married women specifically identified in the tax rolls, marriage did not lead to a change in work.

The impact of children on a woman's work life is difficult to measure. The existence of wet nurses (who would care for infants and toddlers) and the practice of sending older children into service or apprenticeship meant that a woman's work did not always have to be compatible with childcare. The fact that many people in the premodern era, male and female alike, tended to work at or near their homes suggests that work often took place with children underfoot. Add to this the fact that women were often found in occupations traditionally associated with work done for the home. Most of the women identified in the sources for Brittany in this era worked with cloth, clothing, or food. According to the tax records, 62 percent of the women in large cities and nearly 75 percent of the women in small towns and villages did "women's work" in such trades. Their professional work was often compatible with the tasks needed to run a household. Thus, it is not necessarily the case that a woman's work life had to change dramatically once she had children.

Widowhood, a sadly typical life stage in this era, also did not necessarily bring about drastic changes in a woman's work life. This was especially true if she came from an established trade of her own or a shared family business. Such women were often able to continue working until age and illness made work impossible, or, in the case of a family trade, until the children could take over. However, widowhood, solitude, and old age combined brought definite crisis to those who did not have sufficient income or support. Those who had been entirely dependent on a spouse for survival often suffered when forced to live on their own. It should come as no surprise that widows fill up parish charity rolls, or make up the majority of women who reported no specific occupation and reported very low incomes in tax rolls. Widows who did name an occupation in tax rolls frequently identified food sales or textile work such as spinning—work that required little or no training and rarely paid well. Some widows, along with unmarried women of all ages, found roommates in order to share the costs of living. Such an adaptation to circumstance, however, did not usually change the work a woman did. A woman with a long-standing trade of her own was likely to keep it to the end of her days.

LEGAL RIGHTS

Women in the eighteenth century often had fewer legal rights and protections than men. Most women were considered wards of their fathers until they had reached the age of majority, usually set at twenty-five for women, or until they married. Once married, a woman was considered "covered" by her husband's legal status and guardianship. The limitations on a woman's legal status were related to the traditional patriarchal household, of course. Men had the responsibility to care for every member of the household, in most places, and that responsibility came with a certain amount of authority over those who made up their households. Thus, the law codes in operation in this era assumed that most women were under the authority and protection of a man.[10] At the same time, however, laws had to accommodate the many people who were not members of a traditional, male-headed household. The "age of majority," for example, was a concept that recognized that some people might not be married before fully achieving adulthood, and emancipated those people from the control of their parents once they had reached a certain age.[11]

Much of the customary law code of Brittany was somewhat unusual with regard to women. This province was one of only six or seven in France that, along with the central code of Paris, practiced what was known as "partible inheritance," in which brothers and sisters inherited equally from their parents.[12] In other parts of France and in much of the rest of Europe, it was common to favor sons over daughters, or the eldest son over all other children. Inheritance rights determine one's access to resources, and the fact that women in Brittany were assured of a portion of the family's property meant they had some chance of establishing themselves financially. Louise Le Mace, who was identified as "the oldest daughter" in the statement signed by her parents, was living alone in her parents' house after they had died. That property, plus her training and guild membership, likely meant she did not have to even consider marriage unless it appealed to her. Even women from more modest families could hope to improve their lives through inheritance. In 1713 in the city of Rennes, a young woman named Janne Ubedal "left the life of a servant" and sought to remake herself as a merchant by buying the shop of an elderly widow.[13] Ubedal had only been waiting for an inheritance from her parents in the countryside to change her life.

There were disadvantages to the system of partible inheritance, of course. The fact that every child inherited equally often meant that each generation of a family got smaller and smaller portions. Wills from the eighteenth century show that it was not unusual for someone to inherit one room of a house and a section of a garden. If someone died without children, their goods reverted back to their parents or siblings. This sometimes led to complicated legal formulas, such as the one found in the contract outlining what Anne and Francoise Leprieur were entitled to in 1737: "Anne and Francoise Leprieur, both unmarried women in their majority, are each one-eighth heirs to Sieur Jacques Leprieur, deceased merchant of Nantes, their father, and also one-seventh heirs of the late Janne Leprieur, their sister, who was also a one-eighth heir to Jacques, their father, and also one-sixth heirs to their other sister, the late Marie Anne Leprieur, who was also a one-eighth heir to their father and a one-seventh heir to their sister Janne."[14]

This confusing system, meant to protect all lawful heirs, had the potential to leave the uninformed quite vulnerable.[15] Furthermore, heirs were often quick to claim what was theirs, so successful merchants and artisans made sure to distinguish their earned property from their inherited property. That is why Louise Le Mace's parents signed a declaration protecting her goods, and why similar declarations are fairly common in the archives of Brittany. A woman who had earned a living had to know how to protect herself legally, or risk losing everything.

Another unique feature of Breton law was the right of a couple to wait for a year and a day after the wedding to establish "marital community of property." This meant that the bride and groom could each manage their respective properties separately for a time before pooling their resources. Doing so gave each of them time to settle debts and business arrangements before their actions would have any lasting impact on the livelihood of the other. Brides in Brittany could potentially enter a marriage with a guild membership, shop inventory, or property inherited from parents, and the delay in recognizing marital community probably served to avoid unnecessary complications. Women with trades and property could protect their own interests because they could buy, sell, and make contracts regarding their assets without the interference of a spouse. The practice also protected both the bride and groom from assuming responsibility for any debts their spouses might have had at the time of the wedding. Once the couple had established themselves, presumably during that first year of marriage, they would combine their goods, funds, and obligations.

While divorce was forbidden in early modern France, it was possible to obtain a separation. One could either ask for a simple "separation of goods," in which marital community was dissolved but the couple stayed together, or a full "separation of goods and bodies," in which the couple lived apart. Separation was granted only in extreme circumstances, and was somewhat rare. The concept is important in a discussion of the family economy model and women's work identity, however, because it offers yet another way in which the traditional household arrangement did not suit everyone. A full separation was only granted in cases in which the male head of household was both physically violent and financially irresponsible.[16] The law recognized that such a man was not living up to his obligations as a "patriarch," and permitted his wife to get away from him. If a man was merely financially irresponsible, judges preferred to grant a simple separation of goods. This put the wife largely in charge of managing the household and kept her property out of the hands of her husband. In such cases, a woman with a trade of her own or a vested interest in the family business had every reason to assume control of the resources.

Generally speaking, a married woman needed her husband's cooperation, if not his outright authorization, to conduct business of any kind. Legal contracts signed by a married woman often indicated whether or not she was operating with her husband's authorization. Even the contract signed by Louis Le Mace and Louise Calvarin on behalf of their daughter acknowledged that Calvarin was signing with her husband's consent. Men who were going to be absent for long periods of time, like sailors and soldiers, signed documents called "procurations" that gave their wives blanket authority over the household and marital property for the duration. In spite of the need for authorization in almost all matters, however, a woman had the right to work as a merchant "without her husband and without his authorization."[17] The law code assumed that a wife's commerce was separate from that of her husband, and that she alone would be responsible for her debts and contracts. However, if a woman worked as a merchant with her husband's explicit permission, then her debts and contracts became their joint responsibility.

In daily practice, the issues of authorization and a wife's business obligations were probably handled informally. In a strict legal sense, however, there were hundreds of potential pitfalls inherent in this contradiction—that a woman was required to get her husband's consent to make any and all contracts unless she was acting as a merchant, in which case his toleration of her commerce served as implicit consent. This legal paradox made it possible for some couples to manipulate circumstances to their advantage, making whichever claim would be of most benefit to them. In some cases, no doubt, it made more sense to follow the law that set a distinct legal and commercial identity for a wife who practiced her own trade.[18] But even members of well-off two-income households might at times have found it advantageous to nullify "unauthorized" contracts in order to recoup a loss. A wife's independent work identity might have been, therefore, most beneficial as something she could assume or reject at will for the good of the household, and not simply an advantage she used for herself.

FORMAL AND INFORMAL WORK

Women worked in a wide range of formal and informal ways, both inside and outside of the traditional family structure. Most production in the preindustrial era was regulated by the guilds, trade organizations found in almost every European city. Each guild was associated with a particular art, and members worked their way up the ranks from apprentice to master. Most guilds were male-dominated and organized around the traditional family workshop. A master carpenter, for example, would have operated out of a workshop at his home and trained apprentices and journeymen in the craft. The master's wife would have managed the home and shop as a unit, feeding children and employees alike. She might have even dealt with customers or kept the books for her husband's shop. This is why many guilds recognized a master's widow as a member of the association even if she, herself, did not know the art. A widow could often keep her late husband's shop open and preserve it until one of her children could take over. This role for women conforms well to the family economy model.

Not all guilds followed this traditional family structure, however. Depending on the art in question, guilds could support a mixed male-female membership or even, in the rare case, an exclusively female membership. The guilds that admitted women tended to be associated with what might be called "women's work"—that is, work involving food, cloth, clothing, or the care of infants, the sick, and the elderly. It was very uncommon for women to be admitted into guilds that were very prestigious, such as the apothecaries or goldsmiths, or into trades that were connected to the masculine sphere, such as the making of saddles and weapons.[19] As we have already seen, Louise Le Mace was a member of the tailor's guild in Quimper. Tailor's guilds were frequently mixed for a variety of reasons. The care and production of clothing was something women had historically done for their own households, so it was a respectable trade for a woman. Modesty also inspired women customers to seek out women tailors when they needed something made for themselves or their children. Thus, a woman seeking a trade was likely to find training and support as a tailor or in some other art considered appropriate for women.

There were a number of guilds in Brittany that accepted women as members on the basis of their work and not only through marriage to a master. In addition to the tailor's guilds in Quimper, Rennes, and Nantes, the merchant's associations in these cities also admitted women as full members. Female merchants were often petty traders and shopkeepers who specialized in a small number of items: cloth, buttons, and ribbons, for example, or butter and cheese. In Nantes, the presence of women is particularly notable in the guild organization for *fripiers*, or junk dealers.[20] This was a low-ranking trade, and business was easy enough to conduct on a small scale, but literacy was a requirement for guild membership. Dealers in secondhand goods had to avoid accusations of selling stolen merchandise, so their written records had to be especially precise.

Mixed guilds in France did not always admit women as full members, and those that did sometimes placed restrictions on women in the guild. Women could only work on women's and children's clothing in the tailor's guild in Nantes, for example, and could be barred from working if found making men's clothing. The tailor's guild in Paris admitted women only in the specific rank of seamstress-tailor, distinguishing them from male tailors, who were able to work on a wider range of products. In that city, women had a strong enough presence to form a separate guild for seamstresses, making the mixed tailor's guild less of an issue.[21] Many guilds across France prohibited women from serving as officers of the guild or attending assemblies. Furthermore, many guilds stipulated that even a woman who had been admitted on her own merits had to renounce her membership if she married outside of the trade. This was meant to keep the guild and its secrets in tight control, but it was also a recognition that most wives worked to support the work of their husbands. Generally speaking, formal work in the guild system reflected the characteristics of the traditional family economy model.

Guilds may have had the authority to oversee production and retail trade, but they could not maintain control over everything. Training and guild membership were reserved for those with the means to pay for them, and that meant that a good many people worked outside of the guild system. This is especially true for a province like Brittany, where the urban areas tended to be smaller and somewhat more isolated than other French cities. Even Nantes, a port and one of the largest commercial centers in the region, supported a fraction of the guilds found in a metropolis like Paris. Guild officers and market police in Breton towns did their best to reign in unlicensed merchants and artisans, but to no avail. The number of people claiming a formal occupation in the tax rolls always far outnumbered the number of people who belonged to that guild. The tailor's guild in Rennes, for example, only listed forty-two female members in 1777, but the tax roll for that year identified 102 female tailors.[22]

There are many good reasons for workers of both sexes to have remained outside of the guilds. Guild membership carried certain costs, as noted above, and several restrictions. Members had to be certified Catholics and preference was given to those born locally. Migrants from the countryside or from other cities were limited in their formal work options. Guild membership also locked workers into a particular trade when economic reality often called for great flexibility. When the marketplace was overrun with butter vendors, for example, the informal petty merchant could switch to a different product. Informal work could also be performed as needed, for supplemental income when times were hard.

Sources for the port city of Brest reveal that most of the bakers were married women whose husbands were at sea, and that most of them worked too inconsistently for the police to keep track of them all.[23]

Rural areas operated under a different system entirely. Guilds rarely existed outside of the cities and exerted very little control in the countryside.[24] The only possible exception to this rule in Brittany would be the areas devoted to textile production, because rural spinners and weavers had to meet the requirements of the cloth markets in the big cities.[25] It does seem that most rural dwellers worked best as a family unit. Farmers and weavers alike depended on the work of every member of the household to get things done.[26] A sexual division of labor existed as well, ensuring that the work was done efficiently. In a weaving household, women and children did all the spinning so that men could spend as much time as possible at the loom. It took several spinners to produce enough yarn to keep a weaver occupied, and spinning on a simple distaff could be done simultaneously with other tasks.

In the homes of weavers, as in the typical guild-run urban workshop, the family economy model is probably appropriate. A male head of household worked at a particular trade, and the work of all other members of the household served to support him in that trade for the success of the family unit. However, as we saw above, even the small villages of Brittany included a number of households that fell outside of the traditional model: between 20 and 30 percent of households in rural areas were headed by a woman, either widowed or never married. These women must have supported themselves independently through an occupation, rents on inherited property, or a combination of the two sources of income. Even in the village of Roche-Bernard, where the population never topped three hundred people in the eighteenth century, women headed 20 percent of the taxed households. Of these women, 10 percent identified themselves as retailers, 8 percent made clothing, 12 percent were in food-related trades, and a handful were spinners or weavers. The rest did not name an occupation, and likely had some other source of income.[27]

WORK IDENTITY

It is difficult to establish the work identities of women in the past for a variety of reasons. First of all, it is impossible to know with certainty how people felt about their lives. This is true even if they left first-person sources, such as journals and letters—something that women, especially women in the working classes, did not do. Most of the traditional historical sources were written by and about men. Second, "identity" is a complex phenomenon based on multiple factors that change over time. Both men and women probably defined themselves at any given time by their communities, their families, and their language, religion, and ethnicity as much as by the work that they did. Finally, the work that women did was bound up with ideas about what was "appropriate" for them. Most women who identified occupations in the sources were in trades often associated with women's work in the home—food and clothing. This might suggest a real limitation on a woman's ability to choose her work and control her own fate.

In order to study women's work identities, then, we must glean what we can from the sources available. In 1986, Natalie Zemon Davis proposed that work identities for women were much "thinner" than those of men because their work changed so often to meet the needs of the patriarchal household.[28] She identified the masculine work identity using a set of characteristics that included formal training in a profession, public signs of that profession, such as guild membership, and a tendency for men to identify themselves by that trade even if they no longer practiced it. The sources in Brittany attest to the fact that women, too, displayed these signs of a work identity even if most households conformed to the traditional family economy model. Formal apprenticeships for girls may have been less common than those for boys, but they did exist. The mixed guilds of Rennes, Nantes, and Quimper required an investment in training for all of their members.

Women in Brittany clearly made known their work identity. Guild membership itself was a public sign of belonging to a profession, of course, and we have seen that women belonged to certain guilds. Any explicit declaration of status was also a public sign of identity, such as the credentials that certified midwives hung on their doorposts to advertise their services. But perhaps we could accept any self-identification with a trade as a demonstration of work identity. When asked, either for tax purposes or in filling out a legal contract, women identified themselves by an occupation if they had one.[29] Those who maintained an occupation but were not members of any guild defended their right to work when confronted by guild officers and police. Unlicensed tailors and merchants did not lack for a work identity just because their work was informal; they often rejected the authority of the guild to oversee their work, though usually without success.

Finally, just as Davis found for the men in her study of Lyon, the sources for

Brittany reveal some cases in which women identified with a trade that they were not actually practicing for some reason. During an economic downturn at mid-century, for example, merchants of both sexes (*marchands* and *marchandes*) in the village of Broons reported that they did not live "by their commerce, but by odd jobs."[30] A woman named La Duverger identified herself in the tax roll for Rennes in 1777 as "a spinner, selling mustard."[31] Occasionally, women identified with trades that they did not yet practice, signaling an ambition to change. In 1709, the Widow Chevalier in Rennes was taxed as "a spinner, becoming an embroiderer."[32] Anne Letournay, the wife of a musician named Jean Dubois, stated in testimony for the police that she was "becoming a merchant." Two years later, she was identified simply as a merchant.[33] Even those in the process of changing from one trade to another displayed an identification with a particular occupation, giving us a glimpse of how they saw themselves

Only a small percentage of women kept a formally recognized profession from early education through marriage and into widowhood. Thus, even in Brittany, the evidence supports Davis's thesis that women were less likely than men to have a clear work identity. Furthermore, those women who demonstrated the marks of a work identity tended to be found in a very limited number of trades, and only in those identified as "women's work." This could be interpreted as a limitation on women and yet another example of how their lives were shaped by others. However, if true work identities existed primarily in trades accepted as "feminine arts," then perhaps we can acknowledge a distinctly *feminine* work identity that would have been recognized both by the women who worked and by a society that accepted women's work as natural. That is to say, the occupation a woman chose would have been part of her identity as a woman and was not something distinct from her role in the home. A feminine work identity need not be incompatible with the other identities usually assigned to women. The identity of "daughter" or "mother" might also include the ability to work, survive, and support a family. After all, even laundresses and porters had rent to pay and children to feed.

CONCLUSION

Overall, the family economy model is appropriate for understanding the working lives of people in the premodern era. However, as the case of Brittany demonstrates, the model does not tell the whole story. The working lives of women, in particular, are rendered invisible by this model because it leaves no room for the study of those who fell outside of the traditional patriarchal household. Many people lived on their own or with roommates, and even those who were part of a traditional household did not necessarily share in the work of the family unit. A rich and thorough history must account for the variety of life.

Naturally, we historians have viewed women based on readily available sources, and it is true that many premodern and early modern sources seem to define women by their relations to others. Thus, it was easy to conclude that women had no distinct identity. In some tax rolls, for example, married women are invisible and widows are grouped together at the end with no information on their occupations or sources of income. And so, historians wrote about women who had no identity but their marital status. However, a different approach to the sources can reveal much about the hidden identities of women. We must delve deeper into a wider variety of source material. Tax rolls, law codes, contracts, and police reports, by their very nature, give us a cross section of society and are the sort of documents that therefore must include women on their own terms. Only when we have opened our eyes to untapped sources of information can we begin to unearth the stories of those who were invisible in the old models and the typical sources.

It may well turn out that there is no one model that could incorporate or even help us categorize women's experiences in the early modern world. Models can be useful in thinking through general patterns, but at the same time they can obfuscate data and hence distort our understanding of the past. Our aim is to reveal the past to the best of our abilities based on all of the sources available to us, especially when those sources confound our expectations.

NOTES

1. Notarized statement, 4 E 221/120, Archives départmentales du Finisterre, Quimper, France.

2. Clare Haru Crowston, *Fabricating Women: The Seamstresses of Old Regime France, 1675–1791* (Durham: Duke Univ. Press, 2001).

3. Daryl M. Hafter, *Women at Work in Preindustrial France* (University Park: Pennsylvania State Univ. Press, 2007).

4. Janine M. Lanza, *From Wives to Widows in Early Modern Paris: Gender, Economy, and Law* (Aldershot, Eng.: Ashgate, 2007).

5. James R. Farr, *The Work of France: Labor and Culture in Early Modern Times, 1350–1800* (Lanham: Rowman and Littlefield, 2008).

6. Corporate *capitation* tax rolls, C 2146, Archives départementales d'Ille-et-Vilaine, Rennes, France (henceforth, ADIV). The guild's registers for the 1730s and 1740s have been lost.

7. Household *capitation* tax rolls, C 4128 and C 4129, ADIV.

8. Household *capitation* tax rolls, C 4129, ADIV.

9. Household *capitation* tax rolls, B 3583, Archives départmentales de la Loire-Atlantique, Nantes, France (henceforth, ADLA). Some guilds like Rouen's lingères en neuf prohibited mistresses' husbands from participating in their trade. Hafter, *Women at Work,* 99–100.

10. "Authorization" and incapacity of wives in *Dictionnaire raisonné des domains et droits domaniaux,* Tome 1 (Rouen: de L'imp. de Jacques-Joseph Boullenger, 1762), 251.

11. Robert Joseph Pothier, "Division of persons by age and sex," in *Oeuvres posthumes de M. Pothier. Tome second, Contenent les traits des successions, des propres, des donations testamentaires, des donations entre vifs, des personnes & des choses* (Paris: Chez de Bure, 1778), 602.

12. The classic reference is Emanuel LeRoy Ladurie, "A System of Customary Law: Family Structure and Inheritance Customs in Sixteenth-Century France," *Family and Society: Selections from the Annales, économies, sociétés, civilizations,* ed. Robert Forster and Orest Ranum (Baltimore: Johns Hopkins Univ. Press, 1976), 89. Also, commentary in *Coutumes générales du pays et duche de Bretagne* (Rennes: P. Garnier, 1656), Articles 587 and 588.

13. Statement to police, 3 B 1451, ADIV.

14. Notarized testament, 6 E 696, Archives départmentales du Morbihan, Vannes, France.

15. For the confusing nature of inheritance codes, see the tables of fractions concerning succession in Normandy in *Répertoire universel et raisonné de jurisprudence civile, criminelle, canonique et bénéficiale,* vol. 16 (Paris: Visse, 1785), 593–596.

16. Entries on "Séparation de biens" and "Séparation de corps et d'habitation" in *Répertoire universel et raisonné de jurisprudence civile, criminelle, canonique et bénéficiale,* vol. 16 (Paris: Visse, 1785), 205, 225. See also Julie Hardwick, "Seeking Separations: Gender, Marriages, and Household Economies in Early Modern France," *French Historical Studies* 21, no. 1 (winter 1998): 157–180.

17. *Coutumes générales du pays et duché de Bretagne* (1656), Article 448.

18. I develop this more fully in *Women's Work and Identity in Eighteenth-Century Brittany* (Aldershot, Eng.: Ashgate, 2007), 84–87.

19. See the discussion in Locklin, *Women's Work,* 48, and in Hafter, *Women at Work,* 42–43.

20. Locklin, *Women's Work,* 50. Also see the *fripiers'* guild inspector reports for the 1740s, Archives Municipales de Nantes HH 137, nos. 2 and 15.

21. Crowston, *Fabricating Women,* 190, 214.

22. Tailors deliberations and receptions, 1733–1786, 5 E 25, ADIV; compared to household *capitation* tax rolls for 1777, C 4043.

23. Report of the *subdelegué* at Brest to the intendant at Rennes, 1748, C 1453, ADIV.

24. Farr, *The Work of France,* 26–27.

25. Jean Tanguy, *Quand la toile va: L'industrie toilière bretonne du 16ᵉ au 18ᵉ siècle* (Rennes: Éditions Apogée, 1995), 50.

26. Abel Poitrineau, *Ils travaillant la France: Métiers et mentalités du XVIᵉ au XIXᵉ siècle* (Paris: Armand Cole, 1992), 45; Yann Brekilien, *Les paysans bretons aux XIXᵉ siècle* (Paris: Hachette, 1966), 40.

27. Household *capitation* tax rolls, B 3502 (1720) and 3522 (1753), ADLA; and C 4144 (1738), ADIV.

28. Natalie Zemon Davis, "Women in the Crafts in Sixteenth-Century Lyon," in *Women and Work in Preindustrial Europe,* ed. Barbara Hanawalt (Bloomington: Indiana Univ. Press, 1986), 169.

29. For examples, see James B. Collins's essay in this volume.

30. Intendant's report to king, C 1449, ADIV.

31. Household *capitation* tax rolls, C 4043, ADIV.

32. Household *capitation* tax rolls, C 3995, ADIV.

33. Statement to police, B 5851, ADLA.

THE BUSINESS OF BEING KEPT

Elite Prostitution as Work

Nina Kushner

Ⅰ N eighteenth-century Paris, *dames entretenues* (kept women), alternatively known as *femmes galantes,* were women who provided sexual and companionate services to men of the elite in exchange for full or partial maintenance. What distinguished these women from the many others who had extramarital affairs for financial gain was what might best be characterized as the "formal informal" nature of their engagements. Their relations with their patrons were governed by an oral contract whose form was fixed. The contract was not legally binding, but mistresses and patrons followed it nonetheless. It was in part the contract that made dames entretenues professional mistresses. It was also the fact that being kept was what paid the bills and defined the place of these women in society. Femmes galantes moved from patron to patron, driven by unemployment as well as by the possibility of a better employer, one who paid more, demanded less, or who for any reason was a more attractive prospect. Moreover, contemporaries understood being kept as an occupation.[1] The police, for example, who had about one thousand dames entretenues under surveillance over a twenty-two-year period at mid-century, compiled annual lists of kept women and their patrons. Inspector Jean-Baptiste Meusnier wrote in one such report that Demoiselle Rolle "didn't have anybody." By way of explanation, he offered, "she is ugly."[2] Rolle's inability to secure a patron did not compromise her status as a kept woman; it only made her an unsuccessful one.

"Formal informal" might also characterize the market in which kept women sold themselves. Specific conventions governed not just the instrument of exchange, the oral contract, but how these exchanges were tendered, what was sold, and by whom. Yet, like these contracts, none of these conventions had a basis in law. Similarly, the market itself, despite being recognized by contemporaries and being subject to an intense police surveillance, was hardly regulated.

Professional mistresses provide an interesting case study of women and work for a number of reasons. As single women, many were financially successful, at least for a time. Most were able to earn enough to support themselves during their work lives. Some did so in luxury. That success, when it occurred, elevated these women to positions of power within their own families. Yet the earnings of these women were the product of illicit—though not illegal—activity. As the essays in this volume show, so much of women's experiences as economic actors was determined by the legal and regulatory frameworks in which they operated, because these systems shaped labor practices in the Old Regime. In the world of regulated work, women were able to engage in particular economic activities by taking advantage of or manipulating loopholes in regulatory systems designed to exclude them, or they were able to participate directly in those activities because they were specifically granted the right or privilege to do so. Such elasticity makes it difficult to assess women's economic activity within illicit or illegal economies, where regulation was either absent or entirely ignored. What sorts of opportunities did such work—prostitution, smuggling, or street crime, for example—provide for women? What factors shaped or limited their chances? We might wonder still further about the role women played more generally within these "industries."[3]

Using dossiers the Paris police compiled at mid-century on the capital's dames entretenues, this essay looks at the business of being kept and how the particular constructs that regulated the exchange of money and services shaped patron-mistress relationships and contributed to the financial success and agency of professional mistresses.[4]

THE DEMIMONDE: AN OPEN MARKET

Dames entretenues were a fixture in a well-defined, very visible, elite sexual subculture, the demimonde.[5] In using the word "demimonde," I am referring to a sexual market in which certain services were sold, the customs and institutions that shaped that market's operation, and the community of individuals who participated in it. There were a great many eyes scrutinizing the demimonde in the mid-eighteenth century. These included commentators, dramatists, novelists, satirists, and journalists—those compilers of the *nouvelles à la main* (news sheets) like the *Correspondance secrète* and the *Mémoires secrets*—and, of course, the police. In fact, the police devoted an entire unit (the Département des Femmes Galantes) to the demimonde. Part of its mission was to regulate the elite brothels, determining who could operate one and where, and who could work in such establishments. They also expected brothels to be good neighbors, to keep the noise down, and to prevent rowdies from gathering in the street. In exchange for toleration, elite madams were required to supply the police with a steady stream of intelligence on their clients, their workers, and many other men and women in the demimonde. A number supplied weekly reports detailing their brothel operations. Police intervention, however, was less extensive than the rules might suggest. In principle, brothels could not take girls and women from middle- or upper-class families, girls who were too young (twelve seemed to be the bottom limit), or girls who were virgins. In practice, while the police did stop the prostitution of girls from good families and the very young, they stood by and allowed madams to broker virgin sales and to keep women whose parents were looking for them, just as long as these madams kept the police informed of their doings.

Most police efforts, however, were not focused on the brothels, but instead were invested in the surveillance of kept women. From 1749 through 1771, first Jean-Baptiste Meusnier and later Louis Marais, the inspectors successively in charge of the unit assigned to the demimonde, watched about a thousand women, filling thousands of folio pages on their doings. Meusnier built a dossier system, opening files on kept women and adding reports regularly or when he thought something notable. Beyond surveillance, police interaction with kept women was limited, at least compared to the policing of prostitution in the nineteenth century.[6] It is clear that the inspectors readily took advantage of the sexual and possibly financial perks of their positions. But being "policed," in this instance, did not include forcing kept women to conform to standards of sexual decorum external to the demimonde. Rather, these inspectors functioned more as magistrates responsible for making sure the demimonde adhered to its own rules. They mediated between the demimonde and other communities when necessary. And as far as we can tell, all that surveillance, which recorded in exacting detail who exchanged what with whom, was for no specific purpose. It seems to have been part of an expanding effort by the state and the Paris police to make the city more transparent, to know what was happening especially in communities whose members or activities fell outside of natural hierarchies of control. Dames entretenues were often outside the regulation imposed on women in the household, the manufactory, the guild, or the brothel. They were interacting with a portion of the social, political, and financial male elite, which had shifted its center of sociability away from the watchful eye of the king at Versailles to Paris. Collectively, the dames entretenues were the recipients of a great deal of wealth, much of it coming from important families. The police kept track of the demimonde—this elite sex market and community—as they did many other markets and communities.[7]

Effectively, then, kept women operated in what I call an open market. While prostitution was illegal, and the police referred to kept women as prostitutes, they did not treat them as such. Being kept was not illegal; rather, it was illicit, censured by social standards. The police almost never arrested dames entretenues. There are barely a handful of arrests mentioned in the police reports. And when they did, it was for crimes unrelated to prostitution. In fact, while the police forced the brothels to operate by certain rules, they gave dames entretenues a great deal of leeway in their daily activities, watching and doing nothing as these women committed fraud or bankrupted the sons of wealthy families, even as parents tried to stop the financial hemorrhage. Nor is there evidence to suggest that the police tried to limit the total number of kept women, as guilds limited the number of mistresses or masters. Any teenager or woman could contract a patron-mistress relationship, provided she was not too young, or from a "good" family. There was a regular inflow of new women and girls into the demimonde. Some turned to prostitution out of desperation. Others were recruited and proffered by madams and self-appointed pimps, or by parents looking to make a quick livre or establish a new line of income.

Established kept women had to compete for patrons with a constant influx of teenagers, who because of their age and health, and because they were being marketed, were often considered more desirable.[8] Madams competed against each other for access to new sex workers. They were looking for women and girls to staff their brothels, which were fairly small establishments, and for whom the madams could act as agents, brokering them into patron-mistress or other contractual sexual engagements. Most kept women established and negotiated their own relationships, but for the madams, brokering was an important part of their businesses. Kept women worked in a sexual market that had no artificial limits and that was largely unburdened by regulation. It was not a *free* market, however, because of the heavy role of custom in governing exchange.

For one group of professional mistresses, however, there was another set of rules with which to contend. About a fifth of those women under police surveillance were in the theater.[9] They were singers, actresses, and especially dancers in the various Comédies and in the Royal Opera. Some, like Rosalie Astraudi, were stars of the stage. But their positions in the theater should not confuse their status as dames entretenues. With the exception of the Comédie-Française, theater women were paid poorly. A principal dancer might earn as much as 3,000 livres a year, while some had no salary at all.[10] They relied on patrons for financial support, and moved from patron to patron as did other kept women. Their relationships were similarly structured by the contract and with elite men of means. Their position in the theater enhanced, rather than limited, their opportunities as kept women. Theater dames entretenues earned more on average from sex work than those who were not in the theater, and for this reason many kept women worked to get onto the stage. Being inscribed on the Opera rolls also afforded mistresses some legal protection against families or patrons who wished to have them incarcerated. The Opera even lent sums on occasion to help its employees cover debts. What the Opera did not do was police its workers' activities, beyond forbidding women from having sex with their patrons in the actual theater.

SUCCESS, OF A SORT

Within this open market kept women achieved success, of a sort. Those who remained connected to their parents became their family's primary breadwinner; their efforts and not those of the father were the center of the family's efforts and economy. In every case for which we have evidence, these women were eventually able to mitigate familial exploitation and translate their earning power into a position of authority within the family. Often they became the head of household. Many widowed or single mothers came to play support roles, working as cooks, maids, or child minders in their daughters' households. Some kept women, like Demoiselle Astraudi or Louise Règis, a dancer in the Opera, supported their entire families, parents and siblings, paying the rent and the bills. Others lived with sisters whom they similarly employed as domestic help. For a small group of kept women, this was truly a remarkable achievement, having begun their careers in elite prostitution around the age of fourteen as veritable chattel, illegally sold by their parents—usually mothers—to brothels or to patrons.[11]

Dames entretenues had a harder time with husbands. Those kept women who became elite prostitutes after they married were dominated by their spouses, who acted at worst as pimps and at best as financial leeches. Leaving these men was not always easy, as some husbands were disinclined to give up the income a wife's prostitution generated. Marie-Anne Pàges (known professionally as Demoiselle Deschamps) complained to the police that her husband regularly promised to "resume his rights" unless she gave him money, and she always did.[12] Despite damaging behavior like this, I found no evidence of legal separations (*séparation de biens*) among the women. Obtaining a full separation (*séparation de corps et de biens*) could take some time. Hence, while these women were not able to translate their earnings into positions of power within their marriages, most were able eventually to establish their own households, after which they tended to earn a great deal more.

We know less about the marital dynamics of those women who married later, when they were already established as dames entretenues, aside from the fact that they were often wealthier than their spouses. Many of them married men who were unemployed. That these women continued to work suggests it was the wife's career, and not that of the husband, that was the focus of the couple's efforts. But what this meant in terms of their daily life, we simply do not know.

We should not, however, measure success only in terms of family dynamics and the structure of the family economy. In financial terms, these women were successful since they were able to support themselves. Most literature on working women in the eighteenth century has stressed how difficult and unusual this was, arguing that marriage was essential for adult women from lower social echelons. Unmarried women would most likely find themselves impoverished, at best working as servants in the households of siblings.[13] Those industries in which single women could find employment rarely paid a living wage. While this picture still largely obtains, more recently a number of studies have been published, including the essays in this volume, showing examples of women who were self-supporting.[14] Among them, kept women were unusual because under the best of conditions they could live in appreciably better material circumstances than those in which they were raised.

Exactly how much better, however, is difficult to calculate. After death inventories are most useful in this regard. Marie-Joseph Laguerre, for example, had 300,000 livres at her death.[15] But the demimondaine practice of regularly changing names has made such documents difficult to find. Other sources, such as marriage contracts and reports of robberies, function more as snapshots, indicating wealth at a particular moment. For example, in 1762, at the height of her career, Demoiselle Lacour reported a theft of 50,000 livres worth of items, mainly jewelry, including a diamond necklace (11,500 livres) and a pair of earrings (9,600 livres).[16] Yet, these women were rarely as rich as these examples suggest. Like every other Parisian, dames entretenues lived on credit and sometimes owned only portions of those items in their possession. The dancer Marie-Louise Denis, for example, was arrested for debt in October 1768 because she had paid back only 4,200 of the 8,200 livres she had borrowed to buy a pair of earrings.[17] Many mistresses, even the most famous and highest paid, owed rent to landlords. More generally, the material wealth of kept women necessarily expanded and contracted, sometimes dramatically. Rarely were dames entretenues continuously employed, forcing them to pawn items to pay bills. Some were terrible money managers or got caught up in the relentless acquisition of luxury items characteristic of the demimonde. Like the aristocrats they copied, many of these women built material fortunes on platforms of debt. Kept women were obsessed with things. Demoiselle Deschamps, who had been *maîtresse-en-titre* to the duc d'Orléans, bought copiously on credit and was probably able to do so because of the standing of her patrons; the police estimated that she owed 300,000 livres "on the streets of Paris" in 1755.[18] In fact, one hallmark of the most wealthy dames entretenues—the dozen or so hyper elite mistresses like Deschamps who had *hôtels* (urban mansions) and fancy carriages—was their riches-to-rags trajectory.

Moreover, we must also consider the durability of this wealth. When kept women hit their late twenties and reached the age of retirement from elite prostitution, their choices were grim. Few were able to work as dames entretenues for much longer. Some married or found themselves in stable, though irregular relationships. The small minority who had saved opened dress shops or became madams themselves. Others had no choice but to continue working as prostitutes, even as age and disease decreased their sexual capital, forcing them from the top of the prostitution hierarchy to the streets. Hence, any assessment of wealth and thus "success" must consider its duration. Elite prostitutes, unlike many other women workers, necessarily had short careers in an industry that made no provision for them as they aged.

Yet, despite this, many lived in comfort, if not luxury, for the duration of their work lives. The hyper elite mistresses possessed considerable material wealth, owning houses, carriages, sumptuous furnishings, extensive collections of silver plate and jewelry, vast wardrobes, and numerous decorative objects like snuff boxes as well as larger works of art. Almost all were members of the Opera and other theatrical companies. The police reported that the duc d'Orléans and the comte de Coubert each bought and remodeled a house for Deschamps. The financier Auguste-Simon Brissart was rumored to have spent 500,000 livres on her. Coubert paid her a monthly stipend of 2,400 livres, almost four times the average for dames entretenues in this period. The police reported in 1755 that Deschamps showed up at the Opera wearing what they estimated to be 100,000 livres in diamonds and noted in their monthly reports on her that she had been given several carriages.[19] According to her marriage contract, the singer Cecile Rotisset de Romainville had a house, 100,000 livres in cash, silver plate worth 22,045 livres, and an extensive wardrobe. Her entire dowry was worth 100,000 livres.[20]

Often the furniture, at least of the hyper elite, was more expensive than that of court nobles, and they bought and changed their furnishings more frequently. Kathryn Norberg, in a study of the possessions of a few members of this elite group, noted that in 1784 the furniture of the Opera dancer Marie-Madeleine Guimard was worth 27,000 livres, while the Princess Kinsky ordered eighty-five pieces to fully furnish her house at only 11,000 livres.[21] The wealth of kept women was not just in furnishings and jewels. Many of them accrued *rentes* (annuities) from their male protectors. Romainville apparently had 30,000 livres in rente, although usually rente was gifted in increments of 1,500 livres or less, given as the *Étrennes* (New Year's gift) or on the birth of a child.[22] Sometimes patrons gave rentes in larger amounts. The duc de Mazarin gifted 3,000 livres in *rentes viagères* (an annuity paid annually until its owner dies) to Marie Allard, a dancer in the Opera.[23]

By comparison, Christine Adams, in her study of the "provincial professional" Lamothe family, estimated that the total value of their property was 180,000 livres, including 15,000 livres invested annuities and 33,000 livres in furniture, clothing, and jewelry. On the revenues of 5,000 livres a year, all seven could live comfortably. Daniel Roche estimated that in the period 1775 to 1790 the combined value of the possessions of the average Parisian wage earner on his or her death was 1,776 livres, of which the furniture, clothes, linens, and silver were worth 86 livres.[24]

The best indication we have of the wealth and earning potential of dames entretenues, however, comes not from bits of information across a range of sources, but from the systematic reporting within a single source. The Département des Femmes Galantes tried to record the terms of the contracts these women negotiated with their patrons. As we shall see, the particular structure of these instruments enabled not just the accrual of wealth, but a certain measure of agency for women who, as prostitutes, had very little.

PATRON-MISTRESS "CONTRACTS"

The contract was a nonlegal verbal agreement negotiated and assented to by patron and mistress (or sometimes the mistress's parent) that stipulated remuneration.[25] The contract was standardized, and its terms, called *conditions,* were never particularly inventive. They simply settled the details of well-established categories. Future patron and mistress filled in the blanks. The most significant of these blanks were the *honoraires,* a monthly allowance given at the first of each month, usually a month in advance. Use of the word "honoraires" in this circumstance was ironic. It referred to fees given to "persons of honorable professions," such as barristers and medical doctors.[26] In a sample of 100 of these verbal agreements, as reported by the police, the size of honoraires varied from as little as 48 livres a month to as much as 2,400. The median stipend was 600 livres and the mean was 623 livres. Slightly more than three-quarters of these stipends were between 200 and 800 livres a month, with about a third being between 600 and 800 livres. Another fifth were between 800 and 1,200, and only in a few cases was a kept woman paid more than 1,200 livres a month.[27]

Comparatively, honoraires, to the degree that they can be considered wages, were high, especially when measured against what women from such backgrounds could typically earn. Wet nurses were paid 6 livres a month. Clare Crowston found that girls working for mistress seamstresses in skilled and semiskilled positions were paid between 36 and 100 livres a year. The annual salary of a shopgirl (*fille de boutique*) at a *marchande de modes* (fashion merchant) was between 150 and 200 livres. Honoraries were high even in comparison to what men from similar backgrounds earned. Michael Sonenscher estimated that a journeyman in the building trades earned up to 472 livres a year, and at mid-century a master silk maker might bring in 1,800 livres annually. By way of comparison, Robert Darnton reported that when Monsieur and Madame Suard earned an income of between 10,000 and 20,000 livres a year, they had reached the pinnacle of the literary world.[28]

Honoraires tended to remain fixed for the duration of a relationship. This practice was in keeping with the customs of pay in other industries. Michael Sonenscher showed that journeymen hired at a certain rate, whether into a workshop or for a particular project, were paid at that rate until they left, at which point they might be able to negotiate a different wage with a new employer.[29] One difference is that the patron-mistress contract was of an indefinite duration, giving the mistress little chance to push for a raise, at least in her honoraires. However, the complexity of the wage package afforded numerous opportunities for increasing rates of pay.

While honoraires were the foundation of the contract, patrons often contributed to their mistresses' maintenance in other ways. In about a fifth of the cases, new mistresses were given a *pot-de-vin,* a present that marked the beginning of the relationship; it could be considered an early modern signing bonus.[30] A pot-de-vin was received in advance of any sexual activity and generally was worth between five and ten times the monthly honoraires. At the low end (in other words, in contracts with honoraires of fewer than 100 livres), patrons generally offered their mistresses-to-be a dress or two. The powerful aristocrat, military leader, and well-known libertine comte de La Tour d'Auvergne (prince de Turenne), for example, promised the fifteen-year-old virgin Demoiselle Crousol some furniture, a dress, some linen, and some jewelry.[31] At the higher end (contracts with a minimum of 800 livres in monthly honoraires), the pot-de-vin was almost always a large sum of cash, occasionally supplemented by an expensive piece of jewelry.

There were other additional forms of compensation attached to the contract. In slightly fewer than a quarter of the contracts in my one hundred-contract sample, a patron agreed to pay the rent of his mistress's current apartment or to move her to a new one. In a different sample of contracts taken from the *Journal des inspecteurs,* the historian Erica-Marie Benabou found fifty-nine instances in which patrons paid rent at a cost ranging from 100 to 2,400 livres a year. (More than half were between 400 and 700 livres, a bit more than a quarter were between 800 and 1,300 livres, five were between 1,300 and 2,400, and three were more than 2,400 livres.) These figures show that even kept women in lower-end apartments still were housed better than most Parisians. In 1790, more than half of all Parisian residences were rented for between 42 and 200 livres, only 10 percent were between 400 and 600 livres, and 5.6 percent were between 600 and 800. Very few cost more than that.[32]

Rent was not the only additional form of compensation. In about a fifth of the cases in my sample, the patron bought his mistress new furnishings or promised to do so within one term (four months) of the beginning of the contract. Less often, a patron would agree specifically to provision the house, paying the grocery, butcher, wine, and fuel bills as well as servants' wages. Occasionally gifts were included in the contract formally, though neither patron nor mistress specified quantity or value. Sometimes such additional compensation was conditional and on a delayed schedule. Philippe Barthélemy Lévesque de Gravelles, *grand maître des eaux et forêts* (Grand Master of the Waters and Forests) of Touraine, Anjou, and Maine, had Demoiselle Gallodier, the younger, stay under the close watch of a matron, giving her a monthly salary but waiting to see how she behaved before paying off her debts and fulfilling other elements of the contract.[33]

Complex modes of pay, in which wages were combined with other forms of compensation, were standard in the eighteenth century. Many journeymen received meals and lodging. They could be paid both by piece and by time, and they might receive wages, raw materials, and finished products, or some combination of the three. Servants were paid wages and were given food, lodging, and clothes. Provincial actors and actresses were awarded per diems for extended performance runs in other cities.[34] These forms of remuneration were in addition to the rights and protections conferred on individuals by virtue of belonging to a workshop, household, or company.

From the perspective of work remuneration, however, patron-mistress contracts were significant in enabling dames entretenues to accrue wealth for several reasons, the first of which was because they never stipulated total pay. Rather, the agreement determined base pay. Whether "gifts" were formally included, they certainly were expected, and it was not uncommon for the value of gifts to increase as a relationship intensified. Patrons in love with their mistresses notoriously gave so extravagantly that they ruined themselves financially. Many mistresses actively encouraged gift-giving, coercing by whatever means an *entreteneur* (patron) into providing beyond what he had originally intended or expected to provide. This practice actually had a name, "drawing," as in withdrawing from a bank; the verb used was "*tirer.*" Writing about the separation of Monsieur de St. Jean and his mistress Demoiselle Pelissier, Inspector Meusnier speculated that the loss would be quite something for her because in "the space of six months that they were together, she had the talent to draw more than 8,000 livres from him."[35]

Gifts (and furnishings) were often the only means through which kept women could accrue wealth over the course of their careers. Dames entretenues rarely budgeted so as to put aside money from their honoraires. Moreover, their remuneration was designed to help set up and maintain households that were not necessarily for the benefit of the mistress and her financial future, but rather to entertain the patron and sometimes his friends. Gifts, on the other hand, were portable wealth. Patrons gave either material objects—such as dresses and clothing, linens, jewelry, silver plate, additional furniture, decorative objects—or rentes. As we shall see, possession of material gifts could be contested under certain circumstances. Rente, however, was established legally in the name of its beneficiary and, unlike a bowl, could not be retrieved easily. The document in which the duc de Mazarin gifted 3,000 livres in rente viagère to Marie Allard, a dancer in the Opera, declared that they were "for life, pure, simple and irrevocable."[36]

The enormous variety and profit potential in the receipt of gifts stands in sharp contrast to the specificity of payments in kind in other sorts of work contracts. For example, as a result of a dispute in 1786, corporate officials in Nantes's shoemaking guild specified what meals masters had to provide for their journeymen, "an *ordinaire* of two meals a day, with meat on the five *jours gras* and soup on the remaining *jours maigres*." Eventually the masters converted the meals into an extra wage of 10 sous.[37] Whether 10 sous was a fair price for those meals is not clear, but the effort to monetize the benefit, regardless of in whose favor, helps to specify its value. Meals made up a certain defined proportion of the total remuneration of journeyman shoemakers. In the case of patron-mistress contracts, both parties agreed more generally to "gifts" or "furnishings." The vagueness was often the root of serious conflict. If, while negotiating the contract, patron and mistress thought they had an understanding as to what constituted appropriate gifts, they frequently found themselves at odds over the issue within a few months. "Lack of generosity" and "failing to live up to promises" were the most common explanations given by dames entretenues for leaving patrons.

To what did a kept woman agree when she accepted a patron's honoraires and extras? The police never enumerated her responsibilities. This may have been a particular quirk of police reporting, but that is doubtful. It would have been uncharacteristic of the inspectors, who otherwise were focused so tightly on the details of the exchange between patron and mistress and who showed themselves in other instances to be comfortable describing sexual activity.[38] Perhaps mistress obligations were not reported because, unlike those of the patron, they were never spelled out. Rather, once a mistress agreed to accept honoraires, she agreed not to a specific subset of dame entretenue services—say to have sex three times a week—but to every service kept women offered. In other words, she agreed to become a mistress. By the time the police began to devote considerable resources to following kept women around town in the 1740s, *galanterie* (being kept or maintaining a mistress) was a well-established practice. The duties of a kept woman were defined and standardized by convention and tradition, and reified in fiction and satire.[39]

First among these was the duty to have sex. As to what kind of sex, the police reports are rather silent, aside from suggesting that a certain degree of amatory skill was expected, at least of more experienced kept women. Most couples seemed to share expectations of what should happen in bed, as instances in which a couple was reported to have broken up because of sexual dissatisfaction or incompatibility were few. Providing companionship was a second duty of the mistress. The couple spent time together, usually at her residence. Most men saw their mistresses three times a week, often for a few hours in the evening or mid-afternoon. The marquis de Voyer, for example, visited his mistress, Demoiselle Puvigné, a dancer in the Opera ballet, three to four times a week. He visited in the evening but never slept there.[40] Some patrons stuck to schedules or gave advance notice. Others came and went as it suited them. Some couples regularly supped together, but patrons rarely spent the night.

The last service for which patrons paid with their honoraires and extras was fidelity, which it seemed they rarely got. Although patrons cited infidelity more often than any other grievance when breaking off relations with a mistress, expectations of sexual fidelity were complex. Some patrons found being cuckolded humiliating. In his memoirs, the chevalier de Tilly described a friend's reaction to learning that Tilly had slept with his mistress. The man "felt humiliated" and wanted to fight the young chevalier. Instead "all was drowned in torrents of champagne."[41] Most patrons were infuriated. In his typically understated way, the philosophe Jean-François Marmontel reported in his memoirs that his affair with Demoiselle Verrière cost the aspiring actress her patron, the maréchal de Saxe. When Saxe, who had several other mistresses at the same time, found out about the relationship, he swore never to see his mistress or their child again. This was a promise Marmontel claims the military leader kept, more or less, reuniting with his daughter only after the death of her mother.[42]

With time, many cuckolded patrons reconciled with their mistresses. Some even came to resign themselves to their mistresses' infidelity. For example, according to the police, Monsieur de Courval and Demoiselle Aubin broke up repeatedly, not over her infidelity, but over its public nature. At a party marking their reconciliation, Aubin publicly vowed to be more discreet in seeing her *greluchon* (boyfriend), rather than promise never to see him again. Courval, for his part, vowed to be more generous and less violent.[43] Extra-patron affairs were so common that while many men were angered by their mistresses' behavior, few were surprised. And while some kept women went to extraordinary lengths to hide their infidelities, others barely bothered. Clearly, infidelity was more tolerable in some instances than in others.

Expectations of fidelity were always in tension with a counterexpectation that kept women regularly would seek out and engage in extra-patron sex, as though they were constitutionally incapable of doing otherwise. The expectation of cheating was so normal that it challenges the use of words like "infidelity." In fiction and contemporary documents, the dame entretenue was constructed as a woman who was eternally unsatisfied. She might have sex with other men for money because whatever she was earning, it was not enough. Or she might have sex for pleasure, because her sexual desires were thought to be considerable. In police writing, it was only the rare mistress who was both modest and remained faithful to her patron. A closer reading, however, reveals a more complicated situation. Kept women cheated for money, for fun, and for love. Many tried to maintain private intimate lives alongside their professional ones. Others understood that certain forms of cheating helped increase their sexual capital. For many, it may indeed have been part of their professional ethic. In the open market that was the demimonde, most kept women, even those who were paid quite well, eventually turned an eye toward the prospect of a better patron. Landing a new patron often involved some *passades* (paid one-night stands) in advance of a contract.

We can see the various ways in which the demimonde contract reflected wider practices of worker remuneration. It differed, however, in ways that were important in enabling some dames entretenues to achieve financial success. The contract ensured that whatever the personal feelings of patron and mistress, their relationship was fundamentally a financial one. Yet the vagueness of certain parts of the agreement made it a particularly flexible instrument, one through which a patron could express his feelings, whether good or bad, in material or monetary terms. It was in the promise of gifts and furnishings that lay the greatest potential for wealth, because the value of these items was not specified. In principle, they were pay for a job well done, either in satisfying a patron or in having mastered the ability to "draw" additional support from him. In reality, this was not entirely true. Many a patron embellished his mistress to enhance his own status or lifestyle. Whatever the case, under the best of circumstances a mistress could "hit it big," so to speak, through expensive gifts and extras. Of course, unhappy or financially strapped patrons could just as easily leave their mistresses with little more than the base pay stipulated in the contract. But even when things went badly in a particular affair, the fundamental economic basis of these relationships benefitted dames entretenues by stabilizing remuneration, at least for a month, which was more security than many female workers enjoyed.

Ironically, what enhanced the potential for a big payoff was the unilateral structure of the contract, in that it specified the patron's obligations while leaving those of the mistress undefined. In doing so, the contract—the very instrument that made the patron-mistress relationship transactional—had the capacity to downplay its own transactional nature. Failing to enumerate a mistress's sexual duties confused her status and made the relationship ambiguous. It separated her from the prostitute, and in some ways made her closer to a wife. Differentiating the mistress from the prostitute created space to imagine that she was not fully mercenary, laughing at her patron behind his back, but that she might share at least some of the sentiments or attraction that inspired him to spend so much.

The contract conferred respectability on the mistress, making her a better candidate for emotional and financial investment. Yet, the tension over the value and quality of previously unspecified gifts makes clear that mistresses were not necessarily passive parties in either the negotiation or execution of their agreements. It was in the execution of the contract, however, that kept women had the potential to exercise power, even though limited.

CONTRACT AS CUSTOM: SEX AS WORK

The contract may have been a construct unique to the demimonde and one with no legal standing, but it was honored by both patrons and mistresses, as well as by those police and judicial officials who interacted with them. It was not just a question of form or of the necessity of making the agreement before commencing a sexual relationship. Rather, it was a question both of practice and of culture. Both parties agreed the relationship was to be governed by the contract's stipulations. This was the case even when they disagreed, as they often did, as to how to interpret those stipulations or even when one party or the other refused to abide by them outright. The contract functioned as a framework that shaped expectations of what would happen, and hence often served to explain why relationships ended.

Even when patrons reclaimed gifts, which was rare, they explained their actions according to the implicit and explicit assumptions of the contract. What was at issue was whether the mistress had earned the item in question. For example, in March of 1765 the dancer Marie-Catherine Lachau (called Adélaide) accused her patron, comte de Sarmeny, a retired Spanish colonel, of stealing jewelry from her. In the context of the demimonde, the case was a serious matter. Adélaide filed a written complaint (*procès verbal*) with Commissioner Jean-François Hughes in which she stated that Sarmeny had taken a key from her pocket as she slept, emptied out her cabinet, and left a note. Adélaide accused Sarmeny of theft and nothing more. She did not mention their relationship. In response, officers of the *Châtelet,* armed with a warrant, searched Sarmeny's apartment, where they found the missing items.

In his inevitable countercomplaint, Sarmeny made his case: He had already spent a great deal on Adélaide, having paid for the renovation and furnishing of her current apartment, and much else besides. When the dancer asked for diamonds and other jewelry, the colonel doubted he would gain an adequate "return" from such an investment. He was willing to lend her diamonds and the other valuables in question. However, he would not give her their receipts—and hence full ownership, as he construed it—as he had done with the furniture. When she demanded the receipts, he reiterated the point that "he was not suitably satisfied with her to give her these objects." They had supper, slept together, and fought again in the morning, at which point, the colonel claimed, Adélaide was verbally abusive, told him to leave, and gave him back the jewelry.

Sarmeny's defense is telling. Despite his vastly superior status to that of his accuser, he did not simply claim that the items were loaned and expect to be taken at his word. Instead, facing conventions in which mistresses were paid in just such objects, he explained *why* they were only loaned. Adélaide did not please him. As she had not adequately fulfilled her sexual and companionate duties, she did not deserve extra pay. Sarmeny further supported his own case by depicting Adélaide as greedy, ungrateful, and rude, and in so doing he made the assumption that authorities would understand that gifts were a form of payment for certain services, services she had not rendered.[44]

Sarmeny's expectation that the police would understand his particular defense was not misplaced. Despite the ambiguous nature of the contract, it was underpinned by the widely held assumption that sex was a kind of labor a prostitute owned and could sell. This idea pervaded eighteenth-century writing on prostitution in many different genres. It was explicitly theorized in satire. For example, the *Mémoires secrets* published a letter supposedly (though doubtfully) from Marie-Claude Saron in which the Opera dancer explained why having had sex with a notary should have canceled the debt of 1,800 livres she owed him. "Of everything I have, nothing belongs to me more than my favors," argued faux-Saron. "I have the incontestable right to dispose of them freely and by consequence to give them away or sell them." Anyone who saw the notary, she continued, would realize that "nothing could inspire such generosity" in her and that "I sold what I was unwilling to grant for free."[45]

In the demimonde, the idea that the prostitute owned and could sell her sexual labor found its most obvious expression in the convention that sexual services were to be rendered only in exchange for money or goods. The first sexual engagement of a patron-mistress relationship traditionally occurred only after a patron paid his future mistress either an initial gift or her first honoraires. The two transactions might take place on the same night, or within days of each other. Money, then sex. Were the patron to stop paying, his mistress would owe him nothing, regardless of what had transpired between them.

Sarmeny also was drawing on a tradition in which the police, when asked on occasion by the parties involved, would adjudicate patron-mistress conflicts according to the logic of the contract.[46] In one example, Suzanne Elizabeth Le-Grand (known professionally as Demoiselle Beaumont) and the German baron de Wolfdork had such a disagreement. One night after the theater he asked to take her home, presumably to have sex. She assented, and the baron ate and slept at her apartment. A few days later he gave her a small ring containing three diamonds worth 7 or 8 louis (192 livres). When he did not pay her *honoraires* (at 300 livres) on the first of the month, as they had agreed, she stopped sleeping with him. He then asked for the ring back, and she refused. In the meantime, she had set up a "fixed appointment" every Monday with the duc de Grammont. Wolfdork took LeGrand before Commissioner Cadot, who ruled in her favor.[47] Wolfdork was a baron, but LeGrand, a part-time actress and dancer and full-time sex worker, got to keep the ring. In making this ruling, Commissioner Cadot affirmed the custom of the contract, even if it was not a legal instrument. In resolving this case between patron and mistress, the commissioner acted as he did in a thousand other disputes between small-business owners and their clients. Cadot acknowledged that in providing sexual services, LeGrand deserved compensation.

Submitting to the police for mediation, however, was voluntary. While the police investigated what they considered to be legitimate accusations of theft, they would not help a patron or a mistress sort out a property dispute unless asked to do so, and such requests were rare. Some patrons, as we saw in the case of Sarmeny, simply recovered contested items themselves. That patrons could recover such items, including items specifically enumerated in the contract, puts their very ownership in doubt. It emphasizes the degree to which the contract was not binding even if most parties, most of the time, respected it as a convention. There were no legal ramifications and almost no social ones for breaking it. Moreover, we should not forget that, by definition, *dames entretenues* entered into relationships with men who were economically, politically, and socially superior. *Dames entretenues* were extremely vulnerable. If a patron decided to mistreat his mistress, there was often little she or her family could do. It is tempting, then, to argue that the convention could break down under the will of a determined and powerful patron, but what little evidence there is suggests the opposite. In retrieving or trying to retrieve items, patrons did not break the contract; they honored its logic. They claimed that the goods in question had not been earned. In doing so, they admitted that the sexual and companionate services rendered by their mistresses were a form of work, and that these women owned their own sexual labor. This was a claim that kept women also made, both openly and, as we shall see, by their actions.

MISTRESSES, CONTRACTS, AND AGENCY

Mistresses enforced the conventions of pay through negotiating contracts, protesting when patrons failed to abide by the terms, and occasionally seeking adjudication when the ownership of items they considered remuneration was contested. But they also manipulated these conventions. They took on multiple patrons, perhaps for no other reason than to earn more money. In doing so, they asserted ownership over their bodies and sexual labor, and thereby exercised a certain degree of agency. For example, kept women who had more than one entreteneur ranked them. That ranking determined how a mistress related to each of her patrons, who had what kind of sexual access, and whom she might humiliate.[48] A primary patron was the one who had a contract (the terms of which were sufficient to maintain his mistress at a level she accepted) and honored its terms, and who was granted, at least in theory, exclusive sexual access to his mistress. A primary patron always was accommodated. In many cases, mistresses had secondary and even tertiary patrons, defined by the fact that they paid less and that they paid less reliably. Such men rarely were beholden to a contract and hence to the payment of honoraires. They often gave cash and gifts on an irregular but necessarily frequent basis.

But even a patron with a contract could be explicitly denied exclusive sexual access if he did not pay enough. *Fermier Général* (tax collector) Laurent-Réné Ferrand, for example, paid Demoiselle Rossignol fewer than 8 louis (192 livres) a month. Inspector Marais reported that, as a consequence, the tax collector gave his mistress "permission to find a patron who accommodated her better, permission which she used fully in taking all the passades that Brissault [an elite procurer who with his wife ran a famous brothel] could arrange for her." Indeed, Ferrand assumed almost a suppliant position to his mistress. He gave her a gift of 40 louis (960 livres) and a gold tobacco box to "thank her for her attention."[49] Money was the ultimate determinant of patron pecking order and hence sexual access. A poorly paying primary patron, like Ferrand, usually accepted that his mistress might take on other professional engagements to pay the bills. In theory, she would do so discreetly and without inconveniencing him. Secondary patrons, on the other hand, were discommoded openly, a regular reminder of their inferior status.

The conventions of pay, then, created a space in which kept women could exercise power, however limited. But perhaps the best example of this is not the practice of patron-ranking, but rather the custom that allowed mistresses regularly to break contracts so as to take advantage of better offers. In doing so, kept women both exercised agency and increased their sexual capital. The higher their sexual capital, the more they could demand for their sexual services and the greater their choice of patrons. I am defining sexual capital as a personal asset, similar to social, economic, or cultural capital.[50] It was extremely important for all women, not just for professional mistresses, because its core component was virginity. When virginity was lost without marriage, a girl moved from an economy of sexual honor to one of sexual capital and the nature of that capital changed. In the demimonde, the construction of this asset was complicated. Dames entretenues with high sexual capital tended to have certain physical and character attributes valorized by demimondaine society. Or more accurately, they tended to have a high sum total of these qualities, strong areas compensating for weak ones. There were no descriptions of kept women with unattractive faces *and* bodies, or of women who were unattractive *and* insipid. But beyond body and personality, sexual desirability hinged on an equally important second layer of social determination, a self-reflective mechanism by which the demimonde established value. The most desirable kept women were desirable in part because high-status men or important institutions like the Opera identified them as such.

Hence the contract, in particular the honoraires, was a key component of sexual capital, as it represented the value other elite men placed on a particular commodity, in this case a kept woman. While a dame entretenue could not display her honoraires as she did the diamonds that she might have received as gifts, police reporting indicates that the size of these monthly stipends was a subject of demimonde gossip. Some were reported in the *Mémoires secrets*. Honoraires, then, established a kept woman within a certain category of value known to others in the demimonde. Some women had unstable earnings, their honoraires varying wildly from patron to patron, but most did not. What evidence I have from the police reports suggests that in the majority of cases salary remained stable or climbed steadily until reporting stopped. For example, in three years Demoiselle Raye earned 600 livres, 600 livres, and 720 livres, from three separate patrons.[51] Honoraires were a simple (though inaccurate) means of comparing the value of contracts, and hence provided kept women with a way to take advantage of what were perceived as better offers. In tough times, kept women were more inclined to engage in passades to survive than they were to be hired at considerably lower honoraires, which would have damaged their salary histories. In leaving one patron for another who offered higher honoraires, a kept woman increased her own sexual capital. In fact, one could argue that in doing so she actually invested in her own sexual capital. She showed not only that she was worth more, but that she would leave when she could earn more, making her a harder-to-acquire commodity.

CONCLUSION

Let us return, then, to the central question of this essay concerning how illicit economies created opportunities for women. I have made an argument that the "formal informal" nature of the demimonde established a space for women (who might otherwise have died young on the streets from exposure or disease) to achieve a modicum of independence and sometimes more than a modicum of wealth. This was possible because they operated in a largely unregulated market, yet one that was governed informally by a set of customs, one of which was the contract, which benefited kept women in a number of ways. Patrons honored the contract. Perhaps they did so because they had a vested interest in turning the women they paid to have sex with them into something more than bodies for hire. Women, then, were able to earn so much money in this field not despite the fact that they were women, but because of it. Yet, we should remember that their success was not just a function of their anatomy and beauty. Prospering as a kept women required skills—amatory, social, and marketing. The most successful were able to take their earnings and their connections and invest them, building sexual capital, finding new patrons, and creating new opportunities. The demimonde was loose enough in structure that kept women could "grow" their businesses so to speak. However, this is not an argument for the benefits of a free market to women in the eighteenth century. The women in this study had value only because they sold sex and sometimes love, and because as mistresses they could confer status on their patrons. Most did so unwillingly. Most became prostitutes because they were unable to find more socially acceptable means of supporting themselves. And once they were professional sex workers, it was extremely difficult—though not impossible—to reintegrate into more respectable communities. In short, the illicit economy of the demimonde provided women with economic opportunity, but at a very high social cost.

NOTES

1. See, for example, the comments of Alexander Tilly and Jean-François Marmontel in their respective memoirs: Alexandre de Tilly, *Mémoires du comte Alexandre de Tilly, pour servir à l'histoire des moeurs de la fin du XVIIIᵉ siècle,* ed. Christian Melchior-Bonnet (Paris: Mercure de France, 1965), 67,

and Jean-François Marmontel, *Mémoires de Marmontel: Mémoires d'un père pour servir à l'instruction de ses enfants*, ed. Maurice Toureux (Paris: Librairie des bibliophiles, 1891), 1:125–126. Also see Louis Sébastien Mercier, *Tableau de Paris*, ed. Jean-Claude Bonnet (1781–1789; reprint, Paris: Mercure de France, 1994), 3:588–590.

2. Bibliothèque de l'Arensal (henceforth B.A.) ms. 10237, *État present des actrices de l'Opéra*, 1 September 1752.

3. For example, women dominated the business of elite prostitution, as all but one elite madam in Paris at mid-century was female. See Erica-Marie Benabou, *La prostitution et la police des moeurs au XVIIIᵉ siècle* (Paris: Librairie académique Perrin, 1987), 210–267, and Nina Kushner, *Erotic Exchanges: The World of Elite Prostitution in Eighteenth-Century Paris* (Ithaca: Cornell Univ. Press, 2013), 97–128.

4. The dossiers are in B.A. mss. 10234–10244 and 10248, and Bibliothèque Nationale (henceforth B.N.) mss. 11357–11360. The latter have been printed in *Paris sous Louis XV: Rapports des inspecteurs de police au roi*, ed. Camille Piton, 5 vols. (Paris: Mercure de France, 1908–1915), and *Journal des inspecteurs de M. de Sartines: première série, (1761–1764)*, ed. Etienne Lorédan Larchey (Brussels: E. Parent, 1863). For a discussion of how these sources can be used to reconstruct the demimonde, see Kushner, *Erotic Exchanges*, chapter 1. To learn how police files can be used more generally to understand the subjects of policing, see Robert Darnton, "A Police Inspector Sorts His Files: An Anatomy of the Republic of Letters," in *The Great Cat Massacre and Other Episodes in French Cultural History* (New York: Vintage, 1985), 145–189.

5. Besides "demimonde," there is no single term in eighteenth-century sources that describes the world of elite prostitution and mistress-keeping. Referring to a different set of sexual relations than the one under study here, Alexander Dumas *fils* coined the term (as "demi-monde") in a play by the same name in 1855. By the 1870s, however, the term had come to refer to "femmes galantes, entretenues." See Émile Littré, *Dictionnaire de la langue française* (Paris: Éditions universitaires, 1872–1877). It is used in current scholarship in reference to eighteenth-century dames entretenues and their patrons. See L. L. Bongie, *From Rogue to Everyman: A Foundling's Journey to the Bastille* (Montreal: McGill-Queen's Univ. Press, 2004).

6. See Alain Corbin, *Filles de noces: Misère sexuelle et prostitution: 19ᵉ et 20ᵉ siècles* (Paris: Aubier Montaigne, 1975), and Jill Harsin, *Policing Prostitution in Nineteenth-Century Paris* (Princeton: Princeton Univ. Press, 1995), for discussions of the heavy regulation of prostitution in the nineteenth century.

7. This is the argument I make in chapter 1 of *Erotic Exchanges*. Vincent Milliot and Lisa Jane Graham make similar arguments about the development of police surveillance in the eighteenth century. See Milliot, *Un policier des Lumières* (Paris: Editions Champ Vallon, 2011), especially part 2, and Lisa Jane Graham, *If the King Only Knew: Seditious Speech in the Reign of Louis XV* (Charlottesville: Univ. Press of Virginia, 2000), chapter 1. Also see Benabou, *La prostitution et la police des moeurs au XVIIIᵉ siècle*, 161–164. Robert Muchembled has recently argued that Meusnier and Marais used the surveillance system to blackmail kept women and their patrons as part of a vast and organized criminal conspiracy within the police, but his assertions remain unproven. Robert Muchembled, *Les ripoux des Lumières: Corruption policière et Révolution* (Paris: Seuill, 2011).

8. From what I can pull from the police reports, the average age of a girl starting out in the demimonde was fourteen. Casanova called a girl's middle teens "ambrosial," which is especially

significant when we consider that girls reached menarche, on average, at age sixteen. Giacomo Casanova, Chevalier de Seingalt, *History of My Life,* trans. Willard R. Trask (Baltimore: Johns Hopkins Univ. Press, 1997), 3:173. On menarche, see Elise de La Rochebrochard, "Age at Puberty of Girls and Boys in France: Measurements from a Survey on Adolescent Sexuality," *Population: An English Selection* 12 (2000): 55.

9. The reports on kept women of the theater show that 71 percent were in the Opera, 15 percent the Comédie-Française, 7 percent the Comédie-Italienne, and 7 percent the Opéra-Comique.

10. Archives Nationales (henceforth AN), AJ, 13–17 (lists salaries from 1750–1770 for the purpose of the capitation). The highest salaries were for women "in roles" and ranged between 600 and 3,000 livres. Women in the chorus earned between 80 and 300 livres a year. Claude Alasseur found that the principal singers and dancers were paid on average six times more than men and women in the choruses. Opera salaries rose over the course of the century (as did those in the Comédie-Française), so that by century's end principals were earning as much as 6,000 livres and had the opportunity to supplement these earnings with various bonuses. But these salaries still lagged behind those of the Comédie-Française. Martine de Rougemont, *La vie théâtrale en France au XVIIIe siècle* (Paris: Champion, 1988), 202, 193–212. Also see Claude Alasseur, *La Comédie française au 18e siècle: Étude économique* (Paris: Mouton, 1967).

11. For further discussion, see Kushner, *Erotic Exchanges,* 74–82.

12. AN Y 11566, 29 March 1757. Cited in Émile Campardon, *L'Académie royale de musique au XVIIIe siècle: Documents inédits découverts aux Archives Nationales* (1884; reprint, New York: Da Capo Press, 1971), 1:234–235 (henceforth *ARM*).

13. See, for example, Olwen Hufton, "Women and the Family Economy," *French Historical Studies* 9, no. 1 (spring 1975): 1–22, and Olwen Hufton, *The Prospect Before Her: A History of Women in Western Europe, 1500–1800* (New York: Knopf, 1996).

14. Clare Crowston and Nancy Locklin both have found "spinster clusters" and other evidence of single women supporting themselves through work. Clare Haru Crowston, *Fabricating Women: The Seamstresses of Old Regime France, 1675–1791* (Durham: Duke Univ. Press, 2001), 89; Nancy Locklin, *Women's Work and Identity in Eighteenth-Century Brittany* (Aldershot, Eng.: Ashgate, 2007), 43–44, 98. Also see contributions by Nancy Locklin, Cynthia Truant, and Jane McLeod to this volume.

15. *ARM,* 2:55.

16. AN Y 13114, Papers of Commissioner Bernard-Louis-Philippe Fontaine, 28 January 1762 (*ARM,* 2:46–48).

17. Ibid., 11009, Papers of Commissioner Jean-François Hughes, 9 October 1768 (*ARM,* 2:96).

18. B.A. ms. 10236, Dossier of Deschamps (Marie-Ann Pàges), 19 September 1755.

19. B.A. ms. 10236, Dossier of Deschamps (Marie-Ann Pàges), 13 February 1748 through 2 April 1757. For discussion of the total debt, see the entry dated 19 September 1755. Also see B.N. ms. 11358, 9 October 1761, *Notes sur différentes dames entretenues.* Also found in Lorédan Larchey, *Journal,* 43. On the sale of Deschamps's things, see Edmond-Jean-François Barbier, *Chronique de la régence et du règne de Louis XV, 1718–1763* (Paris: Charpentier, 1857) 3:343. On her financial woes, see the judicial and notarial documents reproduced in *ARM,* 1:229–240. Also see Gaston Capon and Robert Yves-Plessis, *Paris galante au dix-huitième siècle: Fille d'Opéra, vendeuse d'amour: Histoire de Mlle Deschamps (1730–1764)* (Paris: Plessis, 1906). Jacques-Samuel-Oliver Bernard (1730–1801), comte de Coubert, was the grandson of the famous financier Samuel Bernard. Auguste-Simon Brissart (1726–79) was

from and married into families of *fermiers généraux*. Becoming a *fermier général* in 1750, Brissart dispensed enormous sums on *dames entrerentues*, especially women in the Opera. Yves Durand, *Les fermiers généraux au XVIIIe siècle* (Paris: Maisonneuve et Larose, 1996), 341.

20. AN Minutier Central, LXXIV, 3333, 2 February 1752, cited in Jean Delay, *Avant mémoire*, vol. 3, *La Fauconnier* (Paris, 1982), 167–168.

21. Kathryn Norberg, "Goddesses of Taste: Courtesans and Their Furniture in Late-Eighteenth-Century Paris," in *Furnishing the Eighteenth Century: What Furniture Can Tell Us about the European and American Past*, ed. Dena Goodman and Kathryn Norberg (New York: Routledge: 2007), 99.

22. Patron reaction to children and pregnancy varied, although it was fully expected that the patron would pay for the birth and provide some initial support for the child, if the mother chose to keep it. The alternative, of which only a minority of kept women availed themselves, was to put the child in the Enfants Trouvés (foundling hospital). A few patrons offered lifelong support and even legally recognized these children. Pregnancy did not stop kept women from working.

23. AN Y 404 (*ARM*, 1:11–12).

24. Christine Adams, *A Taste for Comfort: A Bourgeois Family in Eighteenth-Century France* (Philadelphia: Univ. of Pennsylvania Press, 2000), 69; Daniel Roche, *The People of Paris: An Essay in Popular Culture in the 18th Century*, trans. Marie Evans (Berkeley: Univ. of California Press, 1987), 75 (table 3.4), 81 (table 3.8).

25. The police most often used the term *contrat* (contract) to describe these agreements, but a number of other terms appear in police writing, in fiction, and in satire. These include *les arrangements* (arrangements), *la traité* (treaty), *les appointements*, or even, somewhat rudely, *le bail* (lease), all of which were terms used in contemporary commercial language.

26. *Dictionnaire de L'Académie Française*, 5th ed. (Paris: J. J. Smits, 1798), s.v. "honoraires." The term also appears in fiction. See, for example, [Claude Villaret], *La belle allemande or les galanteries de Thèrese* (Paris, 1755), 66.

27. Erica-Marie Benabou took a different sample and found only slightly different proportions. Benabou counted 517 contracts in the portion of Marais's reports published by Larchey in *Journal des inspecteurs*. Benabou, *La prostitution et la police des moeurs au XVIIIe siècle*, 337–338.

28. Elizabeth Badinter, *Mother Love: Myth and Reality: Motherhood in Modern History* (New York: Macmillan, 1980), 47; Crowston, *Fabricating Women*, 91; Michael Sonenscher, *Work and Wages: Natural Law, Politics and the Eighteenth-Century French Trades* (Cambridge: Cambridge Univ. Press, 1989), 204; Robert Darnton, *The Literary Underground of the Old Regime* (Cambridge, Mass.: Harvard Univ. Press, 1982), 48.

29. Sonenscher, *Work and Wages*, 183–84. In industries based on annual contracts, workers sometimes could negotiate raises during their yearly contract renewal. Lauren Clay found this to be common practice among actors and actresses in the provinces. Lauren Clay, "Provincial Actors, the *Comédie-Française*, and the Business of Performing in Eighteenth-Century France," *Eighteenth-Century Studies* 38, no. 4 (summer 2005): 651–79.

30. It was also called an *entrée-de-jeu*.

31. B.N. ms. 11358, Dossier of Demoiselle Crousol, *la cadette*, 21 November 1760. Also found in Piton, *Paris sous Louis XV*, 3:243–245. This was Charles Godefroy de La Tour d'Auvergne (1706–1771).

32. Benabou, *La prostitution et la police des moeurs au XVIIIe siècle*, 340–341. Her rental statistics were taken from Marcel R. Reinhard, *Nouvelle histoire de Paris, la Révolution 1789–1799* (Paris: Hachette, 1971), 42.

33. B.A. ms. 10236, Dossier of Demoiselle Gallodier, *la cadette,* 13 August 1756. Gravelles held that position from 1753 to 1766.

34. Clay, "Provincial Actors, the *Comédie-Française,*" 661.

35. B.A. ms. 10238, Dossier of Demoiselle Pelissier, 5 January 1754.

36. "entre-vifs, pure, simple et irrévocable." AN Y 404 (*ARM,* 1:11–12).

37. This is taken from Sonenscher, *Work and Wages,* 195.

38. These same inspectors, especially Meusnier, wrote impressively graphic depictions of sex acts engaged in by libertine priests apprehended by the police. See B.A. ms. 10261.

39. By mid-century there were several novels depicting the lives of dames entretenues, including *L'Histoire du chevalier des Grieux et de Manon Lescaut* (1731) by Abbé Prévost.

40. B.A. ms. 10237, Dossier of Demoiselle Puvigné, *fille,* 4 March 1753. In these reports, the inspectors refer to one man as the marquis de Voyer d'Argenson and later as the marquis de Voyer, and then just as Voyer. These titles refer to two different people: Marc-René de Voyer de Paulmy d'Argenson (1722–1782), to whom I think Meusnier was referring, was called the marquis de Voyer and sometimes the comte de Paulmy. Son of the secretary of war, Voyer was made the governor of the Château de Vincennes in 1754. He should not be confused with his cousin, Antoine-René de Voyer de Paulmy (1722–1787), the marquis de Paulmy, who became the third marquis d'Argenson in 1757.

41. Tilly, *Mémoires,* 341.

42. The child was later naturalized as Aurore de Saxe. This incident was not the first time in which Marmontel had an affair with a mistress of the maréchal. The philosophe had also been the lover of Marie-Gabrielle Hévin de Navarre while she was in the pay of the maréchal. Marmontel claims that Saxe was not angry with him over the first affair but was furious about the second. Marmontel, *Mémoires,* 1:125–127. Joseph d'Hemery, the police inspector of the book trade who kept files on many important writers, including Marmontel, gives a different version of the story, claiming that Verrière and Saxe later reconciled. Darnton, "An Inspector Sorts His Files," 170.

43. B.N. ms. 11358, *Notes,* 10 July 1761. Also found in Piton, *Paris sous Louis XV,* 3:330–331.

44. AN Y 11006, Papers of Commissioner Jean-François Hughes, 9, 10, and 11 March 1765 (*ARM,* 1:1–5). Three days after the initial complaint, the colonel had returned almost all of the items to Adélaide, and both parties promised not to pursue their cases against each other, although the commissioner makes no note as to why.

45. *Mémoires secretes,* 14:312 and 21:12 (*ARM,* 2:287–288).

46. Commissioners asked to intervene in these matters tended to record the intervention in their logs, but did not necessarily draw up a *procès verbal,* the paperwork required to start a legal proceeding

47. B.A. ms. 10238, Dossier of Demoiselle Beaumont (*née* Suzanne Elizabeth Legrand), 12 February and 6 June 1750. Meusnier identifies the German noble as Baron Wolf. L. L. Bongie claims he was Baron de Wolfdork, a Lutheran canon from Leipzig. Bongie, *From Rogue to Everyman,* 107.

48. For the ways in which a courtesan's rejection of a patron or client could have social and political ramifications, see Guido Ruggiero, "Who's Afraid of Giuliana Napolitana? Pleasure, Fear and Imagining the Arts of the Renaissance Courtesan," in *The Courtesan's Arts: Cross-Cultural Perspectives,* ed. Martha Feldman and Bonnie Gordon, 280–292 (New York: Oxford Univ. Press, 2006).

49. B.N. ms. 11358, *Notes,* 23 January 1761. From a family of financiers, Ferrand assumed his post in 1751. He was both a friend of, and related to, the Marquise de Pompadour. Durand, *Les fermiers généraux,* 266, 545.

50. The concept of sexual capital is minimally developed in scholarship. Pierre Bourdieu argued that beauty was a form of cultural capital, but he was not concerned with sexuality more generally. Working from Bourdieu's arguments about forms of capital, British sociologist Catherine Hakim developed the idea of "erotic capital," which is conceptually akin to my theory of "sexual capital." Pierre Bourdieu, "Forms of Capital," in *Handbook of Theory and Research for the Sociology of Education*, ed. J. G. Richardson, trans. Richard Nice (New York: Greenwood Press, 1986), 241–258; Catherine Hakim, "Erotic Capital," *European Sociological Review* 26, no. 5 (2010): 499–518; Catherine Hakim, *Erotic Capital: The Power of Attraction in the Bedroom and Boardroom* (New York: Basic Books, 2011).

51. B.N. ms. 11358, Dossier of Demoiselle Raye, *l'aînée*, 14 December 1759, 21 March 1760, 23 January 1761, 21 February 1761, and 2 October 1761.

THE POWER OF WIVES

Managing Money and Men in the Family Businesses of Old Regime Paris

Jacob D. Melish

I n May of 1785, Marie Louise Espec testified to a court and police official (a *commissaire* of the *Châtelet*) that the savings she had been building up from the proceeds of her husband's woodturning workshop had been stolen. She explained that because she "had the ambition both to see her husband become a master in his guild [of woodturners, which would require payment of a substantial fee] and to obtain a small stock of merchandise, [she] had conceived and executed the project of creating a small sum of savings without even her husband knowing." She accused a young man of the theft. Espec stated that "she had taken [him] for a trial period then as an apprentice," and that later "she and her husband . . . had taken him on as a skilled journeyman."[1] Her comments suggest that she was an active player in the affairs of the woodturning workshop even though it, resembling most of the family businesses of the Old Regime, was owned not by women like herself but by men such as her husband. Other testimonies show that her work was part of a broad range of tasks performed by family businesswomen. Those tasks included selling the goods or services, bargaining over prices, collecting the cash from customers, keeping the money safe, deciding issues of day-to-day credit, keeping the accounts, and planning for the long-term development of the enterprise, among other things. To a significant extent, it was women who managed the family businesses that made up the preindustrial urban economy.

Men created a gender hierarchy favorable to themselves in part by enforcing a sexual division of labor in which, with important exceptions, they monopolized work that had higher earning power and status.[2] Many guild regulations were explicit on this point. In most (but far from all) of the more profitable professions, women were not able to own businesses except if, as widows, they were continuing the work of their late husbands.[3] As historians we have rightly tended to associate economic agency among working women during the Old Regime with those who worked independently of any husband, and often outside their homes, for such women were usually better documented and their independence and economic agency are unambiguous.[4] This has meant, however, that women married to and working with male owners of family businesses have been quietly sidelined; they have even been characterized as mere "servants of their husbands."[5] Important work is presently being done that counters this characterization, but much remains to be uncovered about the nature of these women's economic roles. We know about the relative legal status of husbands and wives, the importance of the dowry to business success, some of the commercial responsibilities of each spouse, and working women's roles in regulating domestic violence.[6] The evidence used here contributes to a key aspect of this broad field of research.

The sexual division of labor worked mostly—but not completely—to the disadvantage of women. Despite the handicaps it brought, the division actually made it easier for women to own businesses and run guilds in areas thought of as "feminine," especially those working with textiles.[7] It also led husbands in practically all professions to become dependent on wives for a number of tasks. Husbands who ran workshops or shops outside of certain textile trades usually kept for themselves duties requiring manual skill, heavy physical labor, technical knowledge, travel (whether in the city or beyond), and legal standing; their wives claimed and were given nearly everything else. Business spouses worked in separate, mutually dependent spheres. Most husbands may have had the upper hand in theory, but in daily life the situation was often more complex, and wives were clearly not without agency. The first section of this article looks at the role of family businesswomen in selling the goods and services produced by their husbands, and in collecting and keeping safe the businesses' cash. The second deals with wives' keeping of the businesses' accounts, and the third examines how these responsibilities contributed to wives' broader management, in a sense, of the businesses themselves and of the men within them.

Marie Louise Espec's situation was unusual in two respects: her savings were stolen and she was the only one, besides the alleged thief, who even had known of their existence. That encouraged the magistrate investigating the case to have her testify, and his clerk to include those parts of her testimony that were not legally pertinent but that did lend credence to her claim of having amassed the funds. In practically all other eighteenth-century court cases where a couple had been victimized, the husband was the one to testify, and he did not include details of how the couple divided the management of the business.

To fully understand the role of women such as Espec in the family businesses of the Old Regime, it is important to include court cases from the start of the long eighteenth century, toward the beginning of the personal reign of Louis XIV. At that time the lower rungs of the courts were not as standardized and exclusive, so some clerks transcribed witness testimonies in detail, rather than just making summaries of the legally pertinent parts, and more women were asked to testify.[8] This article is based on a series of seventy-eight such court cases, together with a handful of other cases and published sources from the time. Most of the information from the court cases used here was peripheral to the legally salient parts of the litigation. It consists of snippets of daily life that happened to slip into the documentation, a handful of mentions for each carton of several hundred pages of manuscripts. It does permit, however, even in this preliminary study, an exploration in greater depth than has so far been possible, and an understanding of the significance of the day-to-day economic roles of women who, through marriage, were at the heart of the small workshops and shops that made up the bulk of the preindustrial urban economy.

SELLING THE GOODS, COLLECTING THE CASH, AND KEEPING IT SAFE

The basis of women's informal power in family businesses was that they often brought to the enterprise experience, skill, monies (through a dowry), connections, and credit, and that they were trusted and engaged partners whose work was essential. In day-to-day life this meant that the woman to whom a male business owner was married was the one who usually sold the business's goods or services and received payment from the customers. For example, Antoine Demimuid was a master baker, but (as in practically every other small business) his wife was the one dealing with the customers, selling the bread, and collecting the cash. When she could not be there, she had her mother stand in.[9] Even in four cases where the everyday buying and selling in four different taverns is mentioned, a business where one might expect the husband to be up front and prominent (each tavern was, of course, described as owned by him), one finds the wife dealing with the customers in every case, assisted by her husband in only one, and by a daughter in another.[10] One of the few consistent exceptions to this practice was the butcher's business. Behind the counter, selling, stood the husband, sometimes with his wife, both with blood on their hands. Because many customers wanted their orders custom cut, the husband had to be on hand with his cleavers and knives rather than in the workshop at the back. More typically though, throughout the preindustrial urban economy the wife ruled the front end of the business. The famous eighteenth-century chronicler of Parisian life Louis-Sébastien Mercier noted that in family businesses women sold everything: "the wife of the weapons maker will present and sell you a sword, a gun, a breast plate" and wives of artisans and shopkeepers in general will "weigh you one pound of everything from ground almonds to gunpowder." Two seventeenth-century Italian travelers noted the same in higher-end businesses.[11] Albert Babeau, an historian who published his research in Paris in 1886, drew on literary anecdotes such as these (and perhaps his own experience in the shops and workshops of his day) to conclude that in Old Regime family businesses the wife did the selling. He imagined that she, presumably when dealing with a male customer such as himself, "deployed the qualities unique to her as a woman: she sought to seduce, to attract, to hold on to the buyer; she made one appreciate the qualities of the merchandise."[12]

Selling everything meant family businesswomen were collecting the money for everything, and that meant that they were usually the ones who kept the money safe in a society that did not have banks in which ordinary people could deposit funds. Marie Louise Espec kept her and her husband's money in a green silk purse in a small linen sack closed with a pin, hidden in the straw of her daughter's bed, itself in a small locked room just off the bedroom Espec shared with her husband. The keys wives carried were the symbol of their control over the household's valuables.[13] Even when husbands received earnings, they turned them over to their wives for safekeeping. As one husband put it when speaking of himself and his wife, he "had always given her to guard all the money that came from his work."[14]

When a husband needed money, he often had to go to his wife. For instance, when a heavy goods wagon driver requested his pay from a lock- and blacksmith who had hired him to move several loads, the lock- and blacksmith "turned to his wife" and said, "This man must be paid," for it was she who held the cash.[15] Julie Hardwick's study of domestic violence in Lyon and Nantes underlines the financial management exercised by wives and the tension this could create. Hardwick notes that domestic violence often started when "men asked their wives for money, and the wives turned them down," when "wives refused to provide guarantees for loans," or when wives criticized how their husbands spent their money, as when one husband complained that he and his wife were "'quarrelling because she remonstrated with him about his drinking and gambling.'"[16] This suggests that while wives may well have been the ones keeping the money of a family business, at least some husbands tried to enforce their own will through intimidation and significant levels of violence that were both legally and socially acceptable, as long as they stayed within a few quite wide bounds. Domestic violence does not appear in the examples uncovered for this study, but that does not mean that the silent threat of such violence did not shape the framework within which many women worked.

Domestic violence was not the only way tensions between spouses over money could be expressed. One master market gardener filed a formal complaint stating that his wife, "instead of working well with him had made herself so absolute and the master as much of himself as of all his house that she had refused to give him money when he asked her for it."[17] In another case, a husband complained that his wife had gone even further: she had disappeared with his money and his possessions.[18] Although extremes, both cases suggest that wives were not powerless or without options.

Women also seemed to find their financial and business work not unpleasant. In the few textile professions where gender roles were reversed—those where it was the wife who had the technical skill and knowledge and who did the manual labor, while the husband handled orders and customers—the complaints by husbands were that wives refused to work.[19] By contrast, in all the other professions, where the husband did the manual labor, no husband complained that his wife refused to deal with customers or handle the money. Rather, they complained that wives took too much control or that, more rarely, they spent the money on things of which the husbands did not approve. This difference suggests that, unlike some forms of manual labor, being in charge of selling and of cash, and of the tasks related to them explored below, was satisfying work.

A husband could, in theory, take the money and its management away from his wife, but doing so could have consequences, both personal and professional. A woodseller who took financial control because he felt his wife was making an "outrageous dissipation" of the money was soon complaining that his action "threw [his wife] into a fury so strange that it is not possible to live tranquilly in his home, and that his wife distances all the other businesses from him, and vomits against him insults and damnations."[20]

MANAGING THE MONEY

Collecting and keeping earnings from the family business meant that wives were nearly always the ones who kept the accounts and dealt with issues of credit. When a journeyman stonemason approached the wife of his master and demanded his pay, she verbally walked him through the accounts, which led her to conclude: "We do not owe you anything, on the contrary, it is you who owe us." She twice used the first person plural to convey the unity in the business between herself and her husband; she noted that her words "obliged the journeyman" to drop his demand.[21] When a journeyman baker informed his master that he wished to leave his employ right away, the master baker replied that the journeyman "would have to wait until [the master's wife] had returned from the market, in order to count with her and see if [the journeyman] was owed anything, or if he himself owed [them]."[22] The master baker had no idea of the state of the accounts between him and his journeyman; the sole person knowledgeable in this area was the wife.

Gayle Brunelle has found that even in large business operations in early modern Rouen, when a husband had to defend his business by displaying and explaining his account books in commercial court, one often finds his wife standing in his place, perhaps in part because she kept the account books and knew the most about them.[23] Keeping the accounts here did not require formal training. Julie Hardwick notes that extant early modern account books known to be written by women were nearly always rudimentary in their methods, but were quite adequate for the task at hand.[24]

Women's management of the money in the preindustrial era meant that they were the ones who made the decisions concerning the small loans that kept Old Regime urban economies running.[25] One husband, a cabinetmaker, testified that a male neighbor came into his workshop and asked his wife for a loan of 30 sous (the equivalent of nearly two days' wages for a skilled journeyman) in order to obtain a copy of a legal document. The cabinetmaker was working nearby and heard his wife and the neighbor discuss the matter, and his wife refuse the loan.[26] Both ignored the cabinetmaker himself, for he was irrelevant to the issue at hand, and he presented himself that way in his testimony. He made the cabinets; his wife handled the rest. It was the male neighbor who made the request, rather than his own wife (who was also mentioned), perhaps because most dealings with legal institutions were coded as men's work, and certainly legal officials and the law tended to give more respect and legal standing to men. When such considerations were not in play, men were outside the circuits of small credit altogether, as when, in another case, the same amount of 30 sous was requested of the wife of a leather embroiderer, although this time the person making the request was the wife of a woodturner.[27]

All of these concerned fairly small sums of money and were informal arrangements that did not include charging interest. Wives were also in charge of more serious financial transactions that generated income. A legal commentator of the time noted that "it is the wives who are the usurers" and that "their husbands are agreeable to it, but pretend not to see it." The law that made usury illegal even took the rare step of noting that it applied to "men as much as to women."[28] Women's work in regard to credit was not just limited to urban areas, for Elise Dermineur has found that women peasants invested their savings in rural credit markets (which were very different from their urban equivalents) and played a significant role in the circulation of credit in rural areas before the ascension of capitalism.[29] In practice, each spouse had her or his mostly separate spheres of responsibility and decision making; anything to do with issues of cash, accounts, and credit were usually the wife's purview.

MANAGING THE MEN AND THE BUSINESSES

Collecting, securing, and managing the money led wives to have a deep and gendered involvement in family businesses. Widows who continued to manage the shops or workshops of their late husbands have rightly received considerable attention from historians.[30] Although in Old Regime law they were merely dutiful wives carrying on the work and wishes of their spouses, in our modern view they were independent businesswomen who had the legal power of men (their deceased husbands). Because of that legal status, widows are also well documented. As Janine Lanza has pointed out, it took a lot of knowledge to run such businesses, and business widows probably acquired and honed their commercial and management skills while their husbands were still very much alive. Business widows did not come out of the blue, they came out of married life.[31] This article fleshes out that insight by suggesting how the distinction between wife and widow that is so striking in legal documents may not have been so strong in practice, for wives' dealings with customers and management of the money put them at the structural heart of the business.

The words of Marie Louise Espec—with which this article opened—suggest that as a wife she was doing the long-range business planning. She was thinking of the future of her husband and their business, and perhaps even the future of the young man—the orphan—she had taken on. When hiring him she would have had to take into consideration the impact of the man's wages on, and of the profit he would bring to, her savings and business plans. If her husband were to predecease her, as so often happened, his role in the business (and perhaps even in her personal life) could be filled by another skilled journeyman, as Janine Lanza's work on widows has also shown. The wife was, in essence, overseeing the business.

If the glimpse of Mary Louise Espec's work that has come down to us shows her looking toward the future of what was legally her husband's business, our glimpse of the work of Catherine Frère was rooted in day-to-day management. Her husband, Charles, owned a business transporting heavy goods around Paris with his horses and carts. The work of loading and unloading was often strenuous. A man's world no doubt, but Catherine Frère was at the heart of it. She reported that when she found two male customers by her door who were asking about having a delivery made, she enquired as to what needed transporting (seven or eight four-paned window frames), from where the goods should be collected, and to where they should be delivered. She then "bargained with the said two men," settled on that frequently recurring amount of 30 sous, and sent one of her male assistants to serve them.[32] Her husband was no doubt good at driving and repairing his carts, as well as at loading and unloading, but while he was busy with the manual details, it was his wife who was up front running the show. As one widower noted of his late wife, she "was a great help in his business, about which she had a perfect knowledge."[33]

In some cases, wives' work may have extended into that associated with their husbands. In the witness testimonies used here people rarely had a chance to speak about themselves on this issue, but they did speak about others (usually the litigants). The male witnesses consistently portrayed husbands in family business couples as the ones with the manual skills or the legal ownership, and referred to these men's spouses as merely "the wife of the woodturner" or such. Women whose testimonies were recorded often did likewise, but sometimes they employed another construction that reflected a different understanding. In each of four cases in which husbands were described by their occupation— "woodturner" (*tourneur*), "lock and blacksmith" (*serrurier*), "butcher" (*boucher*), or "house manager" (*principal locataire*), all of these in the male form—a woman among the witnesses, but never a man in the testimonies used here, described the men's wives by using the feminine forms of the same appelations (*tourneuse, serrurière, bouchère, principalle locataire*).[34] Given that the *tourneuse* was last seen holding a plane, a tool used for taking shavings off planks of wood to reduce their thickness or make them smooth, such feminine forms may have sometimes designated wives who were involved in the manual side of the family business as well, and thus suggest the presence of skilled female workers outside of the textile trades, where they were most often found.[35] In some male-dominated professions women's manual involvement could go beyond the day-to-day skilled labor. A woodblock cutter noted that one day his wife made a suggestion that she said would improve his method of work. He noted that he "believed her" and tried it, remarking that it "responded to our desires" and that he thereafter continued to use it.[36]

There were various structural factors (beyond individual character traits or the importance of the wife's dowry for the survival of the business) that affected the roles of family businesswomen and their standing in regard to their husbands. The most important has already been mentioned: the custom of seeing wives as being the ones who usually manage the daily funds of such a business and who sell its goods and services. The implication is that family business husbands may have considered everyday financial management as "women's work" inappropriate for, or even below the dignity of, their conception of masculinity. Also of prime importance was the unstated role of women in the communication networks of each profession, as shaped by guild regulations concerning the admittance of men.[37] Women were, to a certain extent, disempowered in relatively "closed" guilds dominated by sons of masters because guild masters could obtain connections and information from male kin (uncles, brothers, cousins). By contrast, in relatively "open" guilds composed substantially of outsiders, marrying the daughter or widow of a master provided a guild member with tremendous advantages in terms of knowledge and connections, and that likely influenced his relations with his wife in a subtle way. Some guild regulations also explicitly specified the privileges of wives or widows, and that too could affect a woman's standing.[38] Finally, the degree to which customers needed to talk directly to the husband in each profession likewise shaped the standing of the wife, although it is surprising, sometimes even to their husbands, the level of technical detail that wives could negotiate with ease. The sums of money involved may have also been a factor, in that larger sums may have involved the husband more. What is striking though is that, in the examples so far uncovered, the basic structure of women's responsibilities in the family businesses of the Old Regime seems to be roughly similar across a wide range of professions.

DEFUSING TENSIONS BETWEEN MEN

Managing the money meant that wives often managed men in a related area. They dealt with disagreements or conflicts, usually between their husbands and journeymen or temporary hires, for such tensions often revolved around financial issues, of which wives could be the final arbiter. Angelique Buffet saw her husband, a lock- and blacksmith, who was standing near his forge with metal heating in it, get into an argument over pay with a heavy goods cart driver. Her husband threatened him, saying, "Leave my house else I'll give you the staff" (a beating with a thick piece of wood); the driver responded, "It is I who give it to others." At this point Angelique stepped in, took charge, and led the cart driver outside before the men came to blows, thereby avoiding a potentially injurious or even deadly altercation. Her husband, their journeyman, and their apprentice (the latter also her nephew) merely stood by and watched. The cart driver acquiesced to her in part because he likely knew she would be the one with the money, and thus the one who could pay him.[39] From the initial flare up to her intervention very little time had passed. This suggests that she had been keeping an eye on the workshop and the men within it.

Angelique Buffet, and family business wives in general, had strong support when it came to dealing with tensions. A detailed analysis has been done else-where of working women's roles in keeping violence between men in check, the techniques that they deployed, and the multiple forces that strengthened their hands.[40] As a woman, Angelique was by definition outside the world of combative masculinity, allowing the driver to relate to her less defensively, and listening to her provided a face-saving way to avoid the risks of injury and prosecution. He was also no doubt aware that she was protected by her male kin and often by others too. The cart driver was outnumbered, for behind Angelique Buffet stood her husband, her nephew, and their journeyman, all of whom were attached to her by bonds of family, familiarity, or simply by being in her pay. Another family businesswoman testified that when an angry male customer insulted her (she told the commissioner that he had called her "an excommunicated old woman and a blasphemer") and violently threatened her, "many people" (*du monde*) came to her rescue.[41] Journeymen referred to the family business husband as their master (*maître*) and to his wife as their *maîtresse,* which the 1694 edition of the *Dictionnaire de l'Académie française* of the time noted was both the feminine of *maître* and—in a hint of what a woman could accomplish in the male world of the workshop—referred to "girls and women who are sought after in marriage, or who are simply loved."[42]

Family business wives could also use violence to make sure they got the money that was due them. When a visiting Breton nobleman, a social type known for lack of funds, apparently got into a dispute over pay in a cobbler's shop, the cobbler's wife called the noble "a bankrupt" and told him she would take his sword and run it through his stomach. She then threw stones at him, chased him down the street, and gathered other neighbors to her cause. He fled back to his host's house; a servant saw what was happening, held the front door open, then promptly closed it as soon as the nobleman had run inside.[43]

CONCLUSION

Wives were the backbone of the family businesses that made up the Old Regime urban economy. It was the wives of the master artisans and shopkeepers who bargained and sold the goods and services; received the money; kept it in a safe place; kept the accounts; decided on the small loans essential to keeping the economy running; paid employees; planned for the financial future of the business; defused tensions among the men working there, which were often over money; and, when necessary, used force and mobilized that of others to get paid. Wives' financial responsibilities and dealings with customers led them to manage, in various ways, the men in the business, including their husbands, and the overarching framework in which the business ran and developed. Wives were supported in this by the customary sexual division of labor, and their standing was probably influenced by their role in the communication networks of their husbands' guilds. Wives' roles were limited by a number of factors, including that many husbands had the option of using domestic violence or intimidation to enforce their desires without regard for those of their wives. Nevertheless, overall, the assessment of the late nineteenth-century historian Albert Babeau rings true despite his outdated language and his reliance on a few literary references (and perhaps his experience of the family enterprises of his own day). In a brief mention of the husband-and-wife businesses of the Old Regime, he commented that "if the husband was the arms, she was the tongue and the head."[44] In most cases, a man could only hope to run a shop or workshop if he were married; some guilds recognized this explicitly, as did the popular author Louis-Sébastien Mercier. Other research has shown that widows were able to run their late husbands' businesses. This article has fleshed out and extended the insights of others to argue that widows were able to do so because as wives they had, to a significant extent, already been running the family businesses of the preindustrial urban economy.

NOTES

I am grateful to the editors for inviting me to contribute to this volume; to Daryl Hafter for her persistent encouragement, without which this essay would not have been written; to Clare Crowston for her knowledgeable and detailed suggestions; and to the students of my Gender in Europe II course (particularly Courtney Hughes, Jennifer Williams, Jessica Coote, and Lauren Cherry), who critiqued a draft without knowing the author. This is a version of a chapter of my forthcoming monograph concerning working women and gender relations in early modern Paris.

1. Marie Louise Espec's husband was able to run a workshop without being a master because he was based in an area of Paris outside of guild control. Citations to court cases are made in the following format: name of the witness or type of document within the proceedings when relevant; chief defendant in italics; date of case; and call number in the Archives Nationales, Paris (hereafter AN). Complaint, *Girard*, 4 and 9 June 1785, AN Y 9950. The complaint was rendered on 19 May 1785. Due to a technicality, Marie repeated her narrative as a witness on 4 June, and there it says that it was "she and her husband" who had taken the man on for the trial period, then apprenticeship.

2. Katrina Honeyman and Jordan Goodman argue that there were periods of greater opportunities for women alternating with periods of exclusion. See their "Women's Work, Gender Conflict, and Labour Markets in Europe, 1500–1900," in *Gender and History in Western Europe*, ed. Robert B. Shoemaker and Mary Vincent (London: Arnould, 1998), 353–376.

3. Janine M. Lanza, *From Wives to Widows in Early Modern Paris: Gender, Economy, and Law* (Aldershot, Eng.: Ashgate, 2007); Elizabeth Musgrave, "Women and the Craft Guilds in Eighteenth-Century Nantes," in *The Artisan and the European Town, 1500–1900*, ed. Geoffrey Crossick (Aldershot, Eng.: Ashgate, 1997), 151–171; Carol L. Loats, "Gender, Guilds, and Work Identity: Perspectives from Sixteenth-Century Paris," *French Historical Studies* 20, no. 1 (1997): 15–30. A broader and helpful framework is provided by Sheilagh Ogilvie, "How Does Social Capital Affect Women? Guilds and Communities in Early Modern Germany," *American Historical Review* 109, no. 2 (2004): 325–359.

4. The historiography on working women is extensive and, in addition to the contributions to this volume, includes Daryl M. Hafter, *Women at Work in Preindustrial France* (University Park: Pennsylvania State Univ. Press, 2007); Lanza, *From Wives to Widows in Early Modern Paris;* Clare Haru Crowston, *Fabricating Women: The Seamstresses of Old Regime France, 1675–1791* (Durham: Duke Univ. Press, 2001); and James B. Collins, "Economic Role of Women in Seventeenth-Century France," *French Historical Studies* 16, no. 2 (1989): 436–470. The most famous working women of early modern and Revolutionary Paris are perhaps the so-called fishwives. See Katie Jarvis, "Politics in the Marketplace: The Popular Activism and Cultural Representation of the Dames des Halles during the French Revolution" (Ph.D. diss., University of Wisconsin–Madison, 2014), and Rene Sue Marion, "The Dames de la Halle: Community and Authority in Early Modern Paris" (Ph.D. diss., Johns Hopkins University, 1995).

5. Arlette Farge, *La vie fragile: Violence, pouvoirs et solidarités à Paris au XVIIIe siècle* (Paris: Hachette, 1986), 134–135.

6. For the legal standing of husbands and wives, see Clare Haru Crowston, "Family Affairs: Wives, Credit, Consumption, and the Law in Old Regime France," in *Family, Gender, and Law in Early Modern France*, ed. Suzanne Desan and Jeffrey Merrick (University Park: Pennsylvania State Univ. Press, 2009), 62–72; and Sarah Hanley, "Engendering the State: Family Formation and State Building in Early Modern France," *French Historical Studies* 16, no. 1 (1989): 4–27. For the importance of the dowry to a family business, see Julie Hardwick, "Seeking Separations: Gender, Marriages, and Household Economies in Early Modern France," *French Historical Studies* 21, no. 1 (1998): 157–180. For the general responsibilities of each spouse in an artisanal enterprise, as well as the role of the dowry, see Steven L. Kaplan, *The Bakers of Paris and the Bread Question, 1700–1775* (Durham: Duke Univ. Press, 1996). The importance and business skill of working wives is also being uncovered by Gayle K. Brunelle, "Husbands and Wives and the Domestic Economy," paper presented at the annual conference of the Society for French Historical Studies, Tempe, Arizona, April 8–10, 2010.

For domestic violence and women's role in limiting it, see Julie Hardwick, *Family Business: Litigation and the Political Economies of Daily Life in Early Modern France* (New York: Oxford Univ. Press, 2009), 183–221, and Roderick Phillips, "Women, Neighborhood, and Family in the Late Eighteenth Century," *French Historical Studies* 18, no. 1 (1993): 1–12.

7. See, for example, Crowston, *Fabricating Women*.

8. This aspect of legal practice has not been studied. I base my conclusions on a comparison of commissioners' records of the 1670s with those of 1785, as well as more impressionistic comparisons with several other years throughout the eighteenth century. For more general studies, see Alan Williams, *The Police of Paris, 1718–1789* (Baton Rouge: Louisiana State Univ. Press, 1979).

9. *Val,* 21 September 1683, AN Y 12286.

10. *La Mouche,* 18 and 19 February 1670, AN Y 12249; *Dumouches,* 27 May 1664, AN Y 12238; *Meullé,* 25 March 1670, AN Y 12249; *Gargottier,* 20 July 1670, AN Y 12250.

11. Louis-Sébastien Mercier, *Le tableau de Paris,* cited by Albert A. Babeau, *Les artisans et les domestiques d'autrefois* (Paris: F. Didot, 1886), 178–179; Sébastien Locatelli, *Voyage de France: Moeurs et coutumes françaises (1664–1665),* trans. A. Vautier (Paris: A. Picard et fils, 1905), cited in Wendy Gibson, *Women in Seventeenth-Century France* (New York: St. Martin's Press, 1989), 105–106.

12. Babeau, *Les artisans et les domestiques d'autrefois,* 178.

13. Zoë A. Schneider, "Women Before the Bench: Female Litigants in Early Modern Normandy," *French Historical Studies* 23, no. 1 (2000): 27.

14. *Parizot,* 20 August 1683, AN Y 12286.

15. *Remy,* 26 April 1670, AN Y 12249.

16. Julie Hardwick, "Early Modern Perspectives on the Long History of Domestic Violence: The Case of Seventeenth-Century France," *Journal of Modern History* 78, no. 1 (2006): 11.

17. *Parizot,* 20 August 1683, AN Y 12286.

18. *Carré,* 15 May 1683, AN Y 12286.

19. "Détail de tout ce qui s'est passeé," 1774, AN Y 11741, cited by Farge, *Vie fragile,* 101–118. Gay Gullickson, *Spinners and Weavers of Auffay: Rural Industry and the Sexual Division of Labor in a French Village, 1750–1850* (Cambridge: Cambridge Univ. Press, 1986). I am grateful to Clare Crowston for encouraging me to reflect on this example.

20. Farge, *Vie fragile,* 137.

21. Plainte, *Perrot,* 30 December 1670, AN Y 12251.

22. Requête, *Adelaine,* 16 August 1670, AN Y 12250.

23. Brunelle, "Husbands and Wives."

24. Julie Hardwick, conversation with the author, April 10, 2010.

25. Crowston, "Family Affairs," in *Family, Gender, and Law in Early Modern France,* 62–100, shows that wives could contract debt for "household purchases." Such debt was binding on the husband, and could in extreme cases even bankrupt him.

26. Jaris, *Quesnel,* May 12, 1682, AN Y 12283. For the annual wages of a typical skilled Parisian journeyman, see Daniel Roche, *The People of Paris: An Essay in Popular Culture in the Eighteenth Century,* trans. Marie Evans and Gwynne Lewis (Berkeley: Univ. of California Press, 1987), 87.

27. *Grenu,* 16 August 1670, AN Y 12250.

28. Adam Théveneau, *Commentaire sur les ordonnances* (Lyon: Rolin Glaize, 1666), 547.

29. Elise Dermineur, "Female Peasants, Patriarchy and the Credit Market in Eighteenth-Century

France," *Proceedings of the Western Society for French History* 37 (2009): 61–84.

30. See, for example, the article by Jane McLeod in this volume on printer widows and her book *Licensing Loyalty: Printers, Patrons, and the State in Early Modern France* (University Park: Pennsylvania State Univ. Press, 2011).

31. Lanza, *From Wives to Widows in Early Modern Paris*.

32. Frère (née Boudin), *Nolin*, 24 October 1675, AN Y 12266.

33. *Parizot*, 20 August 1683, AN Y 12286.

34. *Grenu*, 16 August 1670, AN Y 12250; *Mathurin*, 11 October 1672, AN Y 12260; *Champagne*, 14 October 1670, AN Y 12251; *Rolle*, tenement no. 12, 22 October 1666, AN Y 12242.

35. *Grenu*, 16 August 1670, AN Y 12250.

36. Jean-Michel Papillon, *Traité historique et pratique de la gravure en bois* (Paris: P.-G. Simon, 1766), 2:74. I am grateful to Caroline Duroselle-Melish for this reference.

37. I am grateful for the suggestions of Clare Crowston here, as in many other places.

38. Many of these questions are dealt with in Clare Haru Crowston, "Engendering the Guilds: Seamstresses, Tailors, and the Clash of Corporate Identities in Old Regime France," *French Historical Studies* 23, no. 2 (2000): 339–371. In Lyon's silk industry, a journeyman might gain mastership quickly, if married to a master's daughter who would teach him her skills. Hafter, *Women and Work*, 133.

39. Nicolas Baudet and Claude Buffet, *Remy*, 26 April 1670, AN Y 12249.

40. Jacob Melish, "Women and the Courts in the Control of Violence between Men: Evidence from a Parisian Neighborhood under Louis XIV," *French Historical Studies* 33, no. 1 (2010): 1–31.

41. *Val*, 21 September 1683, AN Y 12286.

42. "Maistresse," *Le Dictionnaire de l'Académie françoise* [*sic*] (Paris: J. B. Coignard, 1694).

43. *Musnier*, 30 June 1670, AN Y 12250.

44. Babeau, *Les artisans et les domestiques d'autrefois*, 178.

MANY EXCEPTIONAL WOMEN
Female Artists in Old Regime Paris
Cynthia M. Truant

MARY SHERIFF's superb book *The Exceptional Woman: Elisabeth Vigée-Lebrun and the Cultural Politics of Art* is a deep analysis of this painter's outstanding artistic production and her successful negotiation of Old and New Regime society. Vigée-Lebrun (1755–1842) was indeed exceptional. Court painter to Marie Antoinette and a renowned portraitist in her time, she encountered and conquered many obstacles in her long career. Fleeing France early in the Revolution, she traveled widely and with fame throughout Europe. Vigée-Lebrun was openly ambitious about her talent, bold, confident, and able to bridge the space between her private and public lives.

One aim in this essay is to examine some issues that Vigée-Lebrun's career raises regarding other women in the arts in this era—not only the issue of "exceptionalism," but also those concerning identity and socio-legal rights. Vigée-Lebrun was not alone; there were surprisingly many female artists from the mid-seventeenth to the early nineteenth centuries. Even if Vigée-Lebrun was unique in the attention and praise her work received, as Sheriff acknowledges, there were many women who supported themselves in this era through their production of various art forms, from the decorative to the fine arts. One could thus argue that there were many women artists who were exceptional. While they were not numerous in comparison to male artists, there were more of them in the eighteenth century than in previous times. They were women for whom professional achievements were not unusual, nor "unnatural." This is not a critique or reductionist reading of Sheriff, who examines her subject with great perception.[1] I merely wish to explore women artists in some different contexts.

Women artists had critics and faced impediments in the Old Regime. Privilege, which restricted women from some professions, was rooted in customs and laws, although with skill it could be manipulated to some extent. Also relevant

to the experience of the women in this period was the character of work organization and the particularities of their artistic genres, as well as the fluid and
shifting nature of artistic hierarchies. For example, history painting, considered
the pinnacle of the fine arts as well as a traditional province of male artists, was
not a rigid category in this era, particularly among collectors. We must also keep
in mind that as these women established careers in the arts, even in domains
that were traditionally male, they did not radically transgress established norms
of female behavior, even as these norms shifted.

Why was there a relatively large number of women in the arts, especially in
Old Regime France? Why was this cohort able to play an essentially public role in
the arts more generally?[2] Answering these questions, or even simply acknowledg-
ing that women were there, means documenting what we can about their relatively large number, continuing to discuss the question of female exceptionalism,
and exploring the possibility that women chose the arts not only to make a living,
but also as a way to create new identities.

I wish to examine a variety of women artists in the eighteenth century in
order to observe the choices that they made, including those concerning their
professional relations with male painters, art collectors, critics, and vendors. I
shall also look into their relations with and admission to academies of art, their
personal relations with men, women, and children in their families, and finally
their professional successes as well as their failures. To manage this large subject
as succinctly as possible, I begin with a brief overview of average income levels
of these women and then examine three topics: The first concerns women in the
Corporation (guild) of Painters and Sculptors (1381–1777).[3] Its name had changed
over the centuries, like that of many guilds, but it had more or less stabilized by
the mid-seventeenth century. The Corporation, after many hurdles and disputes,
obtained official permission in 1705 to establish its own academy of fine arts,
called the Academy of St. Luc, while simultaneously retaining its original guild
status.[4] The second topic concerns women admitted to the most elite French art
academy, the Royal Academy of Painting and Sculpture (1648–1793). Established
in the reign of Louis XIV, it was the only royal academy that officially accepted
women. I examine its rationale for doing so, and the subsequent contestations
of and amendments to this practice. Finally, I discuss "independent" women artists who were unincorporated, members of neither the Parisian guild (and its
Academy of St. Luc) nor the Royal Academy.

While the vast majority of the women examined here did not earn large incomes or achieve great fame, they were all exceptional in some way, not least

for defying—to some extent—social norms that found the combined words "woman" and "artist" rather unnatural. Like other women who held positions in legally sanctioned corporations or academies, these artists often had their rights restricted and were subject to various prejudices.

INCOME AND SOCIAL STANDING OF WOMEN ARTISTS

Female and male artists who made viable but often modest livings were usually members of the Corporation of Painters and Sculptors, which received its official statutes in 1381. Until it was abolished in 1777, it was one of the few trade organizations that granted both men and women the rights of mastership (*maîtrise*) and eased the path to mastership for both daughters and sons. Women guild artists, often unknown to the public by name, excelled in the decorative arts, painting, and pastels. By the eighteenth century, a number became members of the branch of this Corporation, the Academy of St. Luc; only a few of them (including Vigée-Lebrun) were ever accepted into the elite Royal Academy of Painting and Sculpture, founded by Louis XIV in 1648. Yet, the more these women (even those in the Academy of St. Luc) gained public notice, the more social custom and gossip forced them to defend their morals as well as their artistic reputations.

The different ways in which women artists organized their work lives and the wide range of artistic objects they produced make financial generalizations difficult. Besides oil paintings, women produced exquisitely detailed lace and painted fans, cameos, paintings in various genres, and miniature paintings on snuff boxes, the quality of decoration obviously adding to the price. Thus, income was quite variable, from several livres to hundreds, even thousands of livres. In addition, paintings or other works of fine art were often freely given to royal patrons, a shrewd strategy that enhanced the reputation of the artist and could lead to further commissions. While many women artists may have given art lessons, it is almost impossible to discover how much they charged for them. However, we do know that members (male and female) of the Corporation of Painters and Sculptors earned more or less regular if moderate incomes, and that they gained a relatively important social standing as well. Women probably earned less than did their male counterparts. We know, for example, that their work was valued less, at least post-mortem; the works of deceased women artists, oil painters, and pastellists fetched much less at auction than those of their dead male colleagues, until the twentieth or twenty-first century.[5]

More is clearly known about the earnings of elite women artists who worked for royal or aristocratic families. These women often received regular stipends, pensions, or money for living expenses from their benefactors. Madeleine de Basseporte (1701–1780) is an important example. Traditionally considered to have taught the noted still life artist Anne Vallayer-Coster, she also most likely instructed the daughters of Louis XV. By the early 1740s she was well known and respected as a "painter of miniatures and gouaches specializing in flowers, butterflies, and birds." In 1749 Basseporte was granted a yearly royal pension of 1,100 livres, a substantial sum for any artist, male or female. In 1774 the Crown bestowed on her another annual award of 400 livres, for living expenses. An acclaimed draftswoman, Basseporte became official painter to the king, for both the plants in the royal gardens and in the Jardin des Plantes. This post brought her other commissions, including one in 1750 from the comte d'Argenson, who asked her to go to northern France to paint a rare species of pineapple![6] Despite such accomplishment, Basseporte was not an academician, meaning she was not a member of any academy.

Even women accepted into the Royal Academy were not always well paid or able to live and work where they wished. While most noted male artists were granted studios and living quarters in the wings of the Louvre, only one woman gained this privilege before 1789. This was Anne Vallayer-Coster, patronized by the queen. When it came to payment, Vallayer-Coster, Vigée-Lebrun, and a handful of other women painters with elite patrons could earn up to several thousand livres for a painting.[7] However, Adélaide Labille-Guiard, who became a member of the Royal Academy in 1783 and was greatly respected and favored by Louis XVI's aunts, did not earn large sums for her work in the early phase of her career. And in 1785, when she requested lodgings in the Louvre, she was denied. The official refusal, handed down by the comte d'Angiviller—Louis XVI's chief painter and general director of the buildings and grounds—focused on the fact that Labille-Guiard's studio would double as "a school for young students of her sex." D'Angiviller, in his letter to the king on Labille-Guiard's request, explained that male artists had students as well. Thus there would be "great dangers . . . to get to these lodgings one must go through vast corridors that are often dark; this mixing of young artists of different sexes would be very inconvenient for the decency of your majesty's palace."[8] Labille-Guiard, who was in a straitened financial state, did receive a pension of 1,000 livres in 1785; she had more success during the Revolution.[9] More is known about particular women's earnings, including the famed Italian pastellist Rosalba Carriera, who became a member of the Royal Academy in 1720 during her stay in France.[10]

THE CORPORATION OF PAINTERS AND SCULPTORS
AND ITS ACADEMY OF ST. LUC

A number of female artists are known to us by name because of their membership in the Academy of St. Luc. Many of these artists were also members in the
Corporation of Painters and Sculptors. Whether membership in the Corporation
was a necessary requirement for membership in the Academy of St. Luc is not
yet clear. Guild members, except those with honorary status and those in related
art trades, paid an entry fee upon joining the Corporation as apprentices. In the
Corporation of Painters and Sculptors, the intermediate stage of journeyman was
replaced by that of shop or artist's assistant. All members had to present a masterpiece, a work of art in one's chosen specialty, and it had to be judged worthy
by a jury of masters and/or mistresses in that field. Upon the conferring of the
maîtrise, individuals were legally allowed to produce and sell their goods as well
as direct the work of usually one apprentice. Sons and daughters of masters and
mistresses had certain advantages in their training. Their entrance fee was reduced or waived and they had fewer requirements for advancement. They needed
only "slight experience," as Steven Kaplan states, and not the usual six apprentice
years followed by two further years of work before presenting a masterpiece.[11]

By the mid-seventeenth century, individual artisanal producers and even
large-scale merchants in a number of fields were dissatisfied with the restrictions imposed by the guild system.[12] The problems posed by guild origins became
a contentious and long-standing matter of rivalry between the Corporation of
Painters and Sculptors, who wished to have their own academy, and the Crown
and those artists, sculptors, and art critics who wished to establish a Royal Academy, entirely devoted to the fine arts. The latter group wished to focus on the fine
arts practiced by artists of "genius," none of which had any relation to a "mere"
and allegedly manual craft. This definition of the artist, already adopted in Italy,
was an individual *par excellence,* normally a male, and one not limited by the rules
and regulations of a guild.[13]

There were other aspects of the Corporation's practices that were offensive
to those who wanted to establish a Royal Academy of Art. These opponents disdained the Corporation of Painters and Sculptors because the guild included as
members art dealers, art restorers, and "honorary" members (often art collectors
or art critics). There were also objections to the kind of work some guild members did; some only painted backgrounds or worked only in the decorative arts.
Once it was established in 1648, the Royal Academy of Painting and Sculpture

waged a public relations campaign against the members of the Corporation of Painters and Sculptors, accusing them of lacking genius and imagination. The Royal Academy increased pressure on the court by producing pamphlets, legal briefs, and initiating lawsuits demanding that the "painters' guild" be prevented from establishing an academy of "fine arts." But, as Katie Scott and others point out, although there were growing differences between the Corporation of Painters and Sculptors and the Royal Academy of Painting and Sculpture, there were, in fact, a great many points of similarity for a long time.[14]

The artistic disputes between the Corporation and the Academy can be connected to the guild's admission of female members, although the Academy rarely stated this objection openly. The Corporation did, indeed, have female members. While the Corporation of Painters and Sculptors, at least after the late 1760s, was not opening its apprenticeships to women as frequently as it had in prior centuries, women were not an insignificant part of its membership. Moreover, after this guild had fought and won, by the eighteenth century, the right to have an academy and hold biennial art expositions or salons, many female artists exhibited their work.[15] Yet, Royal Academicians considered only a minority of women in the Academy of St. Luc fine artists; the work of others was still "mere" craft. Nonetheless, the china, fire screens, and particularly the delicately painted fans produced by these women were sought after and prized by the nobility.[16] Indeed, membership in the guild mattered. If these women had not been accepted as mistresses in the Corporation of Painters and Sculptors, their work could have been seized as illegal production.

My research in the notarial archives has yielded figures available for those who became mistresses in the mid-eighteenth century.[17] Between the years 1743 and 1766, sixty-two women and 265 men achieved the maîtrise. (See table 1.) Women thus comprised nearly one-sixth of the total membership in the Corporation of Painters and Sculptors. Furthermore, the numbers of married (or widowed) and unmarried mistresses in this Corporation were roughly equal. Although not all these women were in the fine arts, the percentage of women in the guild was far higher than in the Royal Academy of Painters and Sculptors, which stopped accepting women in 1706. When the ban was lifted in 1770, the Academy allowed only four women to be members at any one time; none were sculptors. I have thus far found only one female sculptor in the Academy of St. Luc; she worked as a sculptor of bas-relief in wood, considered a remarkable talent for a woman.[18] My examination of archival data recording maîtres/maîtresses of the Corporation of Painters and Sculptors in the years 1743–1766 revealed no women serving or nominated for what this institution called *directeurs gardes* (directors-officials). Moreover, thus far I have found only one woman acting as an official after the post-1776 reorganization of any of the Corporations of Arts and Trades, when there was no such restriction.[19] Prior to 1776, women had almost always been barred from corporation governance, except in all-female or sometimes mixed (male and female) trades.

The other branch of the guild of painters and sculptors, the Academy of St. Luc, deserves more scholarly study. Abolished in 1777—under pressure from

TABLE 1. Distribution of Candidates for Maîtrise among Women and Men in the Academy/Guild of St. Luc: Sample of Six Years from 1743 to 1776

Year	Candidates Admitted	Nature of Admission
1743	3 mistress painters 46 master painters 2 master sculptors	presentation of masterpiece[a]
1745	1 mistress painter 1 mistress sculptor 20 master painters	presentation of masterpiece "by experience" (training and work)
1749	12 mistress painters 63 master painters	presentation of masterpiece "by experience" (training and work)
1750	8 mistress painters 27 master painters 9 master sculptors	presentation of masterpiece
1765	7 mistress painters 37 master painters	apprenticeship and presentation of masterpiece
1766	18 mistress painters 61 master painters	apprenticeship and presentation of masterpiece

[a]When the masterpiece alone is indicated, the assumption is that the regular apprenticeship or additional work was waived or shortened because the candidate was a son or daughter of a maître or maîtresse.

the Royal Academy—it gave many women the opportunity to present work in its exhibitions.[20] While the varied genres of work done by women or men who were members of the Academy of St. Luc were often disdained by members of the Royal Academy, there was not yet a rigid genre hierarchy. As the respected art historian Michael Levey points out, many different genres were still highly regarded, including those of "semi-luxury" and "populuxe" goods.[21] Portraiture, miniatures, and decorative work, almost exclusively done by women, were not simple repetition; they were often inspired artifacts, and were praised by art collectors and critics.[22]

THE ROYAL ACADEMY OF PAINTING AND SCULPTURE

The Royal Academy of Painting and Sculpture was the only royal academy to accept women members, albeit few in number.[23] Their admission of women might be explained both by the European tradition in which noted male painters trained their daughters and sisters, as well as by the high level of patronage some women artists enjoyed. Such patronage was not as common in other fields. Sheriff discusses this issue in terms of the importance of "the king's grace"—his will. Yet, as Sheriff says, royal and possibly administrative pressure to include women in the new fine arts academy does not fully explain the exclusion of women from other royal academies. Of course, writers were not members of guilds. Scientists of some types were. But the exclusion of women from these institutions was significant and, given the customary and often official opposition to women in the academies in the nineteenth and even much of the twentieth centuries, needs to be examined more deeply.

The women accepted into the Royal Academy were artistically talented in their own right. Some women, it is true, were the daughters, sisters, nieces, or cousins of male academicians. For example, the Boullongne sisters, Geneviève and Madeleine (the second and third women ever accepted), were the daughters of Louis Boullongne, a well-known and respected member of the Royal Academy. Nevertheless, and perhaps desirous of imitating other Royal Academies, the Royal Academy of Painting and Sculpture banned female members starting in 1706: "Saturday 25 September 1706, the Academy . . . finding that several young women ['Damoiselles'], who have applied themselves to Painting, have planned to present themselves to be received as Academicians . . . the Company, after having seriously reflected on this matter [and] in order to prevent these presentations, has resolved that from hence forward [the Company] will not receive any young woman. . . . This resolution will serve as a general regulation . . . from henceforward. [Unsigned]"[24]

They lifted their ban on 28 September 1770:

Regulation for the Admission of Women into the Academy

The Academy, having deliberated that, in as much as it would be pleasing to encourage the talent of women in admitting several of them into this Body, despite these admissions, foreign in a certain way to its [the Academy's] constitution, should not be excessive in number. The Academy has agreed that it will not admit more than the number of four women . . . [an] extraordinary and distinguished talent [might] move the Academy [. . .] by a unanimous vote, to "crown" such an individual with the great distinction of acceptance. In any event, the Academy does not wish or claim to regularly replace this number of four, and reserves [the right] to make their decisions only when it finds itself convinced by talents that are truly distinguished.[25]

While the British Royal Academy of Art was even more stringent in its rules against female membership, there were other academies of art in Europe and France (for example, Marseille, Toulouse, and Bordeaux) that welcomed the admission of women artists and exhibited their work.[26]

Male members of the Royal Academy were concerned that an excessive number of women might alter the standing and purpose of their Academy, which they thought should be free both from what they considered to be the taint of the guilds and from royal grace. It appears that there were concerns not only about the entry of "too many women" that might link this Royal Academy to the Corporation of Painters and Sculptors, but also about royal favoritism that would be harmful to this academy of fine arts—even though it had originally been sanctioned and established by Louis XIV. This latter issue arises particularly toward the end of the Old Regime, as the concept of the public sphere was becoming more entrenched. There were growing objections over royal pressure on the rights of the Royal Academy of Painting and Sculpture to make decisions independently. This issue became most pronounced over the admission of Vigée-Lebrun in 1783.[27] Acceptance into the Royal Academy was a multi-stage process. After presenting a work in a medium and on a subject assigned by the Academy, all candidates, both men and women, were "provisionally accepted" (agréé). Men, however, often had to present a second work, and had this work subject to a jury, before obtaining full acceptance. For women, the second work was not required and hence they were often fully accepted into the Academy on the same day as their provisional acceptance, although their acceptance did not come with all the rights a male member of the Royal Academy might enjoy. For some women, particularly those who had supportive fathers, husbands, or brothers who were already prominent or had been accepted by the Royal Academy, acceptance may have been easier (for example, there was no review by a jury of academicians). But this was not true for all women who were accepted; some had their work scrutinized by the Royal Academy.

Certainly, there were men with connections to members of the Academy who had a harder time being fully accepted than did women. For men, the usual process was that they were provisionally accepted into the Royal Academy and then worked for years (virtually as apprentices) before being fully accepted. One example is that of Charles-Jacques Clérion, husband of Geneviève Boullongne. While Boullongne was both received and made a member of the Academy on 12 December 1669, her husband had a much longer and more difficult path to becoming an academician, despite his marriage into a family of well-known artists.[28] He was received in 1676 as an apprentice into the Royal Academy and only became an academician in 1689. Little or none of his work is extant and cannot be independently judged at this point.

Women members were allowed to exhibit their art at the salons of the Royal Academy of Painting and Sculpture. But, for the most part, women fully accepted into the Royal Academy did not truly have full membership; unlike male members, they only rarely, if ever, participated in the meetings of the Royal Academy. Women were not voting members of the Royal Academy, nor could they become officials of the Academy. Vigée-Lebrun was again exceptional in attending at least one of the meetings of the Royal Academy, where she defended her admission.

Finally, even women fully accepted into the Royal Academy never swore an oath, as did men (and all women mistresses in guilds), to uphold its regulations. Women simply received a letter informing them of their acceptance into the Royal Academy of Painting and Sculpture. In contrast, women accepted into the Academy of St. Luc did swear an oath to this institution. In addition, when the Academy of St. Luc won the right to hold its own salons, more than just a few of its female members presented their work, at least in the years I have examined, 1751, 1753, 1764, and 1774. Elisabeth Vigée-Lebrun and Adélaide Labille-Guiard exhibited paintings in the salons of the Academy of St. Luc *before* their acceptances into the Royal Academy. Yet, the Academy of St. Luc also seems to have excluded women from their regular meetings and never made women officials. The number of women in the Academy of St. Luc diminished by the late 1760s, although they still admitted women in greater numbers than the Royal Academy (which, as noted, banned the admission of women from 1706 to 1770).

From the start, the Royal Academy's aim was to be the premier Royal Academy of the *fine* arts. While in its early years the Royal Academy permitted the production of decorative arts, its standards became increasingly rigid with time. With this change there was also more emphasis on oil painting, sculpture, and hierarchies of genre. History painting was elevated in status and women were increasingly seen as practitioners of the "lesser" forms of the fine arts, despite the fact that outside of the Royal Academy portraits and still lifes—often produced by women—remained important. Sculpture had long been considered outside the province of women, and it remained so into the era under study.

Certain factors remained constant with regard to the admission of women members. The first four women accepted into the Royal Academy specialized in some form of still life painting, and three of the four probably gained their admission because of their husbands or other male relatives who were influential in the Royal Academy. Sheriff rightly stresses the importance of these factors in the acceptance of the first woman, Mademoiselle Giradon, into the Academy.[29] But I wish to stress the exceptionality of the case of Elisabeth-Sophie Chéron, the fourth woman accepted, whom I have not found to have any male relatives in the Royal Academy, although she did have influential patrons there. There was an engraver, Charles-François Chéron, but he entered the Academy four years *after* Mademoiselle Chéron and there is no indication that they were related. Elisabeth-Sophie Chéron married a Monsieur le Hay, who had no known ties to the Royal Academy or to art in general. She was presented to the Academy in 1672, not by her family, but by one Monsieur Charles (1619–1690), a prominent founder of the Royal Academy (one of the twelve *Anciens*). Charles presented two portraits executed by Chéron. These paintings "greatly satisfied the Company," which deemed her works so extremely rare that they exceeded the "constraints of her sex." The Company (as the Royal Academy of Painting and Sculpture sometimes liked to call itself in its written minutes) resolved to name her an academician, and "ordered that the proper Letters to this effect be expedited to her." In September 1673, Monsieur Montagne, another key member of the Academy (and the subject of one of Chéron's portraits) wrote a letter to the Company, dictated by Mademoiselle Chéron, asking that this portrait remain in the Academy's collection. The Academy "received [his letter] with joy."[30]

Three more women were accepted after Chéron, before the 1706 ban: Anne-Renée Stressor (circa 1649–1713), a painter of miniatures, received on 24 September 1676; Dorothée Massé, *veuve* Godequin (dates unknown), a sculptor in wood, received on 23 November 1680; and Catherine Perrot, *femme* Oudry (dates unknown), a painter of miniatures, received on 31 January 1682.[31]

While both Stressor and Perrot fall into more traditional categories of women artists of this era, Massé, perhaps the only female sculptor in the Royal Academy, should be singled out for attention. This was in part because of the plaudits she received in the minutes of the meeting at which she was accepted (although there is no indication that she was actually present at that meeting). Her work was presented to the assembly by the academician M. Lebrun and was described as ". . . a work of sculpted leaves, encircling a monogram, very delicately carved in wood by Demoiselle *Dorothée Massé*, widow of Monsieur Godequin. . . . The Academy, considering the precision of the work and the virtue of this Demoiselle, have agreed to receive her and found it good to allow her to receive the grace that the King has shown to the Academy in granting her the quality of Academician, *without indicating that this [acceptance] will have any future consequence . . .*" (my emphasis).[32]

Massé received the regular admission letters. Sheriff stresses that the Royal Academy considered Massé's acceptance along with that of Catharine Perrot (1682), the next woman accepted, "not of consequence" and "not to be considered a precedent" for the future admission of female candidates. The denial of further admissions as precedent was codified in the 1706 regulation that prohibited the admission of women to the Royal Academy.

Nonetheless, as was often the case in the Old Regime, there were always possible exceptions. In fact there were six exceptions to the 1706 ban, and three of these may have been allowed because of the international reputations of the women in question. Also in their favor were their connections to influential men in the world of court politics. Rosalba Carriera (1675–1757), admitted in 1720 during her stay in France (1720–1721), is an early case. Carriera was an extremely well-known Italian painter and innovator in pastels. While in France, she painted a number of portraits of noted French men and women, including Antoine Watteau. In 1722 the Dutch still life painter Margueritte Haverman (1693–circa 1750) was accepted into the Royal Academy, albeit with some hesitation on the part of its members. The Academy may have felt safer from the problem (or danger?) of the reception of too many women as long as they accepted foreigners. It would have been a slight not to accept Carriera, a woman who had many French patrons and supporters, who had already been accepted into numerous European art academies, and who had received a number of eminent awards. However, it appears that the Royal Academy may have felt justified in their caution in Haverman's case. Soon after her acceptance she was accused of presenting for her reception piece a painting by Jan van Huysman, her former teacher, and she was expelled a year later. This claim was disputed and now appears groundless.[33] The third woman accepted into the Royal Academy in this era of the ban on women, in 1767, was Dorothea Lisieswska-Therbouche (sometimes known as Therbusch, 1732–1782). Originally from Poland, she lived primarily in Berlin and specialized in portraiture.

Three of the post-1706 exceptions were not foreigners, but were French. The first French woman artist accepted since Catherine Perrot (1682) was Marie Thérèse Réboul (1728–1805), admitted in 1757.[34] She was a skilled painter of flowers and plants, and the wife of the gifted history painter Joseph-Marie Vien (1716–1809). Vien was also an important administrator in the Royal Academy. He directed the Ecole Française de Rome and he eventually became Painter to the King in 1789. Anne Vallayer-Coster (1744–1818) was accepted to the Academy on 28 July 1770. Vallayer-Coster was one of Queen Marie Antoinette's painters; her still life paintings won her lasting fame. Finally, Marie-Suzanne Giroust, a noted pastel portraitist, was accepted to the Academy on 1 September of 1770.[35] There were now four women (including Therbusch) in the Royal Academy. Did these cases have something to do with the Royal Academy's decision on 28 September 1770 to reverse its ban on women members?

The Royal Academy's decision raises many questions, largely because attitudes with respect to gender norms in France were not moving in the same direction. A growing number of upper-class political men viewed privileged and independent women as a potentially negative force in French society. Male and female writers influenced by thinkers like Montesquieu, Diderot, and Rousseau, among others, articulated a view of a virtuous, reformed society, a republic in which certain types of women had no place. Without simplifying the complexity of contemporary constructions of gender, women who put their own aspirations ahead of their domestic and womanly roles were increasingly considered problematic.

Contemporary constructions of gender help us better understand the use of the term "foreign" in the 1770 regulation that allowed women back into the Royal Academy. The adjective "foreign" (étranger—in parentheses in the original) does not simply mean someone who was not French, but rather foreign or strange in some way to the Academy's culture. This idea is quite telling, for the Academy's founding principles of 1648 never directly excluded women nor claimed them as foreign to the Academy's (unwritten) constitution, suggesting an extremely important vision of what nation/nationality/difference might mean for the Academy, if not for France. "Foreign," as it is used in the 1770 minutes, denotes someone considered too different from the accepted norms of the Royal Academy, a person capable of changing the institution's very nature.[36]

Yet, the discussion over gender and foreignness had just begun in the 1770s. The new struggle of the Royal Academy (having now banished its rival, the Academy of St. Luc) was with the Crown over the Academy's right to admit members, particularly women, without royal interference. This disagreement culminated in the early 1780s, with the king and queen's imposition of the candidacy of Elisabeth Vigée-Lebrun on the Academy, much to the academicians' great displeasure. Feelings were so aroused that even the king's supporter, the comte d'Angiviller, stated that while Madame Lebrun *might* be accepted into the Royal Academy, its views were to be respected. Hence, d'Angiviller humbly requested the king "graciously limit to four the number of women who may . . . be admitted to the Academy. This number is sufficient to honor [their] talent; women could never be useful to the progress of the Arts [due to] the modesty of their sex that would prohibit them from the study of nature [in other words, nudes], in a public School founded by Your Majesty."[37] For an ambitious painter like Vigée-Lebrun, her reception in May of 1783, despite the surrounding negative publicity, was extremely important. It raised her social status, her earnings, and her ability to show her works at the salons of the Royal Academy. In her travels in Europe, she remade the fortune her profligate husband had squandered and became a particular favorite of the Empress Elisabeth of Russia.[38]

The dispute between the Academy and the king over what was seen as royal intervention in promoting Vigée-Lebrun led to the Academy's proposal of a counter-candidate, Adélaide Labille-Guiard. During the controversy, a minister of the king wrote strongly worded letters to the Royal Academy, which responded in equally strong terms. In a bold move, Vigée-Lebrun attended a session of the Academy to defend her case. Although both women were accepted into the Royal Academy in 1783, ill feelings remained. Because Sheriff provides such a complete account of the incident, I will not belabor this issue. I will only stress that both artists were distinguished oil painters, primarily portraitists, although each also did some historical painting. Vigée-Lebrun, as the well-known painter of Marie Antoinette, and a supporter of the Crown and nobility throughout Europe, was the more productive and far better known of the two. Yet, Labille-Guiard was unquestionably active as a painter, teacher, and early feminist; she received a number of royal and then Republican commissions.[39]

Disagreement about the admission of women to the Royal Academy continued as the Revolution approached. Jacques-Louis David, for example, wished to accept female students, but the directors of the Academy denied his request, telling him that such a move would harm his career. Later research has demonstrated that several paintings of women attributed to David were in fact painted by women.[40] It is noteworthy that many renowned male painters—Fragonard, Quentin de la Tour, Gérard, and David, among others—had a high regard for women painters and often served as their mentors.

WOMEN ARTISTS WORKING OUTSIDE THE ROYAL ACADEMY OR THE ACADEMY OF ST. LUC

It is possible that some unaffiliated women artists were encouraged by other women and by their own fathers, brothers, and relatives who were painters. During the eighteenth century, many women became students of noted male or female artists. Major male artists gave lessons in painting to women who gained entry to the Academy of St. Luc, who were admitted to the Royal Academy, or who painted independently. These women often sought to further their instruction with male or female artists of note, even to the point of collaborating with well-known artists. Such collaborations and discussions may well have stimulated the talents of these female artists.

There were also new outlets for unaffiliated women artists. Sheriff lists forty-seven women who exhibited their works at the Pahin de la Blancherie's Salon de Correspondance in the 1770s and 1780s.[41] This late eighteenth-century salon was independent of any institutional affiliation, yet was considered notable and was not prohibited from showing works of art periodically. Some women who exhibited works there were members of the Royal Academy (for example, Vallayer-Coster, Vigée-Lebrun, and Labille-Guiard). However, most of those who showed at the Salon de Correspondance were not members of established institutions. Sheriff also lists fifteen women in the 1777 *Almanach historique et raisonné des architectes, peintres, sculpteurs, et cizeleurs*; only two of them, Mademoiselle Navarre and Madame Vien were members of the Royal Academy.[42] Thus, women who did not necessarily seek institutional affiliation may have been encouraged by the examples set by other women artists who had achieved some recognition.

These were women who worked in the fine arts without ever entering an officially established art academy in Paris, such as the Royal Academy or the Academy of St. Luc. For some women, membership in the Academy of St. Luc was never even an option because they were active after it had been dissolved. The number of such women who seem to have been fairly active producers of art in the decades before and to some extent after the Revolution is not necessarily insignificant. I have found some names beyond those listed by Sheriff. (See table 2 for the names of some of these artists.)[43] At least three fairly prolific and talented women among the group listed in table 2 merit further mention. The eldest was Marianne Loir, essentially a portraitist who was well acquainted with one of the earliest eighteenth-century salonnières, Madame Geoffrin (1699–1777). Loir's undated portrait of the mature Madame Geoffrin presents the subject as a welcoming and pleasing woman at ease, without the need for books, papers, or pens around her; she was well dressed, though not ostentatiously. The painting highlights Geoffrin's intellectual intensity. Loir lived in Paris in the mid-eighteenth century and may have studied in Rome with Jean-François de Troy (artist and director, Académie de France in Rome, 1738). Never a member of the Royal Academy, she moved to the provinces after 1760 with a major reputation as a portraitist. In another independent and astute move, Loir became a member of the Marseille Academy and also worked in Pau and Toulouse. She came from an artistic family; her brother was Alexis Loir (1712–1785), a painter-sculptor.

Another of these women, Marie Anne Collot (1748–1821), should be noted for her work as a sculptor, an occupation presumed to be beyond women's capacity. Collot may have studied with her father-in-law, Etienne-Maurice Falconet; if so, she transformed the prevailing opinions on the limitations of women sculptors. Falconet generally sculpted rococo works in full scale. His son (Collot's husband) was also a sculptor, but he did not follow his father's path. Some say that the younger Falconet's most notable achievement was his illustration of his father's article on sculpture in Diderot and d'Alembert's *Encyclopédie*. But, it was his wife who created a striking marble bust of her father-in-law. She brilliantly captured Falconet's strength, pride, and joy. While her family ties likely gave her an entrée into elite circles, Collot's work stands high on its own merits.[44]

Finally, there was Marguerite Gérard, another unaffiliated active female artist. Called a rebel, Gérard came from a respected family of noted painters who tended to paint domestic scenes. Her alleged rebelliousness might be attributed to the fact that she never married or desired to become a member of the Royal Academy, which likely could have been a possibility, given her family connections. Yet she had a successful career for more than forty years, won three important

TABLE 2. Independent Women Artists in the Eighteenth Century

Name	Birth/Death	Genre	Comments
Masson, Madeleine	1646–1713	drawing, engraving	Little known about her
Loir, Marianne	1715–1769	portraiture	Painted portraits primarily of elite women in the mid-eighteenth century, first in Paris. Left Paris in 1760 and served a prosperous clientele in provinces. Was a member of the Marseille Academy of Art. Studied in Rome and was the sister of Alexis Loir III (pastellist and sculptor).
Allen, Anne		printmaking	Was active in the 1760s and worked primarily on delicately colored arrangements of flowers.
Collot, Marie Anne	1748–1821	sculpture	Produced marble busts of Henri IV, Diderot, and Catherine the Great, and completed a highly regarded bust of her father-in-law, Etienne-Maurice Falconet (noted sculptor and director of the Royal Academy). She was married to Pierre-Etienne Falconet, who was not a member of the Royal Academy.
Lemoine, Marie-Victoire	1754–1820	portraiture, miniature	Was possibly a student of Vigée-Lebrun. Was prosperous before and after the Revolution. Painted Atelier of a Painter, possibly a rendering of the studio of Vigée-Lebrun.
Ducreux, Rose Adélaide	1761–1802	painting	Painted in neoclassical style. Exhibited her work in the Louvre's Salon Carré, 1791.
Gérard, Marguerite	1761–1837	rococo genre painting in varied media	Sister of Marie Anne Gérard Fragonard. Collaborated with Gérard, Fragonard, and Delaunay.
Benoist, Marie-Guillemine	1768–1826	portraiture, history painting	Perhaps her most noted work was Portrait d'une négresse (c. 1800). Studied with Vigée-Lebrun and David.
Villiers, Marie Denise	1774–1821	drawing	Active in the 1790s. Identified as the artist of Young Woman Drawing (in the Metropolitan Museum), a significant and innovative work with "dramatic backlighting." Student of the history painter Anne-Louis Girodet Trioson.
Godefroy, Marie Eléonore	1778–1848	portraiture	Primarily a portraitist specializing in the representation of women and mothers and children. Studied with Gérard.

medals (two in Paris), and exhibited work in salons of the 1790s. Napoleon and other luminaries bought her paintings. She also amassed a good deal of wealth and real estate. Gérard was Fragonard's pupil, unofficial apprentice, and one of his collaborators. She also collaborated with her brother, Hénri, and the noted artist Nicolas Delaunay.[45]

CONCLUSION

The many exceptional women I have brought to wider attention in this essay were women of uncommon lives and talent who deserve to receive increased critical study. What strikes me as particularly important in the production of arts in the eighteenth century is that so many women not only worked in the arts, but were often recognized as successful and serious in their own fields of endeavor. Even the more "decorative" female artists of the Corporation of Painters and Sculptors, while not wealthy, made a living and seemed proud of their work and the social standing that their membership in the guild conferred.

Furthermore, some women who became members of this guild's Academy of St. Luc also became fine arts practitioners and exhibited their work in the salons of St. Luc as well as in independent salons. Some of these women even became members of the Royal Academy. Other women artists, often unacknowledged, entered the field of art on their own, with the assistance of family connections, or possibly with the encouragement of established male and female artists. The production of these women allowed them to fulfill their vocation as serious painters and sculptors, and not dilettantes. Yet, one must still recognize the difficulty many female artists faced in establishing their credentials. Their work was sometimes wrongly attributed to famous artists, male and female, or was ignored altogether.

In sum, more than a handful of eighteenth-century women artists can be understood to be exceptional, not only because of their superior and unusual talents, but also because of their determination to overcome institutional and social barriers. They were integral to the world of French art. Accepted or not into guilds or academies, they earned their livings and achieved status by means of such work. Not all were married, although many were, but we know little or nothing of their families. Some of these women thus defied or skirted traditional norms. A fuller understanding of their experiences and skills will add to our knowledge of the range of "women's work" from the mid-seventeenth to the early nineteenth centuries.

NOTES

I deeply thank Daryl Hafter and Nina Kushner for their central role in producing this collection and their valuable advice on my work. I gratefully acknowledge the suggestions of the anonymous reviewer of this essay. Finally, I thank Judith de Groat for her encouragement and insights.

1. Mary D. Sheriff, *The Exceptional Woman: Elisabeth Vigée-Lebrun and the Cultural Politics of Art* (Chicago: Univ. of Chicago Press, 1997); Bryan D. Palmer, "Most Uncommon Common Men: Craft and Culture in Historical Perspective," *Labour/Le Travail* 1 (1976): 5–31. Palmer notes that so-called common crafts were quite complex, requiring high skill levels. Women who acted outside of what was considered the female norm were exceptions, even *lusus naturae* (freaks of nature). I thus hope to examine the many interpretations of the concept of exceptional.

2. My thanks to the reviewer of this essay for raising some of these issues.

3. The French term is *corporation* or *corps des métier*, commonly translated into English as "guild," a term I will use for convenience.

4. Nathalie Heinrich, *Du peintre à l'artiste: Artisans et académiciens à l'âge classique* (Paris: Les editions de minuit, 1993), 64, 83.

5. E. Bénézit, ed., *Dictionnaire critique et documentaire des peintres, sculpteurs, dessinateurs, et gravures de tous les temps et tous les pays* (Paris: Grunde, 1999). Even before her death, many of Vigée-Lebrun's paintings were evaluated at and auctioned for as much as 18,000 francs (Bénézit, *Dictionnaire*, 14:32). Her paintings subsequently dropped in price until the 1880s. Geneviève Boullogne's (spelling varies) case is more common. One of her still life paintings, auctioned in Paris in 1768, sold for 7 francs. Auction prices are hardly the most reliable gauge of a painting's worth, but they do provide useful information on contemporary interest (Bénézit, *Dictionnaire*, 28:654). The same painting sold for 3,000 francs in 1949.

6. Marianne Roland Michel, "Vallayer in Her Time," in *Anne Vallayer-Coster: Painter to the Court of Marie Antoinette*, ed. Erik Kahng and Marianne Rolando Michel (Dallas: Dallas Art Museum, 2002), 14.

7. Ibid., passim.

8. Ibid., 14.

9. Mary Sheriff, "Adélaide Labille-Guiard," in *Dictionary of Women Artists*, ed. Delia Gaze (London: Fitzroy Dearborn Publishers, 1997), 1:47; Vivian Cameron, "Labille-Guiard," in *Concise Dictionary of Women Artists*, ed. Delia Gaze (London: Fitzroy Dearborn Publishers, 2001). For her 1785 and 1795 pensions, her pre-1789 patrons, and her work during the Revolution, see *Concise Dictionary of Women Artists*, 436–437. See Anne-Marie Passez, *Adélaide Labille-Guiard, 1749–1803: Biographie et catalogue raisonné de son oeuvre* (Paris: Arts et métiers graphiques, 1973), 301, for d'Angiviller's denial of Labille-Guiard's request.

10. Vittorio Malamani, ed., *Rosalba Carriera*, vol. 8 of *Monografie illustrate: Pittori, Scultori, Architetti* (Bergamo: Istituto d'Arti Grafiche, 1910). Malamani examined Carriera's accounts, and the following are some examples: in 1710 she earned 16,000 ducats for a portrait done in Venice; for two images painted in Verona, one sold for 700 ducats and the other for 7,500 ducats; and one of her pastel miniatures fetched 100 French francs in 1775. Her work (unlike that of most women artists of her time) sold for very good prices.

11. Steven Kaplan, "The Luxury Guilds in Paris in the Eighteenth Century," *Francia: Forschungen*

zur westeuropäische Geschichte 9 (1982): 257–298, 285–286. Kaplan states that the apprenticeship for fan makers was four years plus two years of work. Entry by experience only, for the low fee of 45 livres, was allowed if the applicant was the daughter of a master or mistress. For apprentices with no guild relations, the fee was 245 livres, and 445 livres for those with no outside support. He also notes that "incompetent sons [and daughters] not only brought the guild little money in fees, but they also risked compromising its reputation."

12. On the nature and criticism of guild production in France in the eighteenth century, see Daryl M. Hafter, *Women at Work in Preindustrial France* (University Park: Pennsylvania State Univ. Press, 2007), especially some of Hafter's telling explanations (chapters 1, 4, 5, and the conclusion). On the rights to grant masterships in all-female and/or many "mixed [male and female] guilds," and to those guilds electing female and male officers (variously called by different names in different trades and in different parts of France), see especially pages 36–50. See also Cynthia M. Truant, "La maîtrise d'une identité? Corporations féminines à Paris aux XVIIᵉ et XVIIIᵉ siècles," *CLIO*, no. 3 (1996).

13. See the work of Heinich, particularly *Du peintre à l'artiste*. Chapters 1–3 discuss this shift in detail.

14. Katie Scott, "Hierarchy, Liberty and Order: Languages of Art and Institutional Conflict in Paris (1766–1776)," *Oxford Art Journal* 12, no. 2 (1989): 59–70.

15. *Livrets des expositions de l'académie de Saint-Luc à Paris avec une notice et une table,* 7 vols. (Paris: Baur et Détaille, 1872).

16. Alfred Franklin, *Dictionnaire des arts et métiers et professions exercées dans Paris depuis le treizième siècle* (Paris: Burt Franklin, 1906), 560. He draws on Abbé Jaubert, *Dictionnaire raisonné des arts et métiers contenant l'histoire, la description, la police des fabriques . . . ouvrage utile à tous les citoyens* (Paris: Les libraires associés, 1743; reprint, Lyon: A. Leroy, 1801), 3:398. Fan makers were not originally part of the guild of painters and sculptors—they were claimed by many other guilds over time. The point is that female fan painters were considered highly skilled and innovative, and were, by the eighteenth century, legally incorporated into the guild of painters and sculptors.

17. The number of mistresses comes primarily from the Archives Nationales series Y. Some are from the "Bons or Avis (notices) de Maîtrise," kept in local police commissioners' offices. The series Y is well organized in registers by trade and year. An archival note in this carton states the "Bons" are poorly organized and do not count all cases. Thus far I have relied most upon Y 9325–9326/p. 190 and Y 9326/pp. 7–28 for 1745; Y 9326/pp. 163–192 for 1749; and Y 9327/pp. 1–22 for 1750. For 1765 and 1766, I counted the "Bons" for painters and sculptors in the series Y 9392.

18. AN, series Y, 9326, fol. 9 verso, 13 June 1745. Marie Anne LeCocq received her *maîtrise* by reason of "experience" (in other words, practice and knowledge of her work in sculpture).

19. AN series V7/438 are records of the *corps des arts et métiers,* primarily debts and taxes from 1744 to 1781. In August of 1781, Veuve Ciety, widow of the deceased syndic Ignace Ciety (a "*directeur computable*"), was named in his place.

20. The work of Charlotte Guichard, *Les amateurs d'art à Paris au XVIIIᵉ siècle* (Normandie: Champ Vallon, 2008), provides much useful information on these exhibitions and on the collectors who bought the works of male and female members of this academy.

21. On the acceptance of genres without extreme regard for hierarchy, see Michael Levey, *Painting and Sculpture in France, 1700–1789* (New Haven: Yale Univ. Press, 1993), 2. By the late eighteenth and early nineteenth centuries, hierarchies became more rigid. See also the following works: Caro-

lyn Sargentson, "The Manufacture and Marketing of Luxury Goods: The *Marchands Merciers* of Late Seventeenth- and Eighteenth-Century Paris," in *Luxury Trades and Consumerism in Ancien Régime Paris,* ed. Robert Fox and Anthony Turner (Aldershot, Eng.: Ashgate, 1998), 99–137, passim; Natacha Coquery, "The Language of Success: Marketing and Distributing Semi-Luxury Goods in Eighteenth-Century Paris," *Journal of Design History* 17, no. 1 (2004): 71–89, especially 82–89 for prices; and Cissie Fairchilds, "The Production and Marketing of Populuxe Goods in Eighteenth-Century Paris," in *Consumption and the World of Goods,* ed. John Brewer and Roy Porter (London: Routledge, 1993), 228–248, especially 230–236.

22. See the important and beautifully illustrated work of Geraldine Sheridan, *Louder than Words: Ways of Being Women Workers in Eighteenth-Century France* (Lubbock: Texas Tech Univ. Press, 2009), on this and other aspects of the wide range of women's work. Sheridan's section "Ornamental and Luxury Products," 83–140, validates the skill, imagination, and difficulty of such production.

23. Much of this data is based on the ten volumes of the *Procès-verbaux de l'Académie Royale de Peinture et de Sculpture, 1648–1793,* ed. Anatole de Montaiglon (Paris: Charavay frères, Libraire de la société, 1889). Sheriff states that during its history (1648–1793) the Academy accepted fifteen women and 450 men. Hence, women made up 3 percent of the academicians. I have found sixteen women that were admitted—hardly a significant difference. See also Reed Benhamou, *Regulating the Académie: Art, Rules and Power in Ancien Régime France* (Oxford: Voltaire Foundation, 2009), 18 n 77. Benhamou essentially paraphrases Sheriff's discussion of the 1706 ban on women members and its 1770 revocation (with the few exceptions I have noted). For Sheriff's more searching thoughts on the question of female admission, see *The Exceptional Woman,* 78–83. In reference to the lifting of the ban, on pages 32–33 she argues that women were accepted based on their connections rather than "unusual talent," as the new regulation required. She mentions (without naming) the last two women accepted into the Royal Academy (before its abolition in 1793), Labille-Guiard and Vigée-Lebrun, stating that "in neither case was talent a consideration." Sheriff discusses at length the politics involved in these acceptances but does not deny the talent of these artists, even if talent was not a consideration for acceptance into the Royal Academy.

24. *Procès-verbaux de l'Académie Royale de Peinture et de Sculpture, 1648–1793,* 4:33–34.

25. Ibid., 8:53–54. The original 1648 statutes of the Royal Academy did not specifically exclude women, but they did not specifically encourage their membership either.

26. The British Royal Academy had only two female members by the late eighteenth century.

27. *Procès-verbaux de l'Académie Royale de Peinture et de Sculpture, 1648–1793,* 9:153, 155, 156, and 158 particularly regarding the discussions and debates over the acceptance of Vigée-Lebrun; see also Sheriff's excellent presentation of this struggle in chapter 3 of *The Exceptional Woman.*

28. *Procès-verbaux de l'Académie Royale de Peinture et de Sculpture, 1648–1793,* 1:344–345, 4:70. There are numerous entries for Clérion—for example, 1:243–245, 2:73, 2:82, 2:285, 2:347, 2:349, 2:353, 2:363.

29. See Sheriff, *The Exceptional Woman,* 80, for information on Giradon, the first woman in the Academy (1663). She was the wife of F. Giradon.

30. *Procès-verbaux de l'Académie Royale de Peinture et de Sculpture, 1648–1793,* on Mlle Chéron, wife of Le Hay, 1:388, 2:12, 3:133.

31. *Procès-verbaux de l'Académie Royale de Peinture et de Sculpture, 1648–1793,* 2:91, 2:107, 2:175–176, 3:317, 3:330.

32. Ibid., 2:175–176.

33. Ann Sutherland Harris and Linda Nochlin, *Women Artists, 1550–1950* (Los Angeles: Los Angeles County Museum of Art, 1976), 36.

34. *Procès-verbaux de l'Académie Royale de Peinture et de Sculpture, 1648–1793*, 7:41

35. Ibid., 7:353–354, 8:48, 8:51.

36. Ibid., 8:53–54.

37. Ibid., 9:157.

38. Elisabeth Vigée-Lebrun, *Souvenirs* (Paris: Des femmes, 1835), 4.

39. On Labille-Guiard's career and goals, see "Adélaide Labille-Guiard," in *CLARA: Database of Women Artists*, http://clara.nmwa.org/8-22-09. Also see Passez's biography of Labille-Guiard: *Adélaide Labille-Guiard, 1749–1803: Biographie et catalogue raisonné de son oeuvre* (Paris: Arts et métiers graphiques, 1973).

40. On the issue of paintings attributed to other artists, such as David or Vigée-Lebrun, see http://www.metmuseum.org/collections/search-the-collections?ft=Eighteenth Century+Women+Painters+in+France (accessed August 25, 2009).

41. Sheriff, *The Exceptional Woman*, 262.

42. Ibid., 263.

43. See the following online sources: National Museum of Women in the Arts; CLARA website; Metropolitan Museum; National Gallery of Art; UK Academy of Art; *Art Cyclopedia*; *Grove Dictionary of Art*; and the Web site of Pomona College. For the names Sheriff lists, see *The Exceptional Woman*, 262–265.

44. "Pierre-Étienne Falconet," Royal Academy of Arts: RA Collections, http://www.racollection.org.uk/ixbin/indexplus?_IXACTION_=file&_IXFILE_=templates/full/person.html&person=15432 (accessed October 11, 2009).

45. "Marguerite Gérard," CLARA: Database of Women Artists, http://www.artcyclopedia.com/artists/gerard_marguerite.html (accessed August 25, 2009).

PRINTER WIDOWS AND THE STATE IN EIGHTEENTH-CENTURY FRANCE

Jane McLeod

IN 1778 the sixty-three-year-old Lyon printer Aimé Delaroche presented a request to the king that his daughter be given the status of a printer's widow and allowed to continue to run the large printing business that he and his ancestors had created over many generations. In his petition he explained that—with a view to keeping the printing business in his family—he had raised his only child, a daughter named Rose-Françoise, in the trade from her earliest years, teaching her everything about the art; he had derived great paternal satisfaction from seeing her run all the operations of the business alone for many years. She was well able to run the printing house until her sons were old enough to apply for printing licenses themselves. The king granted the request, making Rose-Françoise a very rare case of a woman printer who got a printer's license in response to a petition outlining her skill.[1] The skill argument was added because her young husband had died before obtaining a license to be a printer, leaving her with no legal claim to remain in the profession. Had the husband obtained Rose-Françoise's father's license, as had been planned, she would have been one of the many women in eighteenth-century France who became heads of printing businesses as widows of licensed printers. Seven years later, Delaroche sorrowfully reported to the ministry that his daughter had died prematurely at the age of thirty-two, her health ruined by too much hard work in the printing house and by breastfeeding her children. He asked if it would be possible to transfer the printing license to Rose-Françoise's second husband until his grandsons were old enough to take over the business.[2]

Delaroche's two letters imply quite different attitudes toward women printers. The first suggested that it was the most natural of things for his daughter to print. The second, in contrast, intimated that there was something unnatural about it, that by working hard in the printing house so that the business could be passed on to her sons, his daughter had made the supreme sacrifice for her children. We are left to wonder exactly what Aimé Delaroche—the largest printer in Lyon—actually thought about women running printing houses in eighteenth-century France.

Two indisputable realities (not unlike Delaroche's two views) jump out at any historian looking into the place of women in the printing and bookselling trades in eighteenth-century France. The first is that guild statutes, the law, and much eighteenth-century printer rhetoric suggest that women were unsuited to running printing houses or selling books because of their sex. Women were excluded from the printing and bookselling guilds, as they were from many other guilds, and only allowed to run their husbands' businesses as widows—and even then, they were not allowed to train apprentices.[3] In 1789 a Marseille printer, for example, when applying for licenses for his sons, claimed that the sex of his daughters prevented them from sharing in the work of the book trade.[4] On the other hand, if we study practice, we know that women had a huge public presence in the printing and bookselling trades, working in their husbands' and fathers' businesses during their lifetimes and heading these businesses during widowhood. Despite the rhetoric, printers' widows occupied high-profile positions in the French media in the eighteenth century.[5]

HISTORIOGRAPHY AND SOURCES

To tackle this problem we can consult an earlier body of research on the history of women that, by focusing on rhetoric and law, identified a deterioration in the status of women in early modern Europe, often linking these developments to the rise of capitalism, the growth of centralized states, or a developing public sphere that excluded women.[6] We can also consult a body of work by more recent historians that explores the linkages and the discrepancies between rhetoric about women, the laws that governed them, and the actual practices in which they engaged. These later historians found a varied landscape that resists the generalizations of the earlier historiography by identifying examples of remarkable activity, flexibility, and power exercised by individual groups of women: female guilds, artisans' widows, and noble women, to name a few.[7] In this essay I will attempt to examine the lives of women printers and show that their situation fits into these later studies, but should also be understood in light of the insights of cultural and political historians. They see the expansion of both print culture and of the state in the eighteenth century as transformative forces in the social life of early modern French men and women.[8] These developments explain why the rhetoric and the reality of female printers' lives changed in the eighteenth century and why men adopted seemingly contradictory attitudes to the women in their trade.

As sources to explore printers' rhetoric, we shall use the petitions printers addressed to high-level officials in the government in order to obtain printer licenses.[9] For the law, we shall consult guild statutes and a royal order of 1739 that required printers' widows to submit resignations before the family printing licenses could be passed on to successors.[10] To tell us about the practice, we shall consult notarial documents that describe printers' marriage arrangements and wealth, and police documents that reveal their actions as reported to the authorities. The latter keenly supervised printers in the eighteenth century.

From the sixteenth through the eighteenth centuries there were many widows working as printers. In the eighteenth century royal officials conducted many enquiries into the number and identity of printers in the realm, with a view to tightening control of the printed word. The enquiry of 1701, for example, reveals many widow printers and booksellers as heads of businesses. The more precise data of later enquiries show that 39 of the 235 printers in 1764 (16.6 percent) were widows, as were 38 of the 265 printers surveyed in 1777 (14.3 percent).[11] Printers' widows were able to run shops because printers' attitudes to women were conditioned by the guild identity many of them adopted as printing and bookselling spread into urban centers in the seventeenth century. This expansion brought with it forms of corporate organization and thinking. Printers' and booksellers' guild statutes shared two important features with the rules governing many other artisan guilds. First, the profession did not allow women to become masters. Second, a master's widow could work after her husband's death but she could not train apprentices. Thus by law and custom, in operation from at least the early seventeenth century through to the French Revolution, printers' and booksellers' widows were entitled to run their family businesses.

LICENSING

Important changes to the situation of women in the printing trades began to occur when the royal government—increasingly fearful of the printed word—introduced printer licensing and placed quotas on the number of printers allowed in every town in France. This made printer positions very difficult to obtain.[12] The major stages in this shift are the following: In 1667, by order of the Royal Council, new printers were forbidden to set up businesses in the French provinces. Anyone who wanted a dispensation from this law had to apply to the chancellor or keeper of the seals for a royal order allowing him to print (*arrêt du conseil privé*). In the 1680s and 1690s, guild statutes were standardized and the number of printers was fixed in the major towns. For example, in Bordeaux the limit was set at twelve. In Lyon it was set at eighteen, and in Nantes it was four. In 1701, a major survey revealed that there were 360 printers in the French provinces.[13] In 1704, their number was ordered reduced from 360 to 244, and the number of printers allowed in each town in France was specified. Any printer wishing to set up a business had to apply to Versailles for a license. In the very late reign of Louis XIV, the government went so far as to issue official lists naming the printers allowed to print in given provincial towns, effectively purging these towns of what were considered to be excess printers. In 1737, another census of printers was taken, and two years later their numbers were ordered to be reduced to 215. Further cuts were made in 1758 and 1772. Over time, the quotas were respected. A survey in 1764 shows that the number of provincial printers in France had in fact gone from 360 in 1701 to 248 in 1764. By the eighteenth century, the replacement of printers and the enforcement of the ceilings on the numbers was usually supervised by intendants and handled by the Bureau de la Librairie (Royal Office of the Book Trade), which issued licenses in the form of orders of the Privy Council. After this serious intrusion of the central state into their lives, provincial printers worked by virtue of revocable royal licenses.

The procedure to become a master printer after 1704 required that the hopeful hire lawyers and apply to the chancellor or keeper of the seals, usually informing the official that a certain printer had died and then outlining his own qualifications for the license. Requirements for a license included evidence of being a master's son, of having completed an apprenticeship, of adhering to the Roman Catholic faith, and of having knowledge of Latin and Greek. Applications could include letters of support from the bishop or other local officials. Candidates first presented their credentials to the local guild and to the *lieutenant général de police* (head policing official). The latter would assure that there was indeed a vacancy, assess the candidate's skill, inquire if there were any other candidates, and report all this to the Royal Office of the Book Trade. This office would then decide, in consultation with the chancellor or the keeper of the seals, whether or not to issue a new license. The selected candidate would then be sworn in locally. When printers retired they passed their privilege to print "into the hands of the King" or "into the hands of the Chancellor." Many sons did of course follow fathers, but only after applying to Versailles, competing with others, and passing requisite exams. These developments affected printers in many ways, reinforcing their view of themselves as members of the liberal professions or as officeholders. It also created for them a new identity that they used in their rhetoric, an identity that might be described as "pillars of monarchy." This encomium generally represented printers as loyal subjects of the king who were educated, moral, and who were engaged alongside the king in the ongoing battle against evil books and pirating.

HOW DID THESE DEVELOPMENTS AFFECT WIDOWS?

The surveys, the petitions, and the licensing procedures all drew attention to widow printers in an unprecedented way. The guildsmen who provided the information for the surveys, at least in the larger towns, were the first to report on the widows. In the survey of 1701, they represented widow printers in a very specific way, as indigent and ignorant or as a problem, an image that has been highlighted by subsequent historians.[14] Guild officials tried to marginalize women, characterizing the widows as very unimportant to the larger picture. They felt it quite acceptable to argue that there was "only a widow" running a printing business and that widows did not count when assessing whether there were more printers than the quotas allowed. The printers in these towns knew perfectly well that many widows ran big, successful businesses, but, presumably with an eye toward creating openings for their sons, they felt it strategically advisable to suggest that the presence of a widow was almost like saying that there was a vacancy.

Some guild officials listed male masters first in the surveys, including widows only at the end, again implying that the presence of a widow running a shop was in the larger scheme of things somewhere between a filled position and a vacancy.[15] Some guild wardens contested whether or not the widows should be counted when assessing whether a given town had fulfilled its quota of printers.[16] Some guildsmen denounced women who were happily running businesses. When this happened in 1707 to Marie-Marguerite Coquerel, a printer's daughter who had been selling books with her surgeon husband in La Rochelle, she protested that she was the daughter of a printer and bookseller who had been raised in the profession, and that the other booksellers "had no more right than she had to be in the profession."[17] The final, most extreme means by which the liminal status of widows was indicated was the filling of her husband's position with a man while the widow continued to run her family's business. This practice was so frequent in the first generation of licensing that it prompted a new law in 1739 banning it. Aspiring printers and their guildsmen fathers used the category of widows to provide room to maneuver and to soften the impact of quotas.

Licensing encouraged printers' and booksellers' guilds to enhance an already powerful guild discourse against the idea that printing and bookselling licenses could be transmitted through a widow or a daughter.[18] In 1709, the Paris guild made this view very explicit when it insisted on correcting what might be a misinterpretation of its decision to support the bookseller candidate Jacques Douceur, who had married a bookseller's daughter.[19] Douceur offered two arguments to support his request. In the first he acknowledged that his father had been one of those denied a license because of the quotas implemented in 1667, but also claimed that his father's rights had not been destroyed by the new rules of 1667. Rather, he argued, they had only been suspended and consequently could be transmitted to his son. Second, he had married a bookseller's daughter. The guild accepted the first argument but wanted it to be perfectly clear that the marriage to a daughter was irrelevant. Daughters could not pass on the masterships to their husbands and Douceur's license had been granted because he was the grandson and great grandson of established booksellers, "from son to son." The pressures of licensing forced the guilds to articulate a view on gender, something that had not been necessary before. Generally the bank of arguments produced by this discourse did not target the women, but rather took the form of acid attacks on sons-in-law when they tried to enter the trade.

Of the numerous battles waged by guilds and established printers against sons-in-law, one of the most vituperative was against the printer Michel Racle in Bordeaux when he married the daughter of an old and wealthy printing family and tried to obtain the printing license. The guild went to incredible lengths trying to block this member of an old, established legal family in Mont-de-Marsan, hiring lawyers, producing printed legal briefs, writing letters to the intendant and the chancellor. Because he had medical training, the guild called Racle a "tooth puller" (*arracheur de dents*) and decried his incompetence. They grossly distorted Racle's social position, describing him as an ignorant and lowly individual, a claim belied by the presence of the first president of the Parlement of Bordeaux at his wedding.

If the Office of the Book Trade had had to rely on the guild's rendering of a situation such as this, then it would never have come close to the truth of the matter. They discovered the facts when the intendant got involved and explained to the chancellor the real story here, that the daughter "had a good head for the business" and was running it. The guild attacks on Racle's competence were really irrelevant.[20] The Bordeaux printers' and booksellers' guild similarly attacked the credentials of the printer Phillippot and booksellers Merlin and Moreau, all of whom had married printers' or booksellers' daughters.[21] The competence discourse, which these situations generated, implicitly denied that the daughters could run the printing houses. It may have reflected guildsmen's frustration with their loss of control over recruitment as well as their resentment of powerful

families, such as the Brun family, who were often king's printers and monopolized the lucrative business of government printing.

GOVERNMENT RESPONSE

In these situations royal officials sought solutions that favored the daughters
and widows of printers. Take, for example, the numerous instances in which
local printers recommended the closure of widows' shops in the early days of
licensing. The widows who appealed these decisions generally won. One such
example is from Châlons-sur-Marne. In 1704, in response to complaints by the
printer Nicolas Denoux about colleagues printing in defiance of the 1667 ban, a
Privy Council order expelled the Widow Seneuze along with a number of others
from the trade. The Seneuze family was an old, established printing family with
extensive connections to the Office of the Book Trade. When her elderly father-
in-law protested, it took a remarkably short time (eight days) for the expulsion
to be repealed and for the widow and the elderly father-in-law to be granted
booksellers' licenses.[22]

Another example is from Dijon, where the guild warden, Jean Ressayre, made
a major move to enforce quotas and to reduce the competition in his town. He
did this by claiming that there were many evil books and an infinity of unquali-
fied persons selling books and breaking the rules, among them the Widow Fargot.
Ressayre's efforts to seize their books and equipment, however, were opposed by
the local lieutenant general of police, who ordered the goods returned. Ressayre,
therefore, appealed to the Privy Council to help him bring order to the trade,
and morality to the reading of the people of Dijon. Faced with this potentially
dangerous situation, in 1714 royal officials annulled the judgment of the lieutenant general of police and ordered the Widow Fargot and the others closed down.
However, the Widow Fargot immediately appealed and was granted the right to
continue as a bookseller despite the guild's opposition.[23] Widows who appealed
Privy Council orders were generally from families with status, resources, and
patrons, and these factors undoubtedly permitted them to win their appeals.

In many instances when widow printers wanted to marry outside the profession and yet continue their businesses, royal officials agreed, thus strengthening
them against opposition at the local level, which was often motivated by jealous
competitors. When Jaquine Provost, the Widow Augereau, wanted to marry a non-
printer and continue her business in Alençon, she claimed in 1709 that she had
been working on her own as a widow for twelve years and that she had always fol-

lowed the law. Her request was granted and she was still working there in 1730.[24]

In La Rochelle, very shortly after her husband obtained a license, Geneviève Flagé became a widow responsible for the couple's eight-month-old son. Flagé wrote to the chancellor in 1710 requesting a license for Louis Bourdin, a printer who wanted to marry her, and went to great length to outline his qualifications. He had demonstrated his competence in several cities, including Paris, and worked on Greek, Italian, Latin, and French dictionaries. In La Rochelle in 1710 there were already more printers than the allotted number, but Flagé wanted an exception made for Bourdin so that he could marry her, and cited that such an exception had been granted to a widow in Limoges. Printers, their widows, and their lawyers were aware of licensing developments beyond their own towns. The Office of the Book Trade looked favorably on Flagé's request and granted the license, stating that Bourdin could print with the widow and would get the place of the next printer to die in La Rochelle.[25] Given that there was tough competition for positions in La Rochelle and that a mini-purge had taken place in 1707, this was quite a privilege.

In the 1720s the whole issue of widows' rights in La Rochelle was again rather hotly contested. In 1721, Marie-Anne Allain, the twenty-one-year-old widow of Bourdin, complained to the Office of the Book Trade that even though she had her husband's rights, the two other printers in La Rochelle had forced her to appear before the city's magistrates, who ordered her to cease working as a printer and to dismantle her presses within three months. This sentence, she argued, was unjust not only because the statutes gave her the right to continue, but also because her husband had put her dowry into the printing business and, if forced to sell, she would never get the money back. She requested that the king ignore the order of the police and forbid the local printers from interfering in her business (*la troubler*). The Office of the Book Trade came to her aid and issued a Privy Council order granting this request.[26] Once she got this permission she was granted a further request, that she be allowed to marry and the new husband be given a printer's license.[27] Briefly, then, the royal officials in Versailles were extremely receptive to arguments made by widow printers in their attempts to stay in the business.

A Privy Council order in March 1739—while we have no reason to think it was intended to do so—strengthened the position of printer widows in the whole realm. The census of 1737 showed that the policy of cutting the number of printers was not going as well as hoped and that part of the problem was the way widows' businesses were being handled. On the death of a printer, too often men were ignoring the widows; they applied for and received printing licenses, a practice that resulted in two businesses where there previously had been only one.[28] After March 1739, the competitions for the licenses of deceased printers could only take place after the printers' widows had died or had formally resigned their places. No son could postulate for his father's position without a signed copy of his mother's resignation; these documents began to appear in the notarial archives.[29] Royal officials refused to proceed with competitions for printer licenses until they had such a signed resignation in the dossier.

Without underestimating the number of pressures that could be brought to bear on these women by family members or others—such as those placed on the Widow Besse in Narbonne, who wanted to honor her husband's wishes—it would seem that widow printers after 1739 had more control over their children.[30] Sons could no longer set up competing businesses or appreciably sideline their mothers, because their mothers controlled the licenses. A printer's license in the late eighteenth century was a tremendous asset with which to negotiate. We wonder what the ten-year period was like for the son of the Widow Masson in Tours, whose mother started the process of resigning in 1732 but did not complete it until 1742.[31] The transmission of the business to the next generation involved many considerations: extended families depended on the printing houses, dowries needed to be pulled from the businesses, marriages needed to be arranged, and retired widows had to be cared for. Very importantly, the license had to be kept in the family and not lost to a newcomer who might apply for it to officials at Versailles. After 1739, widows were at the center of these decisions.

By the mid-eighteenth century, widows' rights served a number of agendas. They allowed the transmission of the printing business to a member of the family. They protected children's claims on their fathers' businesses, and they allowed royal officials to patronize certain printing families. The idea behind licensing was to create and maintain a small core of educated and wealthy printers who, acting as guardians of print culture in the realm, would have much to lose if caught printing unacceptable materials. Printing families were one of a number of groups with whom royal officials negotiated mutually acceptable arrangements to build absolute monarchy. The women in these families (wives, widows, daughters) were beneficiaries of such developments. Special status and exemptions show up regularly. A mother and daughter in Metz who were running a printing house resigned in favor of their grandson and son but wanted the license returned to them were this man to die.[32] While the Office of the Book Trade refused their last request, it was nevertheless true that licensing significantly transformed corporate ideas about widows' rights, adapting them to a new officeholder identity enjoyed by the realm's printers.

Widows' rights did not, however, fit into the picture of certain reformers, who imagined a more rational eighteenth-century administrative structure that was less reliant on a practice of patronizing certain families in order to secure loyalty and obedience. One such official was Chrétien-Guillaume-Lamoignon de Malesherbes, who, as director of the book trade between 1750 and 1763, undertook a serious critique of the whole censorship apparatus in the mid-century. Malesherbes, who did not believe that the guilds or established printing families worked in the public interest, dismissed their claims to serve the king as guardians of morality and orthodoxy in the burgeoning print culture of the era. Once this fiction was laid to rest, the widows issue looked quite different to him: the law allowing widows to continue their husbands' businesses was a remaining vestige of the idea that printers could succeed their fathers "by right," an idea that had been rejected for men much earlier (at least in theory) by the introduction of licensing.

Malesherbes regretted that this vestige remained because sons, at least, had to possess the specific qualifications and needed to apply for licenses, a requirement that provided minimal control over them; although preference was given to sons, officials would never give a license to a disloyal subject. Widows escaped even this minimal control when they succeeded by right, and could therefore lease their shops to adventurers or disloyal subjects. Malesherbes argued that widows should compete like sons for positions and only those who truly ran shops should be allowed to continue. Widows should be told that "in spite of their sex" they could compete for the positions which, given the right qualifications, they would receive, just as sons almost always got the licenses of their fathers. For Malesherbes it was inconsistent to supervise the entry of men into the printing profession but not that of women. However, he was a voice in the wilderness in the mid-eighteenth century because the procedure for appointing printers, while in theory merit-based, was riddled with patronage. The policy of licensing widows suited both administrators and printing families, who had no intention of listening to Malesherbes on this issue.

GENERALIZATIONS ABOUT LATE EIGHTEENTH-CENTURY PRINTERS' WIDOWS

Let us finish by looking at the lives of the thirty-eight widows who show up in the 1777 survey, the last of the many printer surveys of the eighteenth century.[33] Most importantly, we should note that these widow printers stayed in the business for a long span, an average of 21.5 years. There were male printing house directors, sons, and sons-in-law contributing to these businesses. In some cases these men may have been doing most of the work. Nevertheless, as holders of the licenses, the printer widows were the undisputed heads of the households, and the roles of the men around them were unofficial and nonpublic. Throughout the whole of the eighteenth century, officials dealt directly with the widows and their lawyers in matters of copyright, censorship, and labor law. When the Widow Vatar was informed in 1759 that information sent to Versailles from the Nantes guild had led royal officials to downgrade her license to one that was good only for her lifetime and thus not available to her children, she went to Paris and lobbied officials for the entire summer, sending letters to the intendant and others until she had the decision overturned. When the Widow Besogne and her son were caught engaging in clandestine trade, her son wondered if she could be spared a stay in the Bastille, but was informed that not until she turned herself in could this be discussed.[34] Widow printers dealt with officials when caught in the clandestine trade and generally lobbied government agents just as their male counterparts did.

Our sample of thirty-eight suggests that not only did widows carry on, but that they did so without marrying journeymen.[35] Printing was lucrative in the reign of Louis XVI, and these widow printers were comfortably off bourgeois women from merchant and legal backgrounds. Their maiden names suggest that they were not from printing families, an impression reinforced by a sample of marriage contracts that shows that printers in the larger towns married into local merchant and legal elites.[36] Printers' widows or daughters would have considered marriage to workers quite beneath them. This was probably a view shared by Jeanne Saulnier in the years 1777–1780, when, as a widow of the king's printer in Rennes, she obtained permission to marry not a worker in her shop but an officeholder and lawyer in Rennes who had been helping her with her business for a number of years.[37]

On the few occasions when printers' daughters married printers, it was to members of established printing families and usually only when there was not a son to carry on the business. The daughter of the Faulcon family in Poitiers, for example, had to marry a printer when her brother refused to take over the family business, becoming a judge instead. Far from being a journeyman, the printer she married was a *juge consul* in Poitiers.[38] Many printers' widows or daughters—at least in the larger towns—hired workers to secure skilled help; wider strategic concerns determined their marriages.

Many indicators point to patronage as an enormously important factor in the lives of the last generation of Old Regime printers. While the logic of corporate organization was shaken by the mid-eighteenth century, it was in shatters in the reign of Louis XVI. This was especially manifest during the years 1774–1787, when Armand-Thomas Hüe de Miromesnil was keeper of the seals, at which time competitions were increasingly deemed unnecessary to pass printing licenses on to the sons of the major printing families.[39] It was in this context that Versailles officials began to grant licenses to a few—a very few—female applicants. As we have seen, in 1778 Miromesnil and his director of the book trade, Le Camus de Néville, replied favorably to Delaroche's request that his daughter, Rose, be given a license in Lyon. In 1783, they also replied favorably to the proposal to license Marie-Madeleine-Félicité Malassis, the daughter of Marie-Madeleine-Elizabeth Dumesnil and Jean Malassis, printers in Evreux. Dumesnil had been running the printing house there for many years and wanted the license for her only child, a daughter, whom she had trained in the printing business. Her daughter's health was too delicate to marry, and she would lose her profession on the death of her mother unless she was granted a license.[40] In 1786, the wife of Jacques-Jean-Louis-Guillaume Besongne, a member of a family that had been in the printing business for generations, was given her husband's license, one of the ten allowed to the town of Rouen. Besongne claimed that his wife was in a perfect position to run his printing house and he was resigning in her favor for reasons of humanity and justice.[41] In 1786, Miromesnil allowed the wife of his protégé, the Nîmes printer Pierre Beaume, to openly run the Nîmes printing house when her husband moved to Bordeaux after having obtained a hotly contested printer license there.[42]

The idea that printer positions were considered to be jointly held by couples crept into the petitions in the 1780s. For example, Jean-Baptiste Séjourné referred to the place of "ses père et mère" (his father and mother).[43] In Valenciennes in 1783, Jean-Baptiste Henry referred to the deceased "Jean-Baptiste-Gabriel Henry et Demoiselle Marie-Ignace-Joseph Boulon ses père et mère, imprimeurs libraires."[44] Daughters' rights were acknowledged in 1787 by Miromesnil's successor, Chrétien-François de Lamoignon de Basville, when Pierre Seyer in Rouen sought and obtained a license for the husband of his stepdaughter. In his request he made no effort to hide the role of his wife and stepdaughter in the business. Because of his health and the loss of his wife, he could not continue, and he asked that his stepdaughter's husband be allowed to print because of his *honneté* (honesty, uprightness), morals, knowledge, and because he was married to a woman with *droits* (rights) to the printing house that had been in her family for more than a century.[45] Licensing practices in the reign of Louis XVI reveal that not only had candidates and royal officials adapted a widows' rights notion from their guild identity, but that they had also moved significantly beyond this to recognize more openly the place of privileged women generally in the printing trades.

CONCLUSION

To return to Aimé Delaroche and what he and his colleagues really thought about women running printing houses, we would have to say that the rhetoric, the law, and the practice offer us quite different answers that we should not necessarily try to reconcile. For male printers and state officials who produced most of the administrative documents we study here, gender was a strategic tool around which no consensus was needed. Licensing forced gender on the table in the form of an obstacle that Delaroche had to overcome to have his daughter licensed, and he expected a sympathetic hearing from royal officials. The guild discourse that opposed the transmission of printer rights through daughters could not have been appealing to him. Printers manipulated a significant range of ways of representing themselves (including the women in their families) in the eighteenth century as they dealt regularly with the state bureaucracy, hired lawyers to assist them as they applied for licenses and copyrights, and sought privileges and protections. What seems clear is that in this elaborate positioning both printers and the state officials subordinated gender considerations to other interests, family advancement, ideological control, and market expansion. Licensing extended—and certainly did not diminish—the female presence in the media of eighteenth-century France.

Where do female printers fit into the larger subject of women and work in the eighteenth century? The significant female presence contributes to a literature that focuses on making women visible. As female printers oversaw the printing not only of books but of massive numbers of laws, decrees, *factums* (legal briefs), political pamphlets, and newspapers, they may have been more involved in politics than we think. In Rennes, for example, the printer Garnier's wife was at the center of patriot opposition during the Brittany Affair. The Widow Vatar's shop in Nantes was a patriot center and later a place where priests said mass during the Terror.[46] Female printers also fit into the framework offered by those studies that argue that corporate organization helped some groups of women advance their interests. In establishing the rights of widows to continue their husbands' businesses, something that printers drew from their guild identity and something their barrister friends and relatives could not offer their own wives, corporate organization indisputably placed women inside the expanding world of print culture that is important to our understanding of the eighteenth century. The significance of this cannot be overstated. Yet we also must note that it was guildsmen who tried to marginalize the women in the late reign of Louis XIV, when printer licensing was introduced, making printer places rare and contested. This theme is quite in keeping with an older historiography that presents corporate organization as inimical to women. Finally, this study of printer women fits very well into recent work that argues that the growth of the state benefitted certain privileged groups that included groups of women.[47] Because of the widespread fear of the potentially dangerous influence of print culture, royal officials regulated the book trade more so than many areas of economic life, bringing printers into direct dealing with the bureaucracy at Versailles, which favored certain established families. Like their fathers, sons, and husbands, the women in these families could and did appeal to Versailles and benefit from its backing in many ways.

NOTES

I would like to thank Clare Crowston and Sabine Juratic for their helpful comments.

1. Archives Nationales (hereafter AN) V⁶ 1085, 10 August 1778.

2. AN V⁶ 1085, 10 August 1778; Archives départmentales du Rhône (hereafter ADR) 1C221, 18 December 1784.

3. There are rare instances of widows involved in guild governance. In the small, extremely inactive guild in Aix-en-Provence, the Widow Adibert stepped in as guild warden in 1789 when her husband died. She summoned the printers and booksellers' guild to a meeting to discuss its participation in preparations for the Estates General (Archives Municipale d'Aix-en-Provence HH 57).

4. AN V¹ 552, 28 June 1789.

5. Roméo Arbour, *Dictionnaire des femmes libraires en France (1470–1870)* (Geneva: Droz, 2003); Geraldine Sheridan, "Women in the Booktrade in Eighteenth-Century France," *British Journal of Eighteenth-Century Studies* 15 (1992): 51–69; Sylvie Postel-Lecocq, "Femmes et presses à Paris au XVIᵉ siècle: Quelques exemples," in *Le livre dans l'Europe de la Renaissance: Actes du XXVIIIᵉ colloque internationale d'études humanistes de Tours* (Paris: Promodis, 1988), 253–263. For an examination of the particular circumstances of Parisian printer widows, see Sabine Juratic, "Les femmes dans la librairie parisienne au XVIIIᵉ siècle," in *L'Europe et le livre: Réseaux et pratiques du négoce de librairie, XVIᵉ–XIXᵉ siècles*, ed. Frédéric Barbier, Sabine Juratic, and Dominique Varry (Paris: Klincksieck, 1996), 247–276, and Sabine Juratic, "Marchandes ou savantes? Les veuves des libraires parisiens sous le règne de Louis XIV," in *Femmes savantes, savoirs des femmes du crépuscule de la Renaissance à*

l'aube des Lumières, ed. Colette Nativel (Geneva: Droz, 1999), 59–68. The number of female authors should not be underestimated either. See Carla Hesse, *The Other Enlightenment: How French Women Became Modern* (Princeton: Princeton Univ. Press, 2001). See also Elizabeth C. Goldsmith and Dena Goodman, eds., *Going Public: Women and Publishing in Early Modern France* (Ithaca: Cornell Univ. Press, 1995).

6. Sarah Hanley, "Engendering the State: Family Formation and State Building in Early Modern France," *French Historical Studies* 16, no. 1 (1989): 4–27; Joan Landes, *Women and the Public Sphere in the Age of the French Revolution* (Ithaca: Cornell Univ. Press, 1988); Merry E. Wiesner, "Spinning Out Capital: Women's Work in the Early Modern Economy," in *Becoming Visible: Women in European History,* 2nd ed., ed. Renate Bridenthal, Claudia Koonz, and Susan Mosher Stuard (Boston: Houghton Mifflin, 1987), 221–249.

7. Clare Haru Crowston, *Fabricating Women: The Seamstresses of Old Regime France, 1675–1791* (Durham: Duke Univ. Press, 2001); Janine M. Lanza, *From Wives to Widows in Early Modern Paris: Gender, Economy, and Law* (Aldershot, Eng.: Ashgate, 2007); Daryl M. Hafter, *Women at Work in Preindustrial France* (University Park: Pennsylvania State Univ. Press, 2007); Scarlett Beauvalet-Boutouyrie, *Être veuve sous l'Ancien Régime* (Paris: Belin, 2001). For an overview, see Clare Haru Crowston, "Women, Gender, and Guilds in Early Modern Europe: An Overview of Recent Research," *International Review of Social History* 53 (2008): 19–44.

8. On negotiation between central and local governments, see William Beik, *Absolutism and Society in Seventeenth-Century France* (Cambridge: Cambridge Univ. Press, 1985), and Sharon Kettering, *Patrons, Brokers, and Clients in Seventeenth-Century France* (New York: Oxford Univ. Press, 1986). There is a vast literature on print culture in the eighteenth century that includes the many works of Roger Chartier and Robert Darnton. For special attention to women, see Hesse, *The Other Enlightenment.*

9. The archives of the *Conseil Privé* are in AN V⁶. All applications for licenses in the years 1709–1714, 1719–1724, 1739–1744, 1755–1760, and 1776–1789 have been studied systematically and a number of others added. For excerpts from a number of these documents, see Georges Lepreux, *Gallia typographica ou répertoire biographique et chronologique de tous imprimeurs de France depuis les origines de l'imprimerie jusqu'à la Révolution,* 7 vols. (Paris: Honoré Champion, 1909–1914). For a wonderful guide to the *Conseil Privé* in the seventeenth century, see Albert Hamscher, *The Conseil Privé and the Parlements in the Age of Louis XIV: A Study in French Absolutism* (Philadelphia: American Philosophical Society, 1987). For the impact on widows of increased state regulation of printers in Paris in the reign of Louis XIV, see Juratic, "Marchandes ou savantes."

10. Statutes: Toulouse Statutes, 1623, Article 10, Bibliothèque Nationale (hereafter BN) FF 22127 # 38; *Chartres et statuts des imprimeurs et libraires de la ville de Rennes,* Article 14, BN FF 22125 #115; Statutes for Lyon, 1675–1676, Article 20, Archives Municipales de Lyon HH98; Bordeaux Statutes of 1688, Article 32, in Ernest Labadie, *Notices biographiques sur les imprimeurs et les libraires bordelais des XVIᵉ, XVIIᵉ et XVIIIᵉ siècles* (Bordeaux: Mounastre-Picamilh,1900); *Déclaration du Roi portant reglement pour les libraires et imprimeurs de la ville de Lyon, 1695,* Article 45, BN FF 22173 #77; Claude-Marin Saugrain, ed., *Code de la librairie et imprimerie de Paris ou conférence du réglement arrêté au conseil d'état du roi le 28 février 1723 et rendu commun pour tout le royaume, par arrêt du conseil d'état du 24 mars 1744 avec les anciennes ordonnances . . .* (1744; reprint, Westmead: Gregg International Publishers, 1971), 203–206.

11. For information on widows in 1701, see Claude Lannette-Claverie, "L'Enquête de 1701 sur l'état de la librairie dans le royaume" (Thesis, École Nationale des Chartes, 1964), 266–267. For 1764, see Thierry Rigogne, *Between State and Market: Printing and Bookselling in Eighteenth-Century France* (Oxford: Voltaire Foundation, 2007), 140, and for 1777, see BN FF 21832.

12. On printer licensing, see Jane McLeod, *Licensing Loyalty: Printers, Patrons, and the State in Early Modern France* (University Park: Pennsylvania State Univ. Press, 2011).

13. On the surveys of printers, see Roger Chartier, "L'Imprimerie en France à la fin de l'Ancien Régime: l'état général des imprimeurs de 1777," *Revue française d'histoire du livre* 6 (1973): 253–279. For a detailed analysis of the 1764 survey, see Rigogne, *Between State and Market.*

14. Lannette-Claverie, "L'Enquête," 266–298; Rigogne, *Between State and Market,* 140.

15. Archives départementales de la Gironde (hereafter ADG) C 3771.

16. In 1719, the Nantes guild met and claimed that "they judged that widows should not be counted in the number . . ." AN V^6 847, 23 March 1719.

17. AN V^6 807, 21 February 1707.

18. Until 1777, quotas and licensing were only officially required of printers, but many booksellers applied and obtained licenses to secure their own positions. In 1777, licenses were required by both printers and booksellers.

19. AN V^6 816, 1 July 1709, 2 decrees.

20. ADG C 3314, 25 October 1766; *Mémoire à Monseigneur de Maupeou . . . ,* ADG C 3309; *Mémoire pour Pierre Phillippot et Joseph Brulle au nom et comme syndic et adjoint des imprimeurs et libraires jurés de l'université de Bordeaux, ses membres et suppôts contre Michel Racle, ci-devant dentiste et bachelier en médecine,* Bibliothèque municipale de Bordeaux; *contrat de mariage,* ADG, Notary Séjourné, 7 September 1766. Racle was ordered to close in January 1770 but given a license the following April (AN V^6 1037, 25 January 1770; Archives Municipales de Bordeaux, BB 132, 24 April 1770).

21. ADG C 3309–3314.

22. AN V^6 796, 3 and 11 March 1704.

23. AN V^6 831, 5 February 1714; V^6 832, 25 June 1714.

24. Lepreux, *Gallia,* vol. 3, part 2, pages 38–39; AN V^6 735, 29 November 1709. By this marriage she became Dame Brehein-Brandin.

25. AN V^6 820, 22 September 1710.

26. AN V^6 855, 21 June 1721; V^6 858, 20 May 1722.

27. AN V^6 867, 12 June 1724.

28. Copy of *arrêt,* dated 31 March 1739, in Saugrain, *Code,* 203–206.

29. For example, *cession,* ADG, Notary Loche, 14 July 1755.

30. AN V^6 940, 24 February and 30 March 1744.

31. AN V^6 935, 19 September 1742.

32. AN V^6 934, 30 July 1742.

33. BN FF 21832. The following analysis uses the survey information and biographical data from Arbour, *Dictionnaire,* and others. It is possible that widows in the provinces were more involved in printing activities than in Paris (Juratic, "Les femmes," 268–269).

34. Archives Départementales d'Ille-et-Vilaine, C 1463; Jean Quéniart, *L'Imprimerie et la librairie à Rouen au XVIIIe siècle* (Paris: Klincksieck, 1969), 183–184.

35. On this see Sheridan, "Women in the Booktrade," 57–58. On a more general reluctance of widows to remarry, see Lanza, *From Wives to Widows in Early Modern Paris,* and Beauvalet-Boutouyrie, *Être veuve sous l'Ancien Régime.*

36. A sample of twenty marriage contracts from the last generation of Old Regime printers from Bordeaux, Toulouse, Lyon, Dijon, and Nîmes suggests this, but further research is needed to verify such a claim, especially its applicability to smaller towns.

37. AN V[6] 1079, 26 August 1777. Bruté de Rémur, *directeur des domaines du roi à Rennes, maître es arts en l'université de Paris et avocat au parlement.*

38. Gabriel Debien, ed., *Correspondance de Félix Faulcon* (Poitiers: Société des archives historiques du Poitou, 1939), 1:110; AN V[6] 1114, 23 June 1783.

39. In 1781 the Widow Giroud in Grenoble got permission for her son to be her deputy (*adjoint*) because the license was so important for her family that she could not take a chance on a competition (AN V[6] 1103, 6 August 1781). Other examples: AN V[6] 1126, 19 December 1785; V[6] 1134, 2 July 1787.

40. AN V[6] 1112, 17 March 1783.

41. AN V[6] 1128, 22 May 1786. Besongne's departure may have been connected to a bankruptcy in the family (ADSM 201 BP 552); Lepreux, *Gallia,* vol. 3, part 1, pages 82–83.

42. AN V[6] 1128, 27 March 1786.

43. AN V[6] 1114, 30 June 1783.

44. AN V[6] 1112, 27 January 1783.

45. AN V[6] 1134, 4 June 1787.

46. According to Marion, the printer Garnier's wife was publicly devoted to the Chalotais party and her boutique was its regular meeting place. Marcel Marion, *La Bretagne et le duc d'Aiguillon, 1753–1770* (Paris: Fontémoing, 1898), 568–569; Patricia Sorel, *La Révolution du livre et de la presse en Bretagne (1780–1830)* (Rennes: Presses universitaires de Rennes, 2004), 67–68.

47. Beik, *Absolutism;* Kettering, *Patrons, Brokers, and Clients in Seventeenth-Century France;* Crowston, *Fabricating Women;* Hafter, *Women at Work;* Lanza, *From Wives to Widows in Early Modern Paris.*

WOMEN AND CONTRACTS IN THE AGE OF TRANSATLANTIC COMMERCE

Jennifer L. Palmer

As ships set sail from French harbors, those aboard braved the briny deep and anticipated a place very different from the one they had left. For passengers disembarking in the Caribbean, scorching sunshine replaced the temperate climes of France, and turquoise waters filled with brightly colored tropical fish took the place of chilly waves of gunmetal grey. Yet those making the transatlantic journey left behind more than familiar locales. They also very often left families, including wives and children. The distance between family members separated by the Atlantic meant that they had to devise new ways of apportioning family roles and resources. Such a shift had highly gendered dimensions, simply because men, including married men, often journeyed to the colonies alone to seek their fortunes, taking with them the vague shining hope that one day they would return to France as wealthy men, able to sweep their families into the lap of luxury. This gender imbalance certainly affected the development of colonial society, but it also shaped social and economic practices in the metropolitan cities where male fortune-seekers left their mothers, wives, sisters, and daughters. In a society where their relations to men largely defined women's places in society, the absence of their closest male relatives changed women's position vis-à-vis roles usually reserved for men. This phenomenon was especially notable in the largely masculine arena of transatlantic commerce. Undertaking new positions at the heart of networks on which the wealth of their families was based while their husbands assumed positions on the colonial periphery, women accepted responsibilities as heads of families and businesses at the center of expansive webs of contacts that spanned oceans and empires.

Because neither French common law nor the bureaucratic ideal of the family as the basic political unit took such separations—or their contingencies—into account, families themselves adapted well-established family strategies to manage the long separations and changing family roles necessitated by transatlantic trade. Specifically, they tailored legal provisions in marriage contracts, testaments, and powers of attorney. Families worked to shape these documents to give themselves both flexibility in the event of a transatlantic separation and safety. In particular, such contracts aimed to protect the welfare of women.[1] In the normal course of things, husbands usually represented the interests of married women. This became a significant challenge, however, when an ocean separated husband and wife. This chapter addresses the subject of women who lived in La Rochelle, but whose husbands lived in the Caribbean. Such women were caught between the customary laws of their city and those of Paris, which governed the colonies; the two customs treated women's property and inheritance very differently. Planning ahead, families used contracts to empower women and give them options, particularly at the two moments that most affected all women in the Old Regime, marriage and death. A third moment, a husband's departure, similarly shaped the lives of many women in Atlantic ports.

The explosion of the Atlantic economy did not impel the first instance of marital separation, of course.[2] For centuries, French women had coped when separated from their husbands. However, this practice became quite common in Atlantic ports such as La Rochelle in the eighteenth century, when ship's captains and sailors departed on long transatlantic voyages and other men flocked to France's Caribbean colonies in search of fortune, often leaving their families behind them. Women throughout France routinely managed the quotidian financial challenges of keeping a family afloat, including establishing lines of credit, making purchases, paying bills, and running family businesses.[3] In La Rochelle, however, families often prepared more thoroughly for anticipated absences of husbands by giving wives their power of attorney. This practice was particularly common among seafaring folk, where it extended up and down the social scale, from ship's captains to common sailors.[4] It had the advantage of explicitly empowering the wife, at home in France, with some fiscal and legal authority she might otherwise lack, particularly over joint marital assets. According to the standard formulation of such documents, this included the "power to appear in court for them both [the husband and wife] and their agents, to represent [them] before all judges, commissioners, notaries, clerks, and other public and private persons . . . to make decisions, to govern their goods and affairs either in this town, province, or anywhere else in the manner in which [they see] fit," all with the same authority as her husband.[5] Through powers of attorney such women melded women's traditional obligations to guard, preserve, and augment the family estate for their children with more modern ideas about expanding wealth through engaging in commerce.

This is not to suggest that the advent of transatlantic trade and the absences it entailed ushered in a period of unfettered liberation for wives left behind in France. Rather, their gender limited women's abilities to step neatly into their husbands' roles. Further, when an ocean lay between husband and wife, traditional nuclear family relationships began to change. Spouses formed other attachments, and priorities shifted. Many men in the colonies, less constrained by conventions of sexual propriety than were women, entered into long-term relationships with women of color. As male colonists' families shifted in shape and appearance, wives sometimes had to watch as assets flowed from their husbands' estates to illegitimate mixed-race children. Even with the careful preparation that families put into planning marriage and inheritance, provisions such as these often came as an unwelcome surprise. Such was the case with Jean-Severin and Marie-Magdelaine Regnaud de Beaumont.

This chapter uses a case study of the Regnaud de Beaumont family to explore how families in La Rochelle planned and prepared for transatlantic separations as a matter of course. To do so they used contracts—especially marriage contracts, powers of attorney, and wills—to weave between and around the customary laws of La Rochelle and Paris. In a transatlantic age in an ocean-facing city, individuals often looked to family members in the colonies as business partners, with the assumption that kin shared interests and would safeguard each other's financial welfare. Likewise, in a commercial seaport women often were involved in their husbands' maritime ventures; after all, who could have more interests in common than a husband and wife? However, the assumption of shared marital interests proved to be founded on sand, easily eroded by the waves of the Atlantic as separation redirected the interests of husband and wife into different channels. In such situations, in spite of the protections of common law and the safeguards of contracts, women had little recourse when their carefully laid plans went awry.

COMMON LAW AND CONTRACTS

When Jean-Severin Regnaud de Beaumont and Marie-Magdelaine Royer married in 1735, their families would have been particularly conscious of the significance of strategies of marriage and inheritance. Marie-Magdelaine's deceased father had been a planter in the colony of Saint-Domingue; his father held a royal post in La Rochelle. Jean-Severin himself was a transatlantic ship's captain, a lucrative occupation that often functioned as a stepping stone, as it would for Jean-Severin, to owning a colonial plantation. Both families had amassed a significant amount of capital, and although they were not nobles, they perhaps had ambitions of *noblesse*. If this was their goal, their match was a good one, as it brought together the royal contacts of the Regnaud de Beaumont family with the enormous profit potential of the Royer plantation, which still belonged to Marie-Magdelaine's mother. Yet it was evident to both families that in order to maximize this confluence of assets they needed to take colonialism into account.

Jean-Severin's role as a ship's captain and the prospect of Marie-Magdelaine's inheritance of indigo-laden acres made it almost certain that long separations from each other lay in their future. Marie-Magdelaine's family, with their colonial experience, would have been particularly aware of the challenges such a separation could pose for women. Accordingly, they designed the marriage contract to safeguard Marie-Magdelaine's interests and to open up room for her to exercise choices in the case of a transatlantic separation, or to maximize profits and to protect her from creditors in the case of her husband's death overseas. In doing so, they used the marriage contract to dance around the limitations customary law placed on women's roles.

Managing transatlantic holdings posed distinct challenges. Husbands' personal oversight of colonial interests, while perhaps a sound business move, could entail years, even decades, of separation of husband from wife; during this time she had little sway over his business decisions, even those pertaining to property she had brought into the marriage. Further, transatlantic crossings posed many perils, and colonists faced others: hurricanes and disease both claimed many lives in the sweltering tropics. Were the young bride widowed, particularly without children, she could face difficulties managing or even keeping her property. The Royer-Regnaud de Beaumont marriage contract worked to provide for these very possible sets of circumstances by carefully circumnavigating legal traditions and by writing in provisions that ensured that Marie-Magdelaine Royer would have choices, especially in the event of her widowhood.

The couple's marriage contract, signed and notarized in La Rochelle on 29 March 1735, specified that it would follow the *Coutume de Paris* (the legal code governing Paris) rather than that of La Rochelle.[6] This provision strongly suggests that even upon their marriage, the couple both suspected that a colonial sojourn lay in their future, and recognized the financial importance of Marie-Magdelaine's prospective inheritance of her parents' plantation in Saint-Domingue. The contract thus offered a broad range of options to Marie-Magdelaine in the event of her widowhood, options that drew on both Rochelais and Parisian common law to broaden what either allowed. Inheritance practices were at the crux of the relevant differences between the two.[7] Under Parisian common law, parents had greater testamentary control in naming their heirs or designating a primary legatee, an advantage to those who wanted to keep transatlantic concerns going. This legal tradition also posed some disadvantages for the wife's family of birth, however, because any property wives brought to the marriage, including the dowry, passed into the husband's lineage.[8] In La Rochelle, in contrast, common law somewhat unusually mandated strict testamentary equality for all children, both boys and girls. Should the couple die childless, the wealth a husband brought into the marriage passed back to his family of birth, while the wife's passed back to hers. Any joint property was divided equally between the two lineages.[9]

In the face of these differences, the marriage contract's careful legal navigation makes sense, as the couple married under the jurisdiction of the Custom of La Rochelle, but the Custom of Paris could potentially apply to any inheritance. Numerous families of migrants from France's west coast to the colonies faced this latent legal tangle. A marriage contract could work out possible contradictions ahead of time. Parisian customary law offered some potential advantages to the couple. In particular, the flexibility it allowed in advantaging one heir over the others opened up the possibility that a son or the widow herself could continue operating the family business in the event of the husband's demise. Marie-Magdelaine's colonial upbringing, her merchant father, and her correspondence with her mother about colonial products suggest that this was indeed a very strong possibility.[10] The custom of La Rochelle also offered advantages to the couple, however, in that it allowed them to keep some of their assets strictly separate—at least in theory. These customary laws emphasized lineage through family of birth rather than family of marriage, so many of the couple's personal assets, including real estate property, prospective inheritances, and lump sums of cash, remained strictly separate. Only a few assets specified in the marriage contract and any assets they generated during their marriage became part of their *communauté de biens* (communal property as established by the marriage contract and customarily controlled by the husband). Although Regnaud de Beaumont had some control over his wife's property during his lifetime, in theory at least it was earmarked to pass intact to Marie-Magdelaine's heirs upon her death. He did not have the right to sell it, mortgage it, or alienate it in any way.[11]

This separation of property meant that each spouse maintained a degree of financial autonomy and security. At the same time, only by augmenting their joint property could they better their own social and financial position, and that of their children. While the assets they brought into the marriage remained separate and would be passed discretely to the heirs of each, as per the custom of La Rochelle, any money they made while married would belong to them jointly. Jean-Severin and Marie-Magdelaine thus had strong incentives to work together to increase the property they held in common. This meant that Marie-Magdelaine could play the role of a producer of wealth as well as a bearer of wealth, a role she definitively stepped into during her decades-long separation from her husband while he labored in Saint-Domingue and she remained in France.

In the years between her marriage and her widowhood, Marie-Magdelaine Royer crossed the Atlantic twice, bore eight children, three of whom survived to adulthood, and played a pivotal role in creating and maintaining the trading networks necessary to make a profit from the sale of colonial goods. She did this largely alone; her husband traveled to Saint-Domingue shortly after their marriage, settled there as a planter, and never returned to France. Left as the head of a household and without male relatives in La Rochelle to conduct business in her name or stead, only the *procuration,* or power of attorney, given to her by her husband on their final separation gave her the authority to continue to increase their joint assets. Armed with his procuration, therefore, Marie-Magdelaine Royer, Madame Regnaud de Beaumont, wielded the same power as her husband to make contracts. She used this authority to consolidate her own position, and to attempt to advance her family's wealth.

POWERS OF ATTORNEY

Even during the first years of their marriage Jean-Severin was often absent on merchant voyages.[12] Nonetheless, his wife gave birth at regular intervals, and by the time he left La Rochelle for good, around 1743, he was father to six children. He never met the youngest of these children, his namesake; before the child's birth in 1743, Jean-Severin senior set out for Saint-Domingue.[13] The colony was in the midst of a cash crop boom brought on by an increase in European demand for colonial products, and Jean-Severin did his best to take advantage of it. He managed a plantation, possibly that inherited by his wife from her parents, which specialized in indigo. He also produced some sugar, the quintessential Caribbean cash crop. He saw his wife one last time when she made a final transatlantic journey to Saint-Domingue in the early 1750s, perhaps in response to a long illness Jean-Severin suffered in 1751.[14] A late-in-life son was born to them there in 1753, and Marie-Magdelaine was pregnant again when she left the colony.[15] She gave birth to their eighth and last child on her arrival in La Rochelle in 1755.[16] Although surviving records do not indicate a reason for her return to France, the couple may have found her presence across the ocean necessary for business purposes. Alternatively, they may have found themselves so incompatible they had no wish to remain on the same continent. Whatever the reason, with the exception of these few years passed together in the Antilles, Marie-Magdelaine and her husband spent most of their married lives apart, and she wielded her husband's power of attorney from the time of his initial departure for the colonies in 1743 until his death in 1775.[17]

Holding her husband's general power of attorney gave a wife a greater than usual amount of legal and fiscal control over their joint estate. For the most part, under the customary laws of both Paris and La Rochelle, minor daughters were subject to their fathers or other male relatives; wives' legal identities and fiscal holdings were subsumed into that of their husbands. Even widows, many of whom had broad powers over their own estates, often controlled their late husbands' finances only in custody for minor children. By holding her husband's power of attorney, Marie-Magdelaine Royer Regnaud de Beaumont wielded control over the joint estate she possessed with her husband under the authority of his name, but in her own right. She ran her husband's affairs and her own from her house on the rue des Maîtresses in La Rochelle. She corresponded with merchants in Nantes, Bordeaux, Paris, and Saint-Domingue, arranging for shipment and dispersal of the indigo and other products sent from her husband's plantation, signing contracts and making business arrangements, and filing lawsuits to recover profits from sunken ships or crooked deals.[18] Throughout their separation the couple corresponded extremely rarely, each instead operating independently of the other.

Because of the large number of men who migrated to the Antilles from La Rochelle, on either short- or long-term bases, a woman's wielding her husband's power of attorney became a common legal circumstance in the seaport.[19] However, this created fewer opportunities for women to engage in commerce than one might initially suspect. Although a husband's giving his wife his power of attorney allowed her some measure of authority, this move cannot simply be interpreted as empowering wives with control over family resources equal to that of their husbands. Because of its temporary nature, the power of attorney in fact emphasized husbands' power over their wives' civil life or death. In all cases, men controlled the gateway to their wives' civil authority. They could bestow it, but they could also take it away. For practical reasons, however, many men involved in transatlantic trade chose, during their absences, to legally invest their wives with much of the influence that legally belonged to male heads of household. Such women could testify in court, buy and sell property, and generally oversee their family affairs. In short, they were invested with all the authority they needed to conduct business for their own and their family's profit. Married men on the point of departure very seldom named anyone except their wives as the person who held their power of attorney, emphasizing the assumption that the couple shared a common economic interest. Madame Regnaud de Beaumont, then, found herself in the same legal situation as many other women of varying social statuses whose husbands undertook the perilous sea voyage for the notably insalubrious Caribbean, unsure of their return.

Although possessing a power of attorney conferred legal authority on women, cultural limitations sometimes circumscribed the ways in which they could use this authority. Although shopkeepers might have willingly set up lines of credit for household accounts, businessmen often proved less amenable to accepting shipments of colonial goods or contracting partnerships to outfit merchant voyages with a woman. In entering the male-dominated arena of transatlantic trade, Marie-Magdelaine Royer ran into difficulties that her husband would have been unlikely to encounter. Her agents forestalled her requests, and her letters of credit were not honored. In spite of the indigo and other luxury goods her husband sent to trade from the colonies, she struggled to obtain the necessities required to care for her family; she simply lacked the clout possessed by a man involved in transatlantic trade.

As she strove to muster the influence required to exercise the legal authority the power of attorney gave her, Madame Regnaud de Beaumont turned to personal relationships and drew on the credibility of men besides her absent husband to persuade other merchants she was a force with which to reckon. She looked to a web of associates and acquaintances that stretched from the Atlantic ports of Bordeaux to Nantes, from Paris in the east to the Antillean colonies in the west, with La Rochelle at its center. She called on these contacts as she needed them, acting as a conduit for her husband's authority and empowering them, in turn, to represent her in situations where her femininity made it difficult to represent herself.

THE INCIDENT OF THE *BELLONE*

Madame Regnaud de Beaumont's financial problems did not become evident until 1768, well after she returned from Saint-Domingue and decades after her husband's initial departure for the colonies. Unbeknownst to his wife, Regnaud de Beaumont's indigo enterprise seemed to be struggling. The record is not clear on whether this plantation was the same one promised to Marie-Magdelaine in their marriage contract as part of her eventual inheritance, or what became of this valuable property. The couple, however, cagily diversified their financial holdings and did not rely solely on the vagaries of weather, crop yields, and the market in colonial goods. They also owned an interest in a ship, the *Bellone*. As a former captain himself, Jean-Severin knew firsthand the potential profit margin of transatlantic trade. Accordingly, they went into partnership with several other merchants to buy a vessel, refit it to suit the purposes of the voyage, hire a captain and crew, and gather and load the merchandise to be traded.[20] If the ship returned laden with colonial produce, each partner reaped a percentage of the profits commensurate with the percentage of the capital they had invested in the enterprise. If the ship was lost, each partner lost the money they initially invested, a dispersal of risk that minimized the likelihood that the venture would prove financially ruinous, a possibility even if it was insured. Established merchants owned shares of multiple vessels, thereby increasing the likelihood of returns and decreasing the possibilities of a disastrous loss. The Regnaud de Beaumonts, however, only invested in the *Bellone*. It proved seaworthy, and it regularly brought in profits from the trade in slaves and colonial goods.[21] This venture had the potential to be doubly profitable for the couple, as Jean-Severin provided at least some of the colonial products the ship carried back to France.[22] Marie-Magdelaine, however, little suspected that she would see none of the returns when this profitable partnership was dissolved and the ship sold.[23]

The ship made numerous voyages while it was their property, and Madame Regnaud de Beaumont was active and instrumental in its profitability. Yet when the partners dissolved their association and sold the ship in the late 1760s, the funds remained in the hands of just one of the partners, who lived in Bordeaux and refused to disburse the shares of the profits to the other members of the society. Madame Regnaud de Beaumont had few choices in spite of the power of attorney. How could she, a woman with children and family responsibilities, force a merchant in a different city to yield her family's share of the profits? She had business and family commitments in La Rochelle, and women traveling alone faced both practical difficulties and deep suspicion. Consequently she entrusted her suit to Jacob de Griselles, a merchant and officer of the king in Bordeaux, rather than travel there to take care of the matter herself.

Madame Regnaud de Beaumont's letters to this merchant differ markedly from the usual terse epistles of business associates. Instead, both she and Griselles emphasized their personal connections and wrote the gracious news-filled letters of acquaintances. This departure from common business practice suggests that in this age of letter writing Madame Regnaud de Beaumont used letters to emphasize the importance of personal connections in commerce as in social situations. Griselles reciprocated in kind, even touching on the ways in which personal relationships could ease the path toward a favorable judicial decision as he brought her case to force the disbursement of the profits from the sale of the ship before the Parlement in Bordeaux. He emphasized his own connections with the judges, which he guaranteed Madame Regnaud de Beaumont would help him settle the case in their favor with due speed. He assured her that she should "be very persuaded, Madame, of my zeal and my haste to solicit for myself and my friends the Judgment of the lawsuit that is in our Parlement." By using his connections to gather as much information on the case as he could, he promised that he would gain "a familiarity with this affair to be able to act more effectively."[24] For two and a half years he assured her that their case was about to be heard and that her share of the holdings of the society would be distributed to her forthwith.

Finally, after months of such communication without seeing a single sou of the profits, Madame Regnaud de Beaumont seems to have run out of money or patience. She was involved in other deals for which she needed cash.[25] She finally asked Griselles for an advance on the profits she knew she was owed, drawing on her business acumen to sharply insist on her rights. This move emphasizes the limits she faced in exercising the authority given to her by the procuration. As her letters grew more and more insistent, Griselles finally admitted, "I do not know what to think of his [Monsieur Prevost, a partner in their enterprise who lived in the colonies] delay in getting the capital to me, knowing quite well that he has on hand more than one hundred thousand francs in capital of our society concerning the ship the *Bellone*." He went on to deliver the real blow—that Prevost had already paid her husband the share of the profits that Madame Regnaud de Beaumont thought would be coming to her. As small consolation, Griselles continued, "I do not know if he also remitted to him the seven thousand eight livres that I found owed to Monsieur your husband."[26] Backpedaling somewhat on his extravagant promises to successfully present her case at the Parlement, he offered his sincere regrets on not being able to advance her any of these funds she was owed. Madame Regnaud de Beaumont's special legal rights and privileges came to naught: in spite of her work, her responsibilities, and her best efforts, the hard-earned profits, which she seemed to need desperately, were dispensed directly to her husband, without even a word to her.

This casual assumption of patriarchal privilege shows that while the power of attorney offered Madame Regnaud de Beaumont some practical power, when serious financial matters were at stake other merchants simply dealt with her husband rather than her. She had to use all her business acumen to insist on her own rights. At this point in her correspondence with Griselles, the letters underwent a striking transformation. Perhaps realizing Madame Regnaud de Beaumont's dire financial straits or perhaps responding to her increasingly insistent and detailed queries as to the efficacy of his accounting, the merchant abandoned his avuncular tone and went on the defensive. "I can easily prove to you," he snapped, "that I had in advance for Monsieur your husband from the 25 April 1766 until the 10 February 1767, a sum of more than eleven thousand francs, and from the following 5 October until 5 May 1768 more than sixteen thousand livres." However, because of his own involvement in the enterprise, he said, "I find myself at present his debtor . . . of seven thousand francs."[27] He finally agreed to send her a bill of exchange for two thousand francs which she could draw on a firm in La Rochelle.[28] When she received the bill and took it to the merchant in question, however, he refused to disburse the funds. In Griselles's next letter, he defended himself against what must have been her bitter recriminations. "I will send [another] to you," he said, "in spite of the reasons that I had the honor of sharing with you in my preceding [letter], that must by their validity engage you not to hound me as you do."[29]

Her letters in turn combined careful business accounts of what she was owed with astringent reproaches of his way of conducting business. She berated him, writing, "My last [letter] of the 5 June has been until the present without response on your part, about which I am very surprised." She went on to ask, "What [do] you intend to do on the subject of the sum that you must remit me? You complained wrongly, Monsieur, that I hound you; but I complain rightly that you lead me on, and you mock me in every way." Her indignation rested not only on her want or need for the sum of money, however, but also on careful research and calculations on her part. "I received," she continued, "a letter from my husband, and [another] from M. Prevost, who credited me as having received that sum." She went on to threaten that either he provide her with the sum she asked for—two thousand francs—or she would withdraw all her accounts with him. After giving him a careful statement of any expenses incurred on the lump sum he still held for her, including a bill of exchange he had previously remitted to her, she said, "it still seemed to leave me with 4308 livres." Further, she refused to pay postage for letters he sent on her behalf.[30] Her threats worked; with his next letter he sent her another bill of exchange for 2,000 livres.[31] Having gotten what she wanted, she sent him a very nice note of thanks.[32] In spite of her *politesse*, however, her claims proved only partly successful. The profits from the sale of the ship remained in the hands of her husband, and she received not even half of the additional amount the couple was owed. Although legally they were one unit, the distance between the couple meant that for all intents and purposes Madam Regnaud de Beaumont and her children received little benefit from the sale of the *Bellone*.

This correspondence suggests that the actual authority conferred by the power of attorney was far less sweeping than the text of the document implied. Although the document invested Madame Regnaud de Beaumont with the same rights, privileges, and legal abilities as her husband in a court of law, just getting her case into a courtroom proved to be a trial. Perhaps aware of these difficulties, she first set out to settle her business disputes in more informal ways that were more easily accessible to women, particularly by fostering and trading on personal relationships. Only when this strategy proved unsuccessful did she bring her considerable business acumen to bear; with the evidence of her cold figures, supported by the accounting of her associates, her claim brooked no denial. While the power of attorney gave her claims muscle, it remained in the background, a last resort, and she used it rather to pass along her husband's authority to others than to appropriate and wield it herself.

When at last the case came before the court, she empowered Jacob de Griselles to make her claim. He wrote to her, "I do not fear winning this suit with expenses, if I have merchants for judges, who know all the nuance and force of my presentations; but if it will be magistrates who must judge a question that they do not perhaps consider, as if they were in the place of merchants, in the end we must wait until the time which the judgment is rendered, after which I will sigh heavily."[33] Madame Regnaud de Beaumont no doubt sighed heavily as well when her delicate correspondence with Griselles came to a close. It had been an exercise in carefully negotiating where the responsibility for her business lay, who had authority over her finances, and ultimately the manner in which she lived her life as a woman responsible for a household throughout her husband's long absence. This control was very important in order to maintain the well-being and position of her family.

The incident of the *Bellone* brings into relief one way in which colonialism shaped the lives of women in port cities. Like many other women, because of her husband's extended absence Marie-Magdelaine Regnaud de Beaumont occupied the roles of both wife and head of household. As a head of household, she was responsible for both her own and her children's welfare, and for working to ensure and improve the position of her family. As a wife, not only did she remain under the authority of her husband, he also could—and did—undercut her directives with his own. The long separation of husband and wife therefore caused a rift that affection, if it remained alive, could not surmount. The distance across the Atlantic and the time it took for letters to travel back and forth—six weeks to six months—meant that even in the best of circumstances husbands and wives could not always communicate effectively about their common goals or how they intended to reach them. This particular relationship, however, had strayed so far from either the new companionate ideal or an older pragmatic approach to marriage as a partnership that it had veered permanently off course. The incident of the *Bellone* may have been Madame Regnaud de Beaumont's first inkling that she and her husband, supposedly united in the common goal of increasing their wealth and position for the good of their children, actually had very different intentions indeed. But this was only the beginning of her money troubles, and exactly how far their interests had diverged did not become clear until after her husband's death.

ILLEGITIMACY AND INHERITANCE

When Jean-Severin Regnaud de Beaumont died in 1775 in the town of Léogane, Saint-Domingue, he had been wedded to but physically separated from his wife for most of their forty years of marriage and he had not seen her in over twenty years. In the meantime he had formed another family. This was hardly unusual in Saint-Domingue, where many white men engaged in sexual relationships with enslaved or free women of color. Such liaisons generally remained outside the civil and religious adjudications of family that tended to govern intimate relations in France, and white men had no legal responsibilities to mixed-race offspring born out of wedlock. However, many men, including men who also had legitimate families, made efforts to provide for their illegitimate children of color. Men routinely gave such children gifts of money, land, livestock, or slaves, set them up in business, or provided them with dowries, although there was no legal obligation for them to do so.[34] Regnaud de Beaumont went further than most, however, in that he provided for his mixed-race daughters, Marie-Claire and Marie-Olive, to the exclusion of his legitimate family back in France, a move that went against common law, his marriage contract, and many assumptions about both slavery and the family.[35]

As in France, colonial law mandated that men leave the bulk of their estates to legitimate children or kin. Fathers could not disinherit their legitimate children. Meanwhile, mixed-race children could not lay claim to their white fathers' estates unless their parents married.[36] However, contracts provided means to wiggle around such provisions.[37] Fathers could give illegitimate children gifts of money or property while they were alive, and could leave sizable legacies to them in the form of cash, livestock, personal possessions, and annuities; such gifts in fact contributed to the social and economic power of free colored people in Saint-Domingue.[38] These practices had the potential to wreak havoc among families in France. Jean-Severin Regnaud de Beaumont's loyalty to and wish to provide for his illegitimate "mulatto" daughters drove his legitimate white family apart.

Shortly before her husband's death, Marie-Magdelaine Regnaud de Beaumont realized that something was amiss. Consequently, in 1774, perhaps aware of her husband's ailing health and certainly cognizant of his advancing age, she sent her youngest and only surviving son, Jean-Marie-Olive, to Saint-Domingue, the colony where he had been born twenty-two years before. In the thirty-nine years since their marriage, Jean-Severin and Marie-Magdelaine Regnaud de Beaumont had failed to realize the colonial dream. Jean-Severin had grown old on the land he worked, but his fortune had not increased with his age. While some planters grew rich on colonial products grown by their slaves, his estate, of a promising size at the time of his marriage, had dwindled to practically nothing. He also was deeply in debt; he owed E.-L. Seignette, a transatlantic merchant in La Rochelle, nearly 14,000 livres, and he had other debts as well.[39] Although his wife had also faced financial challenges, his son was shocked to witness the depths to which his father had sunk.

Jean-Marie-Olive's letters to his mother and sisters back in France reinvigorated the ties among the transatlantic members of the family. Perhaps as testament to the difficulties of transatlantic marriage and to the broken trust that lay between them, Monsieur and Madame Regnaud de Beaumont seldom exchanged letters. When young Jean-Marie-Olive arrived in Saint-Domingue, therefore, both his father's poor health and his meager finances came as a surprise. He wrote to his mother, "You would not be able to believe, dear Mother, how my dear Papa is in despair to not have and to not be able to send you any [financial] relief. He has been, and is more than ever, in a physical state which makes it impossible to do it, lacking himself a good number of things, he needs money of which he has been deprived for a long time, and [he] hardly has what is necessary." According to his son, Regnaud de Beaumont found himself "in a situation as critical as that in which we all found ourselves in France, and he has had the worst illnesses, passing whole nights without sleeping, and is even persuaded that he is losing his sight, which is irreparable."[40] The son complained that his father's "linens were already old," suggesting that Regnaud de Beaumont senior could not afford even the most basic necessities.[41]

Regnaud de Beaumont was hardly a figure that inspired reverence or respect for patriarchal authority. He was old, sick, partially blind, and pitifully poor. However, he still had the right and power to make his will. In doing so he decisively undercut his marriage contract, signed forty years before, and the expectations of his legitimate family by leaving legacies that comprised the majority of his estate. For his wife, safeguarded, as she thought, by the marriage contract and customary law, the testament came as one of a series of surprises. First was the revelation of his second family, a woman of color and their two daughters, a common-enough circumstance that she may have surmised but did not seem to know beforehand. Second and most shockingly, in spite of laws prohibiting him from alienating her property, both her husband's entire estate and her own had dwindled to practically nothing. Not even her son's letters had prepared her to learn the extent of her husband's penury. Regardless of the protections of the marriage contract and the customary laws of both La Rochelle and Paris, all of which forbade her husband from alienating her property, it was gone, apparently without her knowledge or consent. Finally, Regnaud de Beaumont had left the pittance that remained of the estate to his illegitimate daughters in the form of legacies, effectively cutting off his three surviving legitimate children completely.

These legacies suggest that Regnaud de Beaumont's emotional connections lay with his family in Saint-Domingue rather than with his legal family in France. He left "a life pension of one hundred livres" to each of his "natural daughters, free mulâtresses" Marie-Claire and Marie-Olive, "daughters of Marie Anne free negress."[42] They were to be paid in installments of fifty livres every six months, beginning on the day of their father's death, and payments were to continue throughout their lives. The girls and their half-brother, Jean-Marie-Olive, also each were to have possession of a mahogany chest filled with their personal belongings, suggesting that the whole family, legitimate and illegitimate, white, mixed-race, and black, lived under one roof—a circumstance the son, perhaps naturally enough, had failed to mention in his letters to his mother. Regnaud de Beaumont specified that his son, still a minor, would stay on the plantation as overseer. He appointed his neighbor, Michel Samuel DeColon, his executor, perhaps hoping that his friend, familiar with life in the colonies, would work to ensure that Marie-Claire and Marie-Olive received their annuities. In principle these legacies were in line with what many mixed-race children could expect:

they provided enough to live on but did not, on the surface, seem overly exorbitant. In this instance, however, so many of Regnaud de Beaumont's assets
had disappeared that these legacies comprised the bulk of his wealth. Even his
plantation was mortgaged to the hilt, and his many debts ate up his lean assets.

Regnaud de Beaumont's burial took place on 27 July 1775 in the parish church
of Saint Rose in Léogane, the same church where his son had been baptized
twenty-two years before.[43] His death precipitated a flurry of transatlantic correspondence and paperwork; his assets had to be valued, his wife had to determine
how to best protect herself and her children from her husband's many debts, and
the estate needed to be portioned out accordingly. Regnaud de Beaumont, never
a good businessman, had proved astoundingly optimistic in judging the value of
his estate; even the annuities he left for his daughters taxed the bounds of his
resources. The unexpectedly small size of his holdings led to conflicts over its
apportioning in disputes that divided parents from children and siblings from
each other.[44]

DeColon, as executor, began the sticky process of liquidating his friend's assets, while keeping the widow informed by letter. His news was seldom good. The
plantation was in "appalling confusion," and what he called the "cursed place"
produced very little revenue in the year between Regnaud de Beaumont's death
and its sale.[45] They hardly had enough to keep body and soul together; DeColon
wrote that "the slaves here are dying of hunger, and all naked." Finally, he wrote,
"I have sold the plantation, the slaves, and the few beasts that remained for the
sum of 34,000 livres," a considerable amount, which, however, included "12,000
livres in letters of credit . . . and 18,000 livres cash."[46] Colonial letters of credit
were notoriously difficult to collect, and the entire sum amounted to scarcely
more than the substantial 30,000-livre dowry Marie-Magdelaine Royer brought
into her marriage.[47] He wrote, "the most difficult thing will be to get paid, and I
fear a terrible suit."[48]

In the end, Marie-Magdelaine Regnaud de Beaumont renounced her right
to her husband's estate.[49] This option, delineated in their marriage contract,
protected her property from her husband's creditors and ended her liability for
his debts. Her younger daughter Marie-Brigitte joined her in her renunciation,
thereby giving up all her claims on her father's estate, although she still would
retain the right to one-third of her mother's. This did not mean, however, that
Marie-Magdelaine could simply walk away. She still had to oversee the appraisal
of the assets and to give authorization for the day-to-day expenses of running
the plantation while the legal battle unfolded. To that end she gave DeColon
her power of attorney, thereby authorizing him to sell slaves and other forms of

property, perhaps in an effort to liquify the assets and to help her children salvage what they could from the estate.[50]

Her other two surviving children, Jean-Marie-Olive and his sister Marie-Magdelaine, more optimistic than their mother or sister, continued to fight for their father's estate. They looked everywhere they could in an effort to recuperate some of the assets their father had lost, and to a limited extent they succeeded. DeColon, acting as their representative, tried to collect debts of over 3,000 livres from a merchant in Bordeaux who had owed money to their father.[51] The siblings also brought suit against a free black man who had owed their father money, and later tried to sue DeColon himself.[52] They appear still to have been trying to recover their father's estate in 1786 when Jean-Marie-Olive wrote his last letter to his mother. In it he complained about his dire financial straits, as he had before, and some of his bitterness about the hopelessness of his situation comes through: "there is no money," he said; "youth passes, and we are no further along."[53] After that the young man disappeared. His aging mother never heard from him again, or learned of his fate.[54]

The provisions of Regnaud de Beaumont's will, the surprising paucity of his resources at his death, and the unexplained disappearance of his wife's property all highlight the difficult contingencies colonialism raised for families, and the lack of options available to women. In the end, when faced with her late husband's near bankruptcy, the result of his own mismanagement, Marie-Magdelaine could only protect the assets over which she had control. She spent her married life legally empowered by her husband, managing business deals and assets, yet as a widow she struggled to recoup any of the fruits of those labors. She had continued operating under the assumption that her husband shared her idea of what constituted a family: a husband and wife legally married and their legitimate children, all working toward the common goal of the betterment of all. He, however, had come to a different understanding of family, one based on shared daily life and, presumably, affection.

CONCLUSION

Establishing an economic foothold in the colonies often occasioned a long separation between husband and wife, which in turn opened up a specific set of opportunities and constraints for women left behind in France. Families tried to prepare for such challenging circumstances through contracts. Customary law, while affording some protections for women, did not account for long marital separations that in ports such as La Rochelle came as a matter of course in the eighteenth century. Families did their best to peer into the future, writing into marriage contracts provisions that would allow a married couple separated by an ocean the flexibility they would need to work singly toward their joint project. Couples continued this strategy on the eve of husbands' departures; powers of attorney, as explained above, offered wives the legal license to continue operating businesses, managing property, and generally contributing toward their mutual assets, even in their husbands' absences. Contracts such as these therefore filled the gaps in customary law while not necessarily undermining or going against it. Both contracts and custom aimed to allow families to accumulate and pass on assets, making provisions for the welfare of women and children, especially in the case of a husband's death.

Testaments generally endorsed this goal, offering the testator an opportunity to indicate appreciation, affection, or benevolence through small legacies, while ratifying the flow of wealth from one generation to the next. However, the case of the Regnaud de Beaumont family demonstrates the power that colonial circumstances had to interrupt this flow, and thus to upset the entire conception of what constituted a family and how families should act, in particular with regard to the accumulation and transmission of wealth. Contracts, therefore, could disrupt as well as protect family assets.

The case of the Regnaud de Beaumont family on the surface seems to suggest a wealth of opportunity opened up for women by the circumstances of transatlantic separation. Marriage contracts wrote in choices, drawing on multiple common law traditions to ensure women maximum flexibility to continue engaging in profitable commercial activity. Powers of attorney gave them the same authority as heads of households, while the absence of husbands gone to the Antilles impelled many women into the thick of business deals. However, contracts proved to be limited tools. Power within the family continued to flow from white French men, who gave women the permission to act in their names, and husbands could take away this authority as well as bestow it. While women's cultural position could stand in the way of their participation in colonial commerce, that of men enabled them, at least on occasion, to alienate their wives' property without raising questions in spite of the multiple prohibitions against this. While women's sexual propriety was of utmost concern in a marriage, men could and did form second families, and sometimes, as here, indicate through their testamentary allocation of assets that their regard for them surpassed the regard they held for their legitimate children. Patriarchal authority, therefore, operated on both sides of the ocean: white women, women of color, legitimate children, and illegitimate children all depended on the will of the father. Other family members could only do their best to protect their own interests and privileges.

NOTES

1. Jean-Claude Perrot, "Note sur les contrats de mariage normands," in *Structures et relations sociales à Paris au XVIIIᵉ siècle,* ed. Adeline Daumard and François Furet (Paris: A. Colin, 1961), 95–97.

2. See Natalie Zemon Davis, *The Return of Martin Guerre* (Cambridge, Mass.: Harvard Univ. Press, 1983).

3. Clare Haru Crowston, "Family Affairs: Wives, Credit, Consumption, and the Law in Old Regime France," in *Family, Gender, and Law in Early Modern France,* ed. Suzanne Desan and Jeffrey Merrick (University Park: Pennsylvania State Univ. Press, 2009), 62–100.

4. "Procuration le Sieur Bidet a Dmlle Delissart son Epouse," [date illegible] 1777, 3 E 1688; "Procuration M Pre Neau a son épouse," 28 April 1763, 3 E 1674; "Procuration Jean Margoteau marinier a son épouse," 25 June 1743, 3 E 2105, all in the Archives Départementales de la Charente Maritime (hereafter ADCM).

5. "Procuration le Sieur Bidet a Dmlle Delissart son Epouse," [date illegible] 1777, 3 E 1688, ADCM.

6. "Contrat de mariage," 29 March 1735, E 513, ADCM.

7. On the *Coutume de Paris* and widowhood, see Janine M. Lanza, *From Wives to Widows in Early Modern Paris: Gender, Economy, and Law* (Aldershot, Eng.: Ashgate, 2007), 32–39.

8. Simon-François Langloix, *Principes généraux de la Coutume de Paris, Où les articles du texte, & les ordonnances qui y ont rapport, sont rangés dans un ordre méthodique, pour en faciliter l'usage,* 3rd ed. (Paris: Prault père, 1746), 148.

9. Charles A. Bourdot de Richebourg, *Nouveau coutumier general, ou corps des coutumes generales et particulieres de France, et des provinces* (Paris: Robustel, 1724), 4:859; Jean Yver, *Égalité entre héritiers et exclusion des enfants dotés: Essai de géographie coutumière* (Paris: Editions Sirey, 1966); Emmanuel Le Roy Ladurie, "Family Structures and Inheritance Customs in Sixteenth-Century France," in *Family and Inheritance: Rural Society in Western Europe, 1200–1800,* ed. Jack Goody, Joan Thirsk, and E. P. Thompson (Cambridge: Cambridge Univ. Press, 1976).

10. For example, her mother refers to the "indigo that I must send to my daughter." Veuve Royer, no name of recipient, 4 August 1735, E 515, ADCM.

11. René-Josué Valin, *Nouveau commentaire sur la coutume de La Rochelle et du pays d'Aunis* (La Rochelle: René-Jacob Desbordes, 1756), 491.

12. He was listed as "absent" at the baptism of their first child. Baptism, St.-Barthélemy parish, Jean-Severin-Nicolas Regnaud, 22 December 1735, GG 251, Archives Municipales de La Rochelle (hereafter AMLR).

13. Baptism, St.-Barthélemy parish, Jean-Severin Regnaud, 21 November 1743, GG 259, AMLR.

14. Bechade to Madame Regnaud de Beaumont, 21 December 1751, E 514, ADCM.

15. Baptism, Sainte Rose parish in Léogane, Saint-Domingue, Jean Marie Renaud, 11 December

1753, 85MIOM/83, Centre des Archives d'Outre-Mer (hereafter CAOM); also "Extrait des Registres de la paroisse de Saint Rose de Léogane Isle et Coste de Saint Domingue," copy made 5 July 1766, E 514, ADCM. She and her son returned to La Rochelle around 15 or 20 May 1755. Bechade to Madame *veuve* Royer, 4 July 1755, E 514, ADCM. The passenger lists for La Rochelle for this period are no longer extant.

16. Baptism, St.-Barthélemy parish, Marie-Severin-Augustin Regnaud, 25 October 1755, GG 276, AMLR. The child's mother was said to have "recently arrived" from Léogane, where her father was a planter.

17. Power of attorney, Notaire Gariteau Fils, 26 March 1743, 3 E 2105, ADCM. A copy was prepared by Notaire Delavergne just a few days later, on 5 April 1743. It was later affixed to a contract for a piece of property she bought on 9 April 1771, E 513, ADCM. Jean-Severin sent his wife a renewal of the power of attorney, 2 December 1772, E 516, ADCM.

18. Receipt from Girard, captain of the ship *Phaeton* bound for La Rochelle from Léogane, for sugar, cocoa, and coffee received from Jean-Severin Regnaud de Beaumont, to be delivered to Madame Regnaud de Beaumont, 14 July 1750, E 512, ADCM.

19. The ship's captain, Pierre Neau, for example, provides a typical example in that he gave his wife his power of attorney when he was "on the point of departing for the Island and Coast of Saint Domingue." He authorized her to make contracts, administer their land, and to buy and sell goods. "Procuration M Pre Neau a son épouse, 28 avril 1763," Notaire Delavergne, 3 E 1674, ADCM.

20. Robert Harms, *The Diligent: A Voyage through the Worlds of the Slave Trade* (New York: Basic Books, 2002), 76.

21. For example, one voyage brought in 246,800 livres from the trade in slaves, with a total profit of 163,703 livres, 8 sols. Summary of profits, no date, E 512, ADCM. Another voyage brought a net profit of 19,379 livres, 8 sols, 6 derniers. "Expenses from the disarmament of the ship the *Bellone*," Camaud, 1 April 1743, E 512, ADCM.

22. Account and repartition, 25 May 1751, E 512, ADCM.

23. The Regnaud de Beaumonts owned a share in the ship from at least as early as 1741 (E 512, ADCM).

24. Jacob de Griselles to Madame Regnaud de Beaumont, 22 October 1768, E 514, ADCM.

25. For example, she purchased a piece of property for 15,000 livres. Notary contract for the purchase of property from Sieur Simon Lazard Didier Boucheron of Niort, 12 May 1770, E 512, ADCM.

26. Jacob de Griselles to Madame Regnaud de Beaumont, 30 December 1769, E 514, ADCM.

27. Jacob de Griselles to Madame Regnaud de Beaumont, 27 April 1770, E 514, ADCM. Francs were an administrative unit of currency equal to livres, the currency that circulated in France and its colonies.

28. Jacob de Griselles to Madame Regnaud de Beaumont, 15 April 1770, E 514, ADCM.

29. Jacob de Griselles to Madame Regnaud de Beaumont, 4 May 1770, E 514, ADCM.

30. Her copy of Madame Regnaud de Beaumont to Jacob de Griselles, 21 July 1770, E 514, ADCM.

31. Jacob de Griselles to Madame Regnaud de Beaumont, 3 August 1770, E 514, ADCM.

32. Her copy of Madame Regnaud de Beaumont to Jacob de Griselles, 7 August 1770, E 514, ADCM.

33. Jacob de Griselles to Madame Regnaud de Beaumont, 18 May 1771, E 514, ADCM.

34. For examples of white men who transferred assets to children of color and the tactics they used, see John Garrigus, *Before Haiti: Race and Citizenship in French Saint-Domingue* (New York: Palgrave MacMillan, 2006), 60–66. On changing attitudes toward illegitimacy in France, see Matthew Gerber, *Bastards: Politics, Family, and Law in Early Modern France* (New York: Oxford Univ. Press, 2012).

35. Similarly, in Brazilian as in French law, illegitimate children could not inherit their parents' estates, although parents could leave them legacies. Linda Lewin, *Surprise Heirs: Illegitimacy, Patrimonial Rights, and Legal Nationalism in Luso-Brazilian Inheritance, 1750–1821*, vol. 1 (Stanford: Stanford Univ. Press, 2003), 71, 75–76.

36. The Code Noir accepted mixed-race children as legitimate if their parents married in the Catholic Church; in that case, it provided that both mother and child were free. Article IX, "Code Noir," March 1685, in Médéric-Louis-Elie Moreau de Saint-Méry, *Loix et constitutions des colonies françaises de l'Amérique sous le vent*, 5 vols. (Paris, 1784–1790), 1:414–424. John Garrigus shows that some white men did in fact marry women of color (*Before Haiti*, 41, 47–48).

37. On property that could be allocated via testament vs. lineage property (*acquets* vs. *propres*), see Ralph E. Giesey, "Rules of Inheritance and Strategies of Mobility in Prerevolutionary France," *American Historical Review* 82, no. 2 (1977): 271–289.

38. Stewart King, *Blue Coat or Powdered Wig: Free People of Color in Pre-Revolutionary Saint-Domingue* (Athens: Univ. of Georgia Press, 2001), 215; Garrigus, *Before Haiti*, 45–49, 65–66. Also see, for example, "donation of Sieur Jean Jacques Renard to Jacques Dominique, free *quateroon*, aged about one year, and to the children to be born to Catherine called Deda, free *mulâtresse*," Notary Beaudould, Port-au-Prince, 26 September 1785, DPPC NOT SDOM 85, CAOM.

39. On Regnaud de Beaumont's debts, see the correspondence between J. LeDuc and Madame Regnaud de Beaumont from 8 May 1771 to 22 February 1772, E 514, ADCM; and E.-L. Seignette to Garesché and Billotteau, in which he lists Regnaud de Beaumont's debts to him as 13,746 l. 3 s. 4 d., 22 August 1780, 4 J 1610, ADCM.

40. Jean-Marie-Olive Regnaud de Beaumont to Marie-Magdelaine Royer Regnaud de Beaumont, 7 May 1774, E 514, ADCM.

41. Jean-Marie-Olive Regnaud de Beaumont to Marie-Magdelaine Royer Regnaud de Beaumont, 18 May 1782, E 514, ADCM.

42. "Testament du Sr. Regnaud de Beaumont homologué le 28 Juin 1775," E 513, ADCM. Hervé de Halgouet refers to a similar case, where a man in Saint-Domingue showed "exorbitant" generosity to his housekeeper, who might have been his natural daughter, at the expense of his wife and daughter in France. Hervé du Halgouet, "Inventaire d'une habitation à Saint-Domingue," *Revue d'histoire des colonies* 21, no. 4–5 (1933): 236. According to the *Coutume de Paris*, fathers could only leave illegitimate children property, including annuities, in usufruct; they could not transmit *immeubles* (real estate) to illegitimate offspring. Langloix, *Principes généraux de la coutume de Paris*, 237.

43. Burial, Sainte Rose parish in Léogane, Saint-Domingue, Jean Severin Regnaud, 27 July 1775, 85MIOM/64, CAOM.

44. Also see Sandra Lauderdale Graham, *Caetana Says No: Women's Stories from a Brazilian Slave Society* (New York: Cambridge Univ. Press, 2002).

45. Michel Samuel DeColon to the Widow Royer Regnaud de Beaumont, 3 February 1777 and 15 July 1776, E 514, ADCM.

46. Michel Samuel DeColon to the Widow Royer Regnaud de Beaumont, 15 July 1776, E 514, ADCM.

47. At least 10 percent of colonists' debts for slaves alone regularly went unpaid. Carolyn Fick, *The Making of Haiti: The Saint Domingue Revolution from Below* (Knoxville: Univ. of Tennessee Press, 1990), 24.

48. Michel Samuel DeColon to the Widow Royer Regnaud de Beaumont, 15 July 1776 E 514, ADCM.

49. Renunciation of Common Goods [no title], 4 November 1775, E 513, ADCM.

50. "Vente d'un négrillon et une négritte par Sieur DeColon," 24 February 1777, DPPC NOT SDOM 1527, CAOM. This contract of sale names DeColon as the *procureur* of Madame Regnaud de Beaumont.

51. "Procuration par Sieur DeColon à M.M. Paul Nairac et fils ainé négociants à Bordeaux," 26 June 1778, DPPC NOT SDOM 1527, CAOM.

52. "Entre les héritiers Regnaud de Beaumont contre le nègre nommé L'Amoureux," 4 April 1778, DPPC Greffes 1, CAOM; "De Colon Dlle de Beaumont," April 13, 1785, DPPC Greffes 2, CAOM.

53. Jean-Marie-Olive to his mother, 6 August 1786, E 514, ADCM.

54. Marie-Magdelaine Regnaud de Beaumont wrote a frantic letter to the priest in St. Marc on 28 July 1789 asking for news of her son. She says that her last letter from him was dated 6 August 1786 and she did not know if he was alive or dead. Also see Regnaud de Beaumont sisters to Buchiére, 19 June 1797, both E 515, ADCM.

WOMEN AND THE BIRTH OF MODERN CONSUMER CAPITALISM

James B. Collins

THE bookseller Siméon-Prosper Hardy often records spectacular bankruptcies in his diary. On 18 December 1769, in a special additional entry—right after his comments on a meteor shower—Hardy reports the massive failures of the Sieur Quérénet, chief treasurer of the Prince of Conti (a loss of 3 million livres), of the Sieur Leroux, sub treasurer of the Estates of Brittany (1.6 million livres), of Billiard, cashier of the postal system (5 million livres), and of the banker Baudard de Vaudésir (900,000 livres). Rumor tied these collapses to the grain monopoly, in this year of the Flour War, another frequent Hardy topic.[1] Hardy then passes to the world of commerce: an "important female fish merchant" (*marchande poissonière*; 80,000 livres) and a female fruit seller (*fruitière*; 25,000 livres), both of the Saint-Germain market.

Hardy here reminds us that women played a major role in Parisian markets. A bankruptcy of 80,000 livres, or even 25,000 livres, marks a merchant of considerable stature, even in Paris. Yet we have largely ignored these women. As in Hardy's journal, they remain anonymous, unlike the male bankrupts, whom he names. The contemporaneous events of the Flour War bring women to the fore once again. In her list of ninety-three women arrested (16 percent of those incarcerated) across France during the riots, Cynthia Bouton found more than a score of professions, including fruit seller, innkeeper, cabaret owner, horse merchant, and even blacksmith's apprentice.[2] The tax rolls of French towns, from a provincial capital like Rennes (population forty thousand), to a middling town, Chalon-sur-Saône (population eight thousand), or a smaller one, Avallon (population forty-two hundred), tell the same story of female labor force participation; their records suggest a considerable eighteenth-century increase in the percentage of women directly involved in the market economy, particularly in smaller and middling towns.[3]

The third edition (2008) of Merry Wiesner's foundational *Women and Gender in Early Modern Europe* makes manifest the extraordinary growth in our knowledge about women in the early modern world. The chapter on women and colonialism illustrates, as well, our changing perspective both on that world and women's roles in it. One element of continuity stands out—the minimal changes in the chapter on women and work. Wiesner wrote, in 1993 (unchanged in 2008), "When we evaluate women's economic role during this period, however, we find that continuities outweigh the changes."[4] This statement echoed the prevailing wisdom of the early 1990s; as Olwen Hufton put it, "Women and work in the early modern era is a sinister chronicle of a struggle for survival."[5] Madeline Ferrières's study on the *mont-de-piété* (municipal pawnbroker) of early modern Avignon illustrates the special financial precariousness of women; every year at least 83 percent (most years 90+ percent) of those pawning an object were women.[6]

Most early modern women, even more than most men, spent their lives struggling for survival, but twenty years of scholarship on women and work in Old Regime France suggests that the time has come to modify the emphasis on the negative and on continuity.[7] Despite the efforts of some scholars, women remain marginal players in the writings of economic historians, especially those focused on big picture issues, such as the rise of capitalism in Europe.[8] This marginalization has one exception: all agree that women drove the revolution in consumption. The available evidence, however, suggests a strong symbiotic relationship between consumption and production in the rise of a consumer society, and of modern capitalism. Early modern French women's contributions must be understood within this symbiotic relationship, not simply on the demand side of the equation.

Thinking about these early modern French families brings to mind my maternal grandparents, George Sullivan and Elizabeth O'Neil Sullivan, who founded the Sullivan Paper Company in 1940. My grandfather initially did all of the production alone; Nana ran the large (nine children) household, supervised work on the two acres of farm, and canned the farm's produce. Seemingly removed from the business, in fact she kept the books, much the way a baker's wife in eighteenth-century France would have done. A talented artist, she created the designs for the paper and for the company logo, a museum-quality piece of mid-twentieth-century industrial art that still adorns its headquarters and website.[9] How many early modern French businesses looked like that? Aside from obvious examples, like bakeries, how can we tell? Reconstructing women's economic activities one notarized transaction at a time provides the micro level view, but fiscal documentation offers us some tantalizing hints about macro developments.

What constituted a modern economy? Jan de Vries and A. M. van der Woude offer the following general comments in making a case for the Netherlands as the "first modern economy": "The high degree of differentiation in this structure of interdependence reflected the early replacement in this region of an autarkic economy with one defined by occupational specialization and market relations. The greater and more differentiated the range of goods available for purchase by rural folk, and the more the city became the source for specialized goods and services, the more citified became the character of rural life and the more self-sufficiency was eroded."[10]

Historians have recognized for over a generation the eighteenth-century revolution in consumption under way in a metropolis like Paris or Amsterdam, or a large provincial city like Bordeaux, or, for that matter, their Chinese counterparts.[11] The physical traces of the connection between the rise of consumption in Paris and in great provincial cities remain: in Bordeaux alone, the royal theatre, designed by Victor Louis, the place de la Bourse, done by Ange-Jacques Gabriel, or the lovely public garden, the first in France, jointly begun in 1746 by the intendant Tourny and the town government. The great park at Bordeaux soon had that ultimate symbol of urbanism, a café. Yet forty years earlier, the local parlementaire Savignac took his wife, his mother, and some friends to the latest sensation, a *limonadier* [seller of cool drinks, like lemonade, but often of ice cream as well]. He drank chocolate and frequented the Café Anglais.[12] One would look far and wide without finding either a café or a limonadier in the small and middling French towns of 1709, which raises the obvious questions: did the inhabitants of such towns participate in the revolution in consumption? If so, when and how did they join? How did changed patterns of consumption affect their distribution of professions?

This revolution had multiple dimensions: consumption, production, culture, and politics. De Vries hypothesizes an "industrious revolution," in which productivity increased, just as Michael Sonenscher and others have emphasized changes in scale of production. Enterprises got larger, whether merchant ships, tailors' shops, or farms in the Île-de-France.[13] This changed scale of activity enabled the development of a key element of modern capitalism, the shift toward maximizing total sales, rather than focusing on profit per sale.[14] Outside of those areas tied intimately to the evolving world economy or to the great cities, however, economies of scale could be difficult to carry out. The proximity of the great Paris market led to rapid agricultural concentration in the Île-de-France between 1625 and 1700, but agricultural consolidation largely failed in Normandy and in the Loire Valley, for example, because landlords could not find ploughmen with sufficient capital resources to lease large consolidated farms.[15]

Late seventeenth-century urban tax rolls demonstrate the contrast between the larger and smaller cities. Four changes accelerated in the early eighteenth century: (1) new occupations, like café owner, came into being; (2) new mass products, like sugar, radically altered certain traditional trades, like pastry making; (3) specialized "luxury" trades became more "populuxe," and spread to smaller towns; and (4) fashionable "taste" penetrated more broadly into outlying areas.[16] The combination of the third and fourth changes produced the greatest shift in small and middling towns, in terms of numbers of people employed in "new" professions. Sixteenth-century Dijon (then with a population of twenty thousand) had plenty of pastry makers, booksellers, and specialized tradespeople. What changed in the eighteenth century is that towns like Chalon-sur-Saône or even Avallon began to have such occupations, too. That had become possible because the regions they served now had a market for these specialized products that was large enough to support a local producer, who was often a woman.

In the countryside, women's economic contributions became ever greater when rural areas became even more closely tied to the international market and shifted to more specialized agricultural production for urban consumers. Much of the rising demand focused precisely on products, such as luxury vegetables, grown in the garden close to the house, almost always the responsibility of the women of the farm. These products brought in cash income, which magnified their economic impact.

In small and middling towns, professions previously known only to larger towns became increasingly important. In Auxerre (population twelve thousand) or Avallon, more than a third of the taxpayers of the 1750s declared a profession that either did not exist in the city in the 1680s, or barely did. At Avallon in 1751 there were six wigmakers (one in 1690), and new occupations such as watchmaker, turner, vinegar maker, chandler, goldsmith, fruit seller, *traiteur* (prepared meals seller), pork butcher (*charcutier*), plasterer, knife maker, and building contractor (*entrepreneur de bâtiments*). A Parisian or a Dijonnais of 1700 would not have turned her head about a traiteur; but by 1750 a traiteur could make a living even in tiny Avallon.

By the 1780s, Avallon had added four wholesale grocers, two cafés, a brandy distiller, two painters, several jewelers, a game piece maker, a bookseller, an architect/urban planner, and two *marchandes de modes* (lit.: female fashion merchant). A larger, richer town like Auxerre already in the 1750s had cafés and the more "modern" professions like coffee merchant, wine broker, lemonade seller, roast meat seller (*rôtisseur*), glazier (urban houses now had many more windows), *ébeniste* (cabinet maker), bookbinder, and *faïencier* (earthenware maker). Auxerre's new professions—commissioner, collector, specialized merchants (wood, wine, iron, cheese)—dot the roll.[17] By the 1780s the city would have a mirror maker, tobacco merchants, brewers, multiple booksellers and grocers, even, by 1788, an organ maker. Autun (population nine thousand) had a half-dozen watchmakers. The watch had become a basic "necessity" of town dwellers, and of the richest ploughmen, too. These local merchants, even retailers, could have broad geographic networks. The merchant Widow Colombo (and her sons), from Nice, for example, had connections in Piedmont, the Swiss cantons, southern France, and even Rouen.[18]

By the 1770s, every one of the thirty-one Burgundian towns with more than one thousand people had a wigmaker; twenty-one had a grocer (*épicier*), thirteen a café owner, and twelve a watchmaker. The four towns with roughly four thousand people—Avallon, Châtillon, Sémur-en-Auxois, and Cluny—all had several of each. Autun had a printer (for the bishop), a bookbinder, a papermaker, four bookstores, five cafés, two ébenistes, thirteen grocers (compared to one in 1692), fifteen wine merchants (zero in 1692), and various other nearly new professions, including thirteen wigmakers (one in 1692). To a similar mix, Chalon added two dancing masters. The roaring seaport of Lorient, seat of the Company of the Indies, had no less than sixteen billiard halls. Such sweeping socioeconomic change affected the State; after the middle of the century, it levied a *vingtième* (5 percent income tax) on "industry."

The small town tax rolls show us as well the spread of professions symbiotically related to public opinion, like booksellers and schoolmasters (less often, schoolmistresses). In larger towns, a broader market meant greater specialization: a "grammarian," sometimes a master writer, who taught the sons of merchants and legal men the basics of proper writing technique, and, in some cases, the wonders of double-entry bookkeeping.[19] By the 1780s we see architects, wine brokers, *feudistes* (specialists in feudal practice), surveyors, and other professions formerly practiced only in the large cities. These professionals formed the new public opinion, which the government felt it "must persuade."[20] Little Quintin (population one thousand) even had a reading room that subscribed to several Parisian gazettes; in their wills, two of the locals left copies of the *Encyclopédie*.[21] As the demand grew for new products—often ones not clearly defined as belonging to the restricted production of a given guild—women stepped forward to produce them, not just to consume them.

The problem of insufficient capital notwithstanding, tax roll data show that in middling and small towns the French economy evolved dramatically between the 1680s and the 1780s. Women played the central role in the spread of the twin revolutions of consumption and industriousness. Their greater role as producers surely helped drive up demand in certain sectors, above all in the prepared food business. Although Pomeranz's argument—that the systematic exploitation of the natural resources of the Western Hemisphere made it possible for Europe to leap ahead of the advanced regions of Asia in the early stages of the Industrial Revolution—explains much of the "great divergence," the considerable increase in integration of women into the waged economy of Europe after 1650, and even more pronouncedly after 1700, might be just as important a factor.

Capitalism generated its start-up capital not simply from Marxian "primitive accumulation" generated from resource extraction in the mines and fields of the Americas, but in the systematic addition of women's wage labor (and that of children) to the stock of surplus value created by European workers in the economically advanced regions.[22] That process is obvious enough in the first stage of the Industrial Revolution, because girls dominated the labor force of textile factories, but the tax roll data from French provincial towns show that it had begun well before spinning jennies transformed European production and consumption of textiles. Dominique Godineau, for example, estimates that two-thirds of the Parisian "luxury goods" workers were women.[23]

English data, at least for London, suggest a similar situation there. In 1700, in a sample of over six hundred women testifying in court, 77.6 percent of the unmarried adult women wholly supported themselves by wage labor, as did 73.2 percent of the widows. An additional 5.8 percent of the "spinsters" and 12 percent of the widows obtained some of their support from wages. A third of married women got most of their support from their own wages, and another quarter got some support from wages.[24] Among married women, two-thirds of them between the ages of twenty-five and fifty-four worked for wages; moreover, only 10 percent of the waged married women worked in the same occupations as their husbands, and nearly half of that group helped run food and/or drink establishments. In London, as in France, the "not employed" women generally came from a higher social group, wives of merchants, master artisans, and professionals. In the first two categories, the wives often helped with the main business. In France, women illegally worked for the state tax bureaucracy. Bourrée, the tax receiver for the district of Coulommiers, for example, preferred to spend his time in Paris. He left the actual work to the capable daughter of his predecessor.[25]

"Revolution in consumption" and "modern economy": what do we mean by these terms? Eighteenth-century European society at large demanded a vast array of new products, from light cotton cloth to sugar, coffee, and tobacco. The varieties of cloth increased. Drab black, brown, and grey became a rainbow. Accessories took on greater importance; people, especially women, from ever more modest economic groups bought them. Every study of these developments, from Roche's pioneering work on the daily lives of ordinary Parisians to Crowston's superb study of the seamstresses who made the new, simpler dresses worn by eighteenth-century Parisiennes, highlights the centrality of women to the process. Crowston's seamstresses played an important a role as producers, a situation emphasized as well in Janine Lanza's recent study of Parisian guild widows and Daryl Hafter's book on women in early modern Rouen.[26] Joan DeJean parallels Crowston's example of change in the seventeenth century with similar change in twentieth-century couture.[27] In both cases, women designers understood the needs of their female clients. The new fashion produced by women designers, in the seventeenth century as much as in the twentieth, was revolutionary because it was intended to be both far more comfortable and far more body conscious than anything the women who wore it had ever known.

The revolution in consumption had its negative side effects. Hardy tells the story of the baker's apprentice, Louis Michel Houlier, who murdered his employer, Jean-Baptiste Raviot (a distant cousin) and his wife, Marie-Antoinette Cousin. Perhaps envious of the material comforts owned by his master, he had stolen "fancy clothes, rags, linens, silverware, jewels, cash, and other effects belonging to the said Raviot and his wife." Hardy later reproduces a ditty that castigated the French for their love of show, comparing them to trees no longer judged by their flowers or fruit, but by the bark.[28]

Women, not surprisingly, often bore the brunt of attacks on the moral ill effects of fashion or style, or conspicuous consumption. That focus, however, ignores the tens of thousands of women who jointly ran family businesses, like a bakery, keeping the books and selling wares made by a husband or, if she was a widow, by journeymen.[29] Louis Berthet's fabulous illustration of "the beautiful *restauratrice*" is just one of the many female food purveyors in Restif de la Bretonne's *Les Contemporaines* (love stories, 1780–1785), whose numbers included "adorable meat-roasting girls" and "fetching pork butchers."[30]

Independent women owned clothing shops in Paris, Rouen, Lyon, and other large cities; seamstresses everywhere followed the Parisian model, taking over the female and child clothing markets from the tailors. By the 1770s, marchandes de modes, ubiquitous in Paris, had spread to provincial towns. Auxerre had three of them by 1785. Avallon had two. Although a marchande de modes like Mlle

Mongeot at Avallon or Mlle Salomon at Auxerre paid the same tax as a poor seamstress, they chose to identify themselves by means of a Parisian term, evidence of the spread of cultural categories from the capital. Some of the marchandes de modes, like Mme Salomon of Chalon-sur-Saône, were important merchants. She paid five times more in taxes than the average shopkeeper or artisan.[31]

More and more single, never-married women appeared on these rolls. When she carried on the business, officials now used the feminine form of a trade (thus *boulangère* for a female baker) to describe the widow of a craftsman, rather than calling her a widow, and then giving the deceased's name and the male term (*boulanger*). At Chalon-sur-Saône in 1751–1752, the documents show such women in twenty-six to twenty-nine different occupations. The women (24.5 percent of the 1,161 taxpayers) concentrated in textiles (seamstress, mercer, hat maker), selling (merchant, regrater, shopkeeper), and food (pastry maker, baker, cabaret owner, *charcutière*), but the town also had a school mistress, a midwife, a hairdresser, and two herbalists. At Avallon, women also sold fruit, made bonnets, and worked as linen drapers (long a female preserve in Paris or Rouen).[32] In Brittany, women in the larger towns had slightly broader employment opportunities than those in small towns, in fields other than textile and food trades.[33] Yet broad categories like "textiles" or "food" disguise dramatic eighteenth-century changes. People still worked in "textiles," but they did so in fundamentally different jobs, especially in the accessories trades. The "food and drink" trade in a late seventeenth-century middling or small town meant a baker, a butcher, or a tavern keeper; in the eighteenth century it could mean a traiteur, a rôtisseur, a pastry maker, a charcutier, a limonadier, a café owner—all occupations unknown in such towns in earlier times. Women often practiced these trades.

De Vries and van der Woude, in making their case about the Netherlands as the first modern economy, focus on specialization.[34] Agriculture became more specialized. In the Netherlands, that meant dairy products for the great urban markets. In France, after 1740, specialization meant luxury wines like the Bordeaux *crus* or Champagne, whose eponymous beverage literally came into being at this time.[35] It also meant a wide range of new vegetables, grown for Parisian consumers.[36]

Although their formula heavily emphasizes economic and concomitant social change—rooted in specialization and market relations—de Vries and van der Woude provide an index of "modern" political and cultural factors for the small towns of North Holland in 1811. They choose seven "specialized functions": religious (a church); economic (retail services, innkeeper, luxury goods makers such

TABLE 1. Distribution of Women's Professions at Chalon-sur-Saône in 1752

Profession	Widow	Single	Wife	"Délaissée"
journalières[a]	37	5	1	1
cabaretières	10			
vendant vin	10	1		1
marchandes	5	1		1
revendeuses	4 (6 l.)[b]	1		
blanchisseuse	1	12		
lavandeuse		1		
mercières	11[c]	8		
couturières	10[d]	15		1
fripières	2	1		
vinaigrières	2	1		
jardinières	1 (24 l.)	1 (13 l.)		
pescheurs	2			
charcutière	1 (Joly 39)			
bouchère	1			
traitteur	1 (Widow Burtin, 53 l.)			
hotelière	1 (widow and son, 35 l.)			
boulangère	1			
herbières	2			
huillière		1 (20 l.)		
ferblantière	1			
maîtresse d'école	1			
fayancière	1 (Delle V Grinzard 35 l.)			
tonnelier	1			
sage femme	1 (V St Michel, 18 l.)			
bourelier	1			
taquier	1			
vitrier	1			
tourneur	1			
avocat	1			
	112	48	1	4
Delle	80	37		1
	192	85	1	5
w/man not husband	6	1 (two *filles* together)		
Insolvables	39	14		3

NOTES:
[a]Among the five single journalières, two had different professions in 1751: one lavandière, one couturière. One woman was described as a "bourgeoise" and as the abandoned wife (délaissée) of the Sieur Lepaige; she paid 20 livres. Thirty-two women were described as a "demoiselle"; there were five listings for "demoiselles." Sixty-two widows lived alone; nine widows lived with a single daughter; two widows lived with daughters; one widow lived with a daughter and a son; seven widows lived with a son.
[b]A few assessments are listed in parentheses to show that, for example, the gardeners were substantial taxpayers, paying far more than the 1 to 3 livres of a day laborer.
[c]With daughter.
[d]Four with daughter(s); one with an unrelated woman.
Source: AD Côte d'Or, C 6641.

as clockmaker, wigmaker, silversmith, *patissier*); medical (doctor or surgeon); judicial (notary, lawyer, or law court); social (a hospital or orphanage); cultural (bookseller, musician, or sculptor); and educational (a Latin school).

How do Burgundian towns of eight thousand to ten thousand people, like Chalon-sur-Saône, Autun, or Auxerre, or those of four thousand, like Avallon or Sémur-en-Auxois, fare on this index? Parallel Dutch towns, in terms of population, might be Edam (population 3,709 in 1795), Hoorn (population 9,551), and Enkhuizen (population 6,803). Edam met six of the seven criteria, lacking only a Latin school; Hoorn and Enkhuizen met all seven. Every Burgundian town of three thousand people or more met all seven of the de Vries-van der Woude criteria by the 1780s; most of them did so in the 1750s. In towns like Avallon or Sémur, some 20 percent of the boys aged ten to sixteen attended the *collège* (Latin preparatory school for adolescents).[37]

Smaller Burgundian towns (fifteen hundred to twenty-five hundred inhabitants) met five or six of these criteria, lacking only the Latin school and the bookseller. In most cases, these towns formed part of a marketing circuit supplied by the booksellers of the nearby larger towns. Saulieu's permanent book peddler, for example, got his wares from the Habert brothers of nearby Avallon. These towns usually had a specialized Latin tutor, who worked with pupils later sent to collèges in larger towns. The level of instruction in these schools varied dramatically. Aside from Avallon, which had a *collège de pleine exercice* (full range of classes), the Burgundian towns of between thirty-five hundred and six thousand inhabitants all had a humanities collège (two or three years of instruction); even in the group of fourteen towns between two thousand and thirty-five hundred, half had a collège, and all but one of the others had at least a Latin tutor. Some textile towns, like Quintin in Brittany, wanted a more modern curriculum; in 1757, the town syndic requested the creation of professorships in drawing, mathematics, and hydrography "to respond to the needs of this region [*contrée*] oriented toward commerce and industry."[38]

These schools, like the one in Tournus, marketed themselves in terms familiar to modern universities: in 1766 a circular boasted about fancy new dormitories, careful grooming by servants, and a wide range of humanities, including both Latin and French language.[39] Although the students in this school might be all male, women worked as instructors and as support staff. In 1784, the "grammarian" Clément, seeking a contract to run the school at Marcigny (population twenty-five hundred), told the town fathers they would get a two-for-one deal in hiring him. Mme Clément, it seems, was "a virtuous woman whose handwriting cedes nothing to that of the finest scribes of large cities." They provided a sample of her excellent calligraphy.[40] Other towns had female scribes. At Rennes, in 1784, Demoiselle (a term of social respect) Boissel was one of the nine writing masters. No woman could be found among the five Latin professors or three in mathematics, but the city had twelve schoolmistresses (four of them widows), as against six schoolmasters. The Demoiselle Tadier, a widow, listed herself as a "mistress of a pension" (school) and employed a preceptor and a domestic servant. Her tax assessment of 25 livres was more than double that of any teacher. In rural villages large enough for separate schools (most educated boys and girls together, royal edicts and Church rules to the contrary notwithstanding) a woman taught the girls. She was often the schoolmaster's wife, in an arrangement much like that promised by Mme Clément.[41]

Who attended these collèges? The mayor of Louhans, in arguing for the establishment of classes in philosophy in their collège, noted that the town had many "bourgeois, title searchers, surveyors, surgeons, goldsmiths, jewelers, twenty barristers, nine notaries and fifteen solicitors, seven royal bailiffs and numerous sergeants."[42] Such were the people, in his view, whose children would need a respectable education. In an important administrative town like Coutances, in Normandy, 20 percent of the lay male heads of households worked for or in the court system.[43]

Far beyond their concern over taxes, urbanites demanded better municipal services, what Guy Saupin has called "the expansion of competencies." They wanted the main street of town paved, then lighted. They wanted better access to water and improved sanitation. They wanted, like the mayor of Louhans, education for their children, and like the syndic of Quintin, an education related to the economy of the town. In the large cities, like Rennes, they had an even greater agenda, one reflected in the vast increase in that town's municipal budget, spent almost entirely on public works (and royal debt).[44]

In 1784, for example, Rennes had a budget of 200,000 livres, excluding its special taxes raised for royal debt. The city spent small amounts on traditional charities, and somewhat more on gifts for the captain of the fire department and his men (675 livres), for the new police force (2,400 livres), and even for the heirs (583 livres) of the Sieur Duclos, who had helped create the inventory of the city's archives.[45] The big spending went to communication and to amelioration of public spaces: 24,000 livres for a year's illumination of the streets; 25,000 livres more for eminent domain costs, related to tearing down houses to build a new street leading to the theater and other new roads; 26,000 livres for new paving stones; 33,000 livres for work on the Vilaine River; 2,400 livres to the Sieur Even, town engineer. These two categories added up to more than 100,000 livres.[46]

Rennes, a city of perhaps forty thousand inhabitants, thus resembled small Burgundian towns with respect to changes in the urban space. With respect to economic structures related to gender, the parallels remain strong. Large administrative cities like Rennes, of course, had scores of taverns and cabarets, hundreds of people working in the law, multiple booksellers and musicians and jewelers.

How does a large provincial city look in this new world? How had the city changed since 1702?[47] Little wonder that with all that spending on urban infrastructure, Rennes now had eight engineers and two sub-engineers (there had been only one engineer in 1702), an architect, a surveyor, two archivists, and an *appareilleur*, who specialized in checking the accuracy of stones cut for buildings or the town walls. Reaching the specialization stratosphere, the roll listed "the one called Genouin, barometer maker," who paid the considerable amount of 25.65 livres in taxes. This phrase, highly unusual for a man paying such a sum, suggests he was new to the city, and little known to the assessors. Yet barometers had a Breton market: the late eighteenth-century inventories after death of linen merchants in Quintin regularly show possession of one.[48]

Rennes had fire and police departments, and a large postal service. The postal service employed directors, lessees (*fermiers*), sub-lessees, postmasters, postilions, drivers, couriers, clerks, stableboys, apprentice saddlers, a nail maker, and domestic servants. The number of doctors and apothecaries remained stable, but Rennes had added a dentist. The tax roll now recognized female medical practitioners as a profession. Rennes had ten midwives (six as "*sage-femme*," three as "*matrone*," and one "*accoucheuse*") and a wet nurse. Midwives certainly delivered babies in 1702, yet the tax roll did not recognize their work as a profession at that time. Both schools and hospitals had female staff. They cleaned, cooked, and maintained.

Among the *droguistes* (sellers of household goods), whose overall numbers remained stable, in 1784 we find three women: two widows, one of them the Demoiselle Widow Chevillard, assessed at 33.65 livres, and the third the wife (*épouse*) of the Sieur Mesnay, *procureur* (solicitor) at the Presidial court. The roll describes Mme Mesnay as a "*marchande droguiste*" (they paid 20 livres). She was one of the few women on the roll described as an épouse, rather than as "femme," the usual term for a wife. The assessors reserved the term *épouse* for the wives of men of high status, very few of whom had a separate profession.

In 1784, most of those identified as *femme* had an occupational listing separate from that of the husband, a stark contrast to the tax roll of 1702, when only a tiny minority had enjoyed such a distinction.[49] This pattern held throughout the social spectrum, from the "one called Tizon, apprentice bookbinder, his wife fishmonger" (joint assessment, 1.3 livres), to the "Sieur Bloudel, bookbinder, his wife hairdresser" (5.35 livres), to the Sieur Fauvel, dancing master, his wife "small merchant" (8.5 livres), to the "Sieur Thuillier, sub-engineer, his wife *marchande*," and their domestic servant (20 livres).[50] In some cases the two occupations might blend seamlessly, as in the case of the Sieur Vincent, cook, whose wife was a grocer, or of another cook whose wife sold knives. The Sieur Thiery, wood merchant, had a wife who sold paper (20.5 livres). The wife of the Sieur Pierre, ébeniste, was a merchant-grocer on her own (8.35 livres). The Sieur Bouttier the elder, a master glazier, had a merchant for a wife; they paid 61 livres, putting them in the top echelon of the city's commercial elite. The roll referred to her as "femme," rather than "épouse," as would have been normal for a couple of their stature.

The roll included the extraordinary power couple of Renée-Jeanne Le Saulnier du Vauhello, widow of François-Pierre Vatar, bookseller (*libraire*), épouse of the Sieur Pierre Bruté de Rémur, barrister and royal officer.[51] She printed under the name of the "Widow Vatar" and then, after the death of her second husband, as "Widow Vatar and Bruté." She was printer for the king, for the Parlement, for the bishopric, and for the duke of Penthièvre. When she died in 1823, at age eighty-seven, she left the business to her granddaughter. The Vatar family women had a long tradition of running their printing business. At the start of the eighteenth century, Jeanne-Marie de la Fontaine, widow of François Vatar, who died in 1700, had also been the printer of the king, Parlement, and the local collège. She had two presses and employed two journeymen and two apprentices.[52] Shortly after Mme Fontaine's death, another widow, Jeanne-Renée Guerre, ran one of the other three printers of Rennes, the Garnier house, from 1725 to 1758.

In 1778, Widow Vatar, when she married Bruté, took the precaution of getting an *arrêt* from the King's Council confirming *her* status as royal printer. She published Rennes's first newspaper, the *Affiches de Rennes*, from 1784 to 1791. She paid 121 livres in taxes for herself, her female agent (*faitrice*), and a domestic. Bruté paid a separate assessment of 110 livres for his enterprises and 62.5 livres more as director of the royal demesne. The other members of the Vatar family of printers and booksellers included—each valued along with his or her single domestic—Demoiselle Vatar (libraire, 23.65 livres), Sieur Julien Vatar (printer, 50.65 livres), Sieur Paul Vatar, (printer-libraire, 42.8 livres), and the Demoiselles Vatar, (libraires 118.4 livres); these last were presumably the widows of Nicolas and Guillaume Vatar, who had petitioned the government in the 1770s.

Women did not run any of Rennes's four cafés or six billiard parlors in 1784, but the Widow Tourel ran the café inside the theater and five women sold coffee in the street. Thirty-two women—including twenty-one wives of artisans, four widows, four "filles" (young adult, single women), and one pair of women sold galettes (*crêpes*) in the street, as did six married couples and a lone bachelor. Women played a lesser role in the candy trade: only one of seven, the wife of the *maître d'hôtel* of the count of Gouyon. Rennes had scores of innkeepers, cabaret owners, and hoteliers, many of them women. In textiles, Rennes was more forward. It had nine marchandes de modes and a tenth woman worked as a *faiseuse de mode* (maker of fashion). Their number included several poor women, some of them doubling as hairdressers, but also the Demoiselle Maugendre, who rented furnished rooms on the side, and paid 61.5 livres. The Demoiselles Artault, surely just seamstresses seeking greater respect, together paid only 1.8 livres. Five of the nine listings involved more than one woman, including the single listing for the La Vallée sisters and the Demoiselle Du Gué, marchandes de modes and hairdressers (together, 13.7 livres).

Some other female merchants paid far more. The Widow Maisonneuve, marchande, had a live-in clerk and a servant. She paid 107 livres, one of the highest assessments in the city. Demoiselle Lucerie, a merchant potmaker on her own, had a servant and paid 63.5 livres, while the marchande Massard sisters paid 51 livres. The Widows Couarde and Menard each had a live-in factor and a servant. Each paid just over 40 livres. Some women practiced highly specialized trades. The Bougueil sisters, for example, described themselves as "children's tailors." They paid 8.9 livres.

Many women (and men) simply sold given items; the tax roll listed them as "selling X." These products included salt, clothes, cider, tobacco, candles, pigeons, buttered bread, canes, honey, milk, umbrellas, bricks, cod, fruit, vegetables, resin, leather, linens, sabots, paper, *toques* (a kind of hat), soap, stockings, hats, spoons, and quicklime. To this number, we might add the two women selling faïence, an industry that had taken hold in the city. One of the largest producers (of the fifteen listed) was the wife of the wine merchant Fouquet. She and her husband paid 35.65 livres. Among the two full-scale merchants selling faïence was the wife of the Sieur Bouttier, master glazier. They paid 25 livres.

What about smaller towns? If we take the list of key "modern" professions listed by de Vries and van der Woude, many of which served precisely this new public, we can highlight the following: innkeeper-tavernkeeper, clockmaker, wigmaker, silversmith, pastry maker, doctor, surgeon, notary, lawyer, bookseller, musician, and sculptor. By the 1780s, even a town like Avallon had someone identified on the tax roll for each of these professions.[53] At Chalon-sur-Saône in 1752, we find thirty-five men and twenty-two women keeping taverns or inns. Men ran fifteen of the sixteen hotels.

A French town like Chalon in 1752 had a dazzling array of specialized professions and purveyors of services. The city had a hospital and a large medical establishment: eight doctors, five surgeons, three apothecaries, or for those dubious of "modern medicine," a choice of two female herbalists. The six educators included a master and a mistress for both the girls' and the boys' primary schools, two grammarians for the Latin school, and two master writers. Thinking of buying a ruined chateau and its estate? You could hire a specialist in feudal rights to check the deed, then pick from among five architects to remodel, and hire a sculptor or a painter to embellish the house. You could stock your library at the bookstore of the Sieur Antoine Lespinasse. Hungry? You could hire one of the three professional cooks or buy food from a traiteur, like the Widow Burtin. Having a party? You could take dancing lessons, and then hire musicians. Bored at home? Head out to the café of Claude Terme, or get some exercise at the tennis court run by Pierre Guyot and his son. Had you lived in Chalon in 1667, in contrast, you could not have found *anyone* in *any* of these professions.

With the exception of Saulieu, every Burgundian town with twenty-five hundred or more people had at least two doctors and two surgeons. Saulieu had a single doctor, but four surgeons. In the fourteen towns with twenty-five hundred to five thousand people, eleven had at least one professionally trained midwife. The six largest towns in this group also had an apothecary, and five of them had two. Tax rolls from the second half of the seventeenth century in these towns show a much smaller medical establishment; only the larger towns had doctors and apothecaries. As for booksellers, fifty-eight French towns (average population forty-eight hundred) got their first libraire between 1761 and 1782.[54]

Everywhere we see movement. Women, especially, had newfound mobility. Many rural women moved to cities to work as servants and amass dowries. The less fortunate among these female servants often had to resort to prostitution. In both Normandy and Champagne, widows moved to work as servants, to live in town suburbs, or to move in with one of their children.[55]

Agricultural growth rates lagged behind industrial ones, but even in agriculture, from 1720 to 1756, per capita growth ran to 0.3 percent a year, an unusually high long-term level for the preindustrial European economy.[56] More and more we can see the influence of the market on provincial France and the growth of a consumer class sufficiently large and wealthy to sustain a host of new commercial activities and products. By the end of the Old Regime, the linen merchants of tiny Quintin regularly owned Chinese porcelain (and Sevrès and English), barometers, tapestries, musical instruments, fine furniture, paintings, tea services, coffee pots, and even, in five cases, bathtubs.[57] Radical changes happened even to basic furniture. In Alsace, for example, only 10 percent of inventories after death listed a chair in 1700, as against 59 percent in 1789; inventories with an armoire rose from 20 to 54 percent.

High-quality products from otherwise isolated areas found distant markets within France: aged wine, knives from Langres or Thiers, linens from Laval.[58] The rise of brokers in the Burgundian wine business introduced a new profession into towns like Auxerre, where these brokers paid some of the highest tax assessments after the 1750s.[59] Such wines formed part of an entirely new pattern of consumption focused on refinement and the exotic. Market gardeners could focus on luxury vegetables like artichokes for urban tables; farmers in Draguignan could export fruits, and those in Fréjus their olive oil. The surviving business records show women actively involved in all these trades.

Not surprisingly, given that more and more women worked outside their homes, one of the growth sectors of these urban economies was the prepared food business; the Widow Burtin, traiteur, and pastry maker Claude Jacquemot paid the second and third highest assessments (53 livres) of any artisan in Chalon in 1752. The rest of the top echelon among artisans came largely from food trades: the Widow Joly, charcutière (39 livres, which was double a typical artisan's tax); a pastry maker (39 livres); a traiteur (35 livres). The widow seamstress "fille Clerget," jointly assessed with her nephews and niece, paid the highest tax of any artisan (61 livres). At the edge of the artisan-merchant divide one found the Demoiselle Salomon (28 livres), or Demoiselle Bridon (33 livres), both female mercers. The richest group of taxpayers, a handful of merchants, royal officers, and lawyers, included women like the sisters of the Sieur Mercier, bourgeois (all three together, 175 livres), and the Widow Bonnabel, bourgeoise, and her daughter (103 livres).[60]

Let us return briefly to Chalon to compare its twelve hundred taxpayers of 1667 and of 1752. In 1667, 19.5 percent of those listed on the roll were women; in 1752 they made up 24.5 percent. We can see dramatic differences in the status of widows. In 1667, only 5.3 percent of them had a professional qualification, such as boulangère; in 1752, nearly 55 percent of the widows carried such a listing. Two-thirds of the widows of 1667 carried only the notation "widow of." In 1752 that had dropped to a third, and most of them were widows of high-status men in fields like the legal profession.

Single, never-married women, just 18.6 percent of the female taxpayers in 1667, were now nearly a third of them. These single women clustered almost exclusively in textile production (fifteen seamstresses), in marketing (eight mercers), or in bleaching (twelve women). Widows, in contrast, could be found across the economic spectrum: twenty-two in textiles, twenty-nine in food, eleven in retailing, and thirty-seven day laborers. In 1667, among those not classified as "demoiselle," the tax roll listed a third of the single women simply by name, with no listing for occupation. In 1752 all forty-eight unmarried women not classified as a "demoiselle" had a trade. Even the fourteen single women listed as "insolvent" called themselves either a seamstress or a laborer.

Working widows could have substantial means at their disposal. Judging from the tax assessments, the largest charcutier and largest traiteur in Chalon were both women. Three of the four largest bakeries had women on their listings—one widow on her own, and two running the shop with a son-in-law. Women played major roles in tavern-keeping and the local manufacture of faïence, such as the Widow Grinzard, assessed among the top 10 percent of artisans.

Leaving aside the law, in which they could not participate (lawyers' widows contributed a substantial portion of the town's taxes and often bought government annuities), women had important roles in five of the six remaining "modern" categories. In Chalon, they were absent only in the cultural sector—painters, sculptors, booksellers—in part because this sector involved so few people: one bookseller, two sculptors, one painter, one musician. We know such was not the case generally in the book trade. Women ran roughly 15 percent of France's print shops throughout the eighteenth century.[61] Lorient, with a single printer who often worked for the Company of the Indies, offers a common example: in thirty-seven of the seventy-five years between 1728 and 1803, a widow ran the business. At Vannes, Guillaume Lesieur printed from 1683 to 1725, at which point Jeanne Le Couriault, his widow, took over running the business. She managed it for the next twenty-five years. In mid-century, Jean-Nicolas Galles lasted only five years (1758–1763), but his widow, Jacquette-Françoise Bertain, lasted a dozen.[62]

Hardy makes regular reference to his female competitors in the book trade: on 11 December 1766, the Widow Amaulry, who had a shop in the Palais de Justice in Paris, and her daughter, Dame Lemoine, were among those arrested for distributing the *Journal de tout ce qui s'est passé en Bretagne depuis un an*. They were sent to the Bastille. Amaulry would remain there until 26 January 1767, when she was released with the injunction "to be more circumspect in the future."[63] The next day, an associate of Widow Duchesne, a bookseller on the rue St-Jacques, went to the Bastille for possessing copies of contraband political works. In Bordeaux, a few years later, the authorities suspected Marie Dubois, widow of Pierre Calamy, of counterfeiting foreign periodicals. Mme Dubois had a "very important commercial activity"; she ran her three presses from 1745 to 1777 and did collaborative business with the Parisian printer P.-G. Simon and the Berlin printer Chrétien Frederic Voss.[64]

CONCLUSION

The royal government recognized the dramatic economic changes taking place in France prior to 1750. The historiography focuses on the obvious ones, like the burgeoning colonial trade, but we have ignored others just as important. These include the related processes of greater specialization in the small and middling towns, due to growth in markets—particularly the growth of local clienteles sufficiently large to provide a ready market for local producers and sellers—for hitherto luxury goods, and broader female labor force participation. The changes in housing architecture for the better-off urban dwellers, with the creation of new rooms, with new types of eponymous furniture like *bibliothèque* (library; bookshelf), and the rise of new types of storage units such as armoires and commodes, gave business to trades such as turners and ébenistes. Owners of the new display furniture filled it with products such as the faïence produced by Mme Grinzard. Women as producers and marketers, and not just as consumers, drove much of French economic growth in the eighteenth century.

The government spotted this trend early, as we know from a November 1666 letter of the intendant of Alençon to Colbert: "Filles never pay the *taille* until they are married; the infirmity of the sex that cannot defend itself from oppression which might be done to it makes the law favorable [to them] on this occasion. But experience has made known to us that several of them, by their commerce, are in a position to pay the *taille*, and since His Majesty above all wants to engage his subjects to get married, that it be ordered that girls at the age of 20 pay the *taille* according to their ability."[65]

The government already collected taxes from such women in urban areas, but, judging from the tax rolls, the practice became universal in rural ones, too.

If Colbert was willing to take seriously the economic contribution of women in the construction of a modern French economy, perhaps it is past time we did. Women had long worked in the wage economy, and run shops such as bakeries, but their numbers as shop owners and as workers in the waged economy grew dramatically in the late seventeenth and early eighteenth centuries. They pioneered production and consumption of new products, such as the *manteau* dress, mirrors, and porcelain plates, and participated actively in the creation of a new sensibility, made manifest in demands for paved and lighted streets and greater urban amenities.

If we can come back to Pomeranz's argument about the "Great Divergence" between the advanced economic regions of Europe and China, we might see the differences in women's eighteenth-century economic participation as a key variable. Twenty-five years ago, Philip Huang argued that "the most important factor" in China's early failure to modernize its economy was that "a substantial portion of the productive labor force—especially women—remained outside of it." Although China had economic growth similar to that of Europe until the late eighteenth century, based as it was on greater commercialization, cotton textiles, and greater mobility related to new job opportunities, the evidence suggests that China seems to have gone in the opposite direction from Europe with respect to women's labor.[66] Given the contrast between Chinese and French (and British) women, perhaps the time has come to ask if the dramatic rise in female labor force participation rates and female creation of capital provides, at least in France, the key to understanding the roots of modern capitalism.

NOTES

1. Siméon-Prosper Hardy, *Mes Loisirs, ou Journal d'événemens tels qu'ils parviennent à ma connaissance*, vol. 1, (1753–1770), ed. Daniel Roche and Pascal Bastien (Québec: Presses universitaires de Laval, 2008), 360–361, entry of 18 December 1769.

2. Cynthia A. Bouton, *The Flour War: Gender, Class, and Community in Late Ancien Régime France* (University Park: Pennsylvania State Univ. Press, 1993), appendix 1, analyzes the grain riots of 1769–1770.

3. Wayne Snyder, "Occupational Evolution in XVIIIth and XIXth-Century France," *Journal of European Economic History* 35, no. 3 (2006): 585–598, offers a fascinating look at the declared professions of nearly five hundred thousand people in the periods 1695–1720, 1790–1820, and 1856–1872. The use of the Revolutionary period for the second sample causes some problems of comparison between Snyder's figures and mine, and partly explains why I found far more women on tax rolls than Snyder did.

4. Merry E. Wiesner, *Women and Gender in Early Modern Europe*, 3 editions (Cambridge: Cam-

bridge Univ. Press, 1993, 2000, 2008), 111 (1st ed.), 133 (3rd ed.). Thanks to my colleague Amy Leonard for lending me the third edition, and for discussing this article.

5. Olwen Hufton, "Les femmes et le travail dans la France traditionnelle," in *Femmes et pouvoir sous l'Ancien Régime*, ed. D. Haase-Dubosc (Paris: Éditions Rivages, 1991), 273.

6. Madeleine Ferrières, *Le bien de pauvres: La consommation populaire en Avignon (1600–1800)* (Paris: Champ Vallon, 2004), 75.

7. Women invariably predominated among the poorest of the poor: James B. Collins, "The Economic Role of Women in Seventeenth-Century France," *French Historical Studies* 16, no. 2 (autumn 1989): 436–470. Because of the different taxable populations on types of tax rolls, the percentage of women on different types of tax rolls could vary sharply for the same place and time; the rolls of the main royal direct tax (*tailles*) are the most comprehensive.

8. Some of these "women," such as most early factory textile workers, were girls. On child labor, see Jan de Vries, *The Industrious Revolution: Consumer Behavior and the Household Economy, 1650 to the present* (Cambridge: Cambridge Univ. Press, 2008). On girls specifically, see Clare Haru Crowston, "An Industrious Revolution in Late Seventeenth- and Eighteenth-Century Paris: New Vocational Training for Adolescent Girls and the Creation of Female Labor Markets," in *Secret Gardens, Satanic Mills: Placing Girls in European History, 1750–1960*, ed. M. J. Maynes, B. Soland, and C. Benninghaus (Bloomington: Indiana Univ. Press, 2004); for context, see also the essays in *Secret Gardens, Satanic Mills* by Maynes and by D. Simonton.

9. http://www.sullivanpaper.com/.

10. Jan de Vries and A. M. van der Woude, *The First Modern Economy. Success, Failure, and Perseverance of the Dutch Economy, 1500–1815* (Cambridge: Cambridge Univ. Press, 1997), 509.

11. Daniel Roche, *A History of Everyday Things: The Birth of Consumption in France, 1600–1800*, trans. Brian Pearce (Cambridge: Cambridge Univ. Press, 2000). For the global dimension, see Kenneth Pomeranz, *The Great Divergence: China, Europe, and the Making of the Modern World Economy* (Princeton: Princeton Univ. Press, 2000).

12. *Chronique du Bordelais au crépuscule du Grand Siècle: Le mémorial de Savignac,* ed. Caroline Le Mao (Bordeaux: Presses universitaires de Bordeaux, 2004), July 1709. Gabriel is most famous for the Place de la Concorde in Paris.

13. De Vries, *The Industrious Revolution*; Michael Sonenscher, *The Hatters of Eighteenth-Century France* (Berkeley: Univ. of California Press, 1987); Robert Darnton, *The Great Cat Massacre and Other Episodes in French Cultural History* (New York: Vintage, 1985); Jean-Marc Moriceau, *Les fermiers de l'Ile-de-France XVᵉ–XVIIIᵉ siècle* (Paris: Fayard, 1994).

14. The rapid expansion of the service sector in places like Paris or London paralleled the national growth in the manufacturing sector; neither Paris nor London had heavy-duty industry, even in 1850.

15. Brigitte Maillard, *Les campagnes de Touraine au XVIIIᵉ siècle: Structures agraires et économie rurale* (Rennes: Presses universitaires de Rennes, 1998). James B. Collins, "*Translation de domicile*: Rethinking Sedentarity and Mobility in the Early Modern French Countryside," *French History* 20, no. 4 (2006): 387–404. Local customary law also could make it difficult to change tenants. See Liana Vardi, *The Land and the Loom: Peasants and Profit in Northern France, 1680–1800* (Durham: Duke Univ. Press, 1993).

16. Cissie Fairchilds, "The Production and Marketing of Populuxe Goods in Eighteenth-Century

Paris," in *Consumption and the World of Goods,* ed. John Brewer and Roy Porter (London: Routledge, 1993), 228–248.

17. A *commissionaire* was a government-mandated, licensed intermediary in the wine business; the practice spread to other trades. See Thomas Edward Brennan, *Burgundy to Champagne: The Wine Trade in Early Modern France* (Baltimore: Johns Hopkins Univ. Press, 1997).

18. Guillaume Daudin, *Commerce et prosperité: La France au XVIIIᵉ siècle* (Paris: PUPS, 2005), 125–127. Cotton cloth ("indiennes") provided its most dynamic growth in this trade.

19. At Chalon, in 1752, the *maître d'école,* Claude Cuniot (13 livres), carried no honorific on the tax roll. The two *grammariens* received the coveted "sieur": le Sieur Pernette (15 livres) and le Sieur Boutteloys (24 livres), further evidence of their higher status. Archives départementales of the Côte d'Or (ADCO), C 6641, for all Chalon tax rolls. Claude Nières, *Les villes de Bretagne au XVIIIᵉ siècle* (Rennes: Presses universitaires de Rennes, 2004), indicates Masonic lodges in eight of the eleven largest Breton towns; ten of the eleven had an academy or learned society.

20. Michael Kwass, *Privilege and the Politics of Taxation in Eighteenth-Century France* (Cambridge: Cambridge Univ. Press, 2000), 39, citing the Keeper of the Seals Miromesnil, in 1761.

21. Jean Martin, *Toiles de Bretagne: La manufacture de Quintin, Uzel et Loudéac, 1670–1830* (Rennes: Presses universitaires de Rennes, 1998), 248–249. Quintin's size is a bit misleading because it was the center of a large nesting of quasi-urban villages manufacturing linen.

22. Much of this labor, as will be discussed below, came in luxury trades. See William Sewell, "The Empire of Fashion and the Rise of Capitalism in Eighteenth-Century France," *Past and Present* 206 (February 2010): 81–120, especially his remarks on page 84 about the production of luxury goods and the accumulation of capital. I read Sewell after completing the article, and I am struck by the similarity of our conclusions. My thanks to Clare Crowston for pointing out Sewell's essay.

23. Dominique Godineau, *Les femmes dans la société française, 16ᵉ–18ᵉ siècle* (Paris: Armand Colin, 2003), 62. Women owned very few of the workshops.

24. Peter Earle, "The Female Labour Market in London in the Late Seventeenth and Early Eighteenth Centuries," in *Women's Work: The English Experience, 1650–1914,* ed. Pamela Sharpe (London: Arnold, 1998), 121–149, tables 5.8 and 5.9, quotation from 130. By way of contrast, in 1911, in England as a whole, only 10 percent of married women worked for wages.

25. No woman could hold such an office. A. de Boislisle, *Mémoire de la généralité de Paris* (Paris: Imprimerie nationale, 1881), 719. The subdelegate does not give the woman's name. See also: Monica Chojnacka, *Working Women of Early Modern Venice* (Baltimore: Johns Hopkins Univ. Press, 2001), and Sheilagh C. Ogilvie, *A Bitter Living: Women, Markets, and Social Capital in Early Modern Germany* (New York: Oxford Univ. Press, 2003), who show both women's expanded opportunities and the legal and social restrictions holding them back.

26. Daniel Roche, *La culture des apparences: Une histoire du vêtement (XVII–XVIIIᵉ siècle)* (Paris: Fayard, 1989); Clare Haru Crowston, *Fabricating Women: The Seamstresses of Old Regime France, 1675–1791* (Durham: Duke Univ. Press, 2001); Janine M. Lanza, *From Wives to Widows in Early Modern Paris: Gender, Economy, and Law* (Aldershot, Eng.: Ashgate, 2007); Daryl M. Hafter, *Women at Work in Preindustrial France* (University Park: Pennsylvania State Univ. Press, 2007); Daryl Hafter's many articles; Guillaume Glorieux, *À l'enseigne de Gersaint: Edme-François Gersaint, marchand d'art sur le Pont Notre-Dame, 1694–1750* (Paris: Champ Vallon, 202); Natacha Coquéry, *Tenir boutique à Paris au XVIIIᵉ*

siècle: Luxe et demi-luxe (Paris: Éditions du comité des travaux historiques et scientifiques, 2011).

27. Joan DeJean, *The Essence of Style: How the French Invented High Fashion, Fine Food, Chic Cafés, Style, Sophistication, and Glamour* (New York: Free Press, 2005), 37.

28. Hardy, *Mes Loisirs,* on Houlier, entries of 11 February and 20 March 1765. Houlier was apprehended near Chartres after selling a gold watch for 36 livres; ditty in entry of 25 May 1770.

29. Steven L. Kaplan, *The Bakers of Paris and the Bread Question, 1700–1775* (Durham: Duke Univ. Press, 1996). Medieval French bakeries, like those of 2014, usually had/have a man baking the bread and a woman selling it, often to a female customer, as in medieval illustrations. Women played a lesser though still important role in the meat trade: Sydney Watts, *Meat Matters: Butchers, Politics, and Market Culture in Eighteenth-Century Paris* (Rochester: Univ. of Rochester Press, 2006).

30. Reproduced as figure 1 in Rebecca Spang, *The Invention of the Restaurant: Paris and Modern Gastronomic Culture* (Cambridge, Mass.: Harvard Univ. Press, 2001), 56.

31. See Fairchilds, "The Production and Marketing of Populuxe Goods in Eighteenth-Century Paris," for how the term "marchandes de modes" sometimes referred to women who sold only fashionable clothing and hence were actual predecessors of modern couture, yet sometimes referred to women who were selling a wide range of luxury products.

32. ADCO, C 6641, tax rolls for Chalon; ADCO, C 6453, tax rolls for Avallon.

33. Three-quarters of working women in small towns, as against two-thirds in large ones. See Nancy Locklin, *Women's Work and Identity in Eighteenth-Century Brittany* (Aldershot, Eng.: Ashgate, 2007), 6, and later tables. See also her essay in this volume.

34. De Vries and Van der Woude, *The First Modern Economy,* figure 11.1 on 512–513 for their modernization index.

35. On specialization, Jan de Vries, *The Dutch Rural Economy in the Golden Age* (New Haven: Yale Univ. Press, 1972); Brennan, *Burgundy to Champagne.*

36. Reyald Abad, *Le grand marché* (Paris: Fayard, 2002).

37. Christine Lamarre, *Petites villes et fait urbain en France au XVIIIᵉ siècle: Le cas bourguignon* (Dijon: Editions universitaires de Dijon, 1993); Nières, *Les villes de Bretagne au XVIIIᵉ siècle*; T. J. A. Le Goff, *Vannes and Its Region* (Oxford: Oxford Univ. Press, 1980), table II-6, shows that because the number of male-headed households steadily declined, women were 24.4 percent of the taxpayers in 1704, but 35.7 percent in 1783.

38. Martin, *Toiles de Bretagne,* 247.

39. Lamarre, *Petites villes et fait urbain en France au XVIIIᵉ siècle,* 359. Of towns under two thousand inhabitants, only Noyers-sur-Serein had a collège.

40. Lamarre, *Petites villes et fait urbain en France au XVIIIᵉ siècle,* 363, reproduces the sample.

41. Karen Carter, "'Les garçons et les filles sont pêle-mêle dans l'école': Gender and Primary Education in Early Modern France," *French Historical Studies* 31, no. 3 (2008): 417–443; Karen Carter, *Creating Catholics: Catechism and Primary Education in Early Modern France* (Notre Dame: Univ. of Notre Dame Press, 2011).

42. Lamarre, *Petites villes et fait urbain en France au XVIIIᵉ siècle,* 366.

43. *L'intendance de Caen en 1700: Édition critique des mémoires rédigés sous la direction de Nicolas-Joseph Foucault,* ed. Pierre Gouhier (Paris: Éditions du CTHS, 1999), 424–431.

44. James B. Collins, "Le pouvoir municipal et l'écroulement de l'Ancien Régime: Question

sociale ou question politique?" (paper presented at the conference "L'exercice du pouvoir municipal de la fin du Moyen Age à 1789, Rennes, December 2009"). Nières and Lamarre offer many examples of such expenditures.

45. Most of Rennes burned to the ground in 1719, so the city was precocious in its concern for fire safety. "Sieur" was a term of social respect. It initially meant a man who owned a rural estate that did not include judicial rights, but by the eighteenth century the term had been extended to most professional men in towns.

46. Archives Municipales de Rennes (henceforth AM Rennes, CC 1070.

47. AM Rennes, CC 773 (capitation, 1784), CC 711 (capitation, 1702).

48. Martin, *Toiles de Bretagne,* 251.

49. Locklin, *Women's Work,* 15, found precisely this situation in six Breton towns in the mid-century.

50. All figures are joint assessments. The townspeople chose their own tax assessors, even for royal levies. Until the middle of the eighteenth century, assessors relied on general knowledge of the community, but they insisted on increasingly detailed records beginning with the *vingtième* re-intro-duced in 1749. For landed property, for example, they demanded to see copies of lease agreements. In much of France, local tax officials, called the *élus,* heard cases, without right of appeal, about tax assessments below a certain level (the level varied over time). Above that level, the taxpayer could appeal to the Cour des Aides (sovereign tax court) holding jurisdiction in her or his area. Differ-ent types of taxes—tailles, capitation, vingtième—had different rules: on the capitation rolls, for example, the head of household had to pay an assessment for his or her servants. Rolls of the tailles are the most complete; rolls of the vingtièmes, in contrast, exclude many people, such as beggars, who are found on the rolls of the tailles. Because so many beggars were widows, the percentage of women on a roll of the tailles will always be higher than the percentage of women on a roll of the vingtième for the same parish.

51. The Rennes tax roll also included the category of used book seller, among whom one could find the Demoiselles Champion, with a domestic, assessed at 23.65 livres. Wealthy merchants' wives often had no listing of a profession, even if they helped run the business. See Martha Howell, "The Gender of Europe's Commercial Economy, 1200–1700," *Gender and History* 20, no. 3 (2008): 519–538.

52. Roméo Arbour, *Dictionnaire des femmes libraires en France, 1470–1870* (Geneva: Droz, 2003), 514. See also Locklin, *Women's Work,* 38–39, and X. Ferrieu, "Les Vatar ou trois siècles d'imprimerie à Rennes," *Mémoires de la société d'histoire et d'archéologie de Bretagne* 62 (1985): 223–284.

53. As Madeleine Ferrières shows, a *mont-de-pitié* in Avignon (not then legally part of France) played a role similar to one found in Italy or Holland (Ferrières, *Le bien des pauvres.*) Small-scale credit functioned differently in France, so towns had no pawnbrokers. Wigmakers offer an excellent example of the difficulty of comparing samples here with those of Snyder, "Occupational Evolution": with the Revolution, the number of wigmakers dropped precipitously, so figures starting in 1790 would not reflect the considerable growth in numbers between 1695 and 1788.

54. Thierry Rigogne, *Between State and Market: Printing and Bookselling in Eighteenth-Century France* (Oxford: Voltaire Foundation, 2007), 174.

55. Collins, "Rethinking Sedentarity."

56. Philip T. Hoffman and Gilles Postel-Vinay, *Priceless Markets: The Political Economy of Credit in Paris, 1660–1870* (Chicago: Univ. of Chicago Press, 2000). Guillaume Daudin, *Commerce et prosperité: La France au XVIIIᵉ siècle* (Paris: Presses universitaires de Paris-Sorbonne, 2005), 32, graph 2, shows woolen production rose 1.2 percent a year in value and 0.7 percent in volume; cotton rose 3.8 percent a year. Commercial indices, such as local tolls, suggest growth rates of 1 to 1.5 percent a year as a whole.

57. Martin, *Toiles de Bretagne,* 251. Moriceau, *Les fermiers,* table on 759, shows that by the 1750s these wealthy peasants owned clocks (80 percent, as against 10 percent prior to 1709), watches (45 percent versus 8.5 percent), books (80 percent versus 23 percent), and card tables (60 percent versus zero).

58. Thomas Le Roux, *Le commerce intérieur de la France à la fin du XVIIIᵉ siècle: Les contrastes économiques régionaux de l'espace français à travers les archives du Maximum* (Paris: Nathan, 1996), 222–223, see also 225–230.

59. Brennan, *Burgundy to Champagne,* on the structural changes; *taille* rolls in ADCO, C 6351.

60. ADCO, C 6641. "*Bourgeois(e)*" was a legal category, meaning someone who lived off the return from their capital, and did not practice a profession. In common practice, the term could have many meanings; as far back as the fourteenth century, documents used the terms "bourgeois" and "citizen" interchangeably, to cite only one example. The self-descriptions could vary from year to year, thus the Demoiselle Salomon, mercer, assessed for 28 livres in 1752, had described herself as a merchant in 1751.

61. See Jane McLeod's essay on printer widows in this volume.

62. Georges Lepreux, *Gallia typographica,* tome IV (Paris: Honoré Champion, 1914), 267–268.

63. Arbour, *Dictionnaire des femmes,* has biographical details; Susan Broomhall, *Women and the Book Trade in Sixteenth-Century France* (Aldershot, Eng.: Ashgate, 2002); Dena Goodman and Elizabeth C. Goldman, eds., *Going Public: Women and Publishing in Early Modern France* (Ithaca: Cornell Univ. Press, 1995). Dorothy Ko, *Teachers of the Inner Chambers: Women and Culture in Seventeenth-Century China* (Stanford: Stanford Univ. Press, 1994), offers fascinating comparative material about China's rapidly growing elite female reading public and female writers.

64. Bordeaux had a tradition of powerful widow printers, running from Marie Lacombe, daughter of the intendant's secretary and widow of Raymond Brun, who printed for the king, the intendant, and the Academy of Bordeaux in the late seventeenth century to her daughter-in-law, Marie Laroche, who ran their four presses from 1752 to 1759. Brun originally bought the business from yet another widow printer, Anne Dache. Louis Desgraves, *Dictionnaire des imprimeurs, libraires et relieurs de Bordeaux et de la Gironde: XVᵉ–XVIIIᵉ siècles* (Baden-Baden: Editions V. Koerner, 1995), entries 136, 139, and 152.

65. Edmond Esmonin, *La taille en Normandie au temps de Colbert, 1661–1683* (1913; reprint, Geneva: Mérgariotis Reprints, 1978), 284.

66. Changes in the late Qing textile industry "by and large displaced women as weavers; women were deskilled, and their contribution to textile production was devalued, marginalized, or subsumed within male-headed household production." Francesca Bray, *Technology and Gender: Fabrics of Power in Late Imperial China* (Berkeley: Univ. of California Press, 1997), 237; Philip C. Huang, *The Peasant Economy and Social Change in North China* (Stanford: Stanford Univ. Press, 1985). Susan Mann, *Precious Records: Women in China's Long Eighteenth Century* (Stanford: Stanford Univ. Press,

1997), 174, stresses the "crucial role" of more efficient female household labor in this economic growth. Janet M. Theiss suggests the "cult of chastity," which peaked in the eighteenth century, played a major role in women's loss of economic opportunities. *Disgraceful Matters: The Politics of Chastity in Eighteenth-Century China* (Berkeley: Univ. of California Press, 2004). Thanks to my colleague Carol Benedict for bibliographic assistance on China.

FRENCH INDUSTRIAL GROWTH IN WOMEN'S HANDS

Daryl M. Hafter

I F we walked into a preindustrial manufacturing center in the eighteenth century, we might expect to see a workforce of men and to hear a clatter of male voices. What would be our surprise if, instead, we saw only a few men and heard the talking of dozens of women? That is how the concentrated, large-scale, outdoor manufacturing centers of eighteenth-century France sounded. Unlike our traditional idea of the early modern labor force, the production of yesteryear employed many more women than men.[1] In Lyon, an observer declared that the female workers were so numerous they reminded him of a "swarm of bees." What were their jobs? In virtually every industry, women were responsible for preparing the raw materials and for doing even complex tasks that were considered unskilled. The reason for employing them is obvious: most women workers earned less than half the salaries of men. Hiring female workers was an important way to reduce the cost of manufactured goods, and thereby increase the entrepreneur's profit.

Scholars have not ignored women's work, but they have too often added the topic as an afterthought, while the major part of a publication was shaped to discuss male workers. Economic historians assumed that men were responsible for industrialization, since heavy industry—considered fitting for men—was the bedrock of the Industrial Revolution. Many scholars of women's history have emphasized domestic crafts and their effect on the household without exploring the wider background into which the domestic work fit. And we have been schooled to understand that urban ateliers had no more than twenty male workers. Emphasis on guilds as the main producers also overlooked women's work, since most guilds did not admit women to the mastership.

By contrast, this essay will contribute to the historiography of women's work by calling attention to the role of female workers and children in large-scale preindustrial production. It will show the breadth of women's work from being street scavengers and wood carriers to household spinners and operators in large textile companies, doing work that was as high in quality as that of male workers. This chapter will scan the various areas that women and children occupied in preindustrial France such as rural industry, the urban *fabrique,* and enclosed industry. In conclusion, it will explore the conditions of work, the significance of working with machines, and how women's work became a precursor of the Industrial Revolution.

In the era before the steam engine (before 1815)—the period this article describes—work was ubiquitous. It was an economy of scarcity, unlike our current economy of surpluses, and every hand was needed to help fashion goods. The heart of fabricated production was the individual handicraft artisan, making items for home consumption or local sale in the family workshop or farm cottage. In my usage, the term "artisan" refers to any handicraft worker, not just to those in domestic industry. Domestic craft evolved into concentrated groups of urban workers in guilds in some cities, and then changed further as skilled tasks remained in cities and less careful work was outsourced to nonguild rural workers. Jan de Vries and A. M. van der Woude have signaled this development as the beginning of the modern economy, showing how workers became beholden to merchants and entrepreneurs through their control of raw materials and markets.[2] Of course, many towns in France and elsewhere did not have guilds, and their economic development might have taken different paths. But in those that did have guilds, entrepreneurs gradually sought to overcome the restrictions the guilds exerted on technology and the number of workers. As the European and transatlantic consuming public increased through the course of the sixteenth to eighteenth centuries, some manufactures embraced a variety of larger formats.

In France, the variety of work structures overlapped. Many large-scale manufactures consisted of an urban center of skilled workers, supplied by a field of outlying workers many times larger who produced the basic product, which was then finished and sold in the city. Contemporaries called such units fabriques. But they also applied the term *fabrique* to an entire region that produced one kind of item, even if the town center was only the marketplace, not a productive center. The lacemaking region of Puy-en-Velay was one such example: women and girls in the Auvergne hills created enough lace to be worth some 2 million livres in export sales. Glass, metal, and paper manufacture, located entirely in the countryside, also counted as fabriques. French historians have currently also called a group of city workers, both guild and nonguild together in small ateliers, an urban-fabrique. For our purposes, all three—(1) the large-scale city manufacturer linked to country workers, (2) the region producing one product, and (3) the guild and nonguild workers in one city—were considered fabriques. Since France did not begin generally to use steam power—the key of modern industrialization—until late in the eighteenth century, its industry remained hand powered, preindustrial. Preindustrial activity, however, did not mean without mechanical devices, and so this article also discusses machines.

Historians have already studied the large role that women played in cottage production, but few writers have paid attention to the incorporation of new productive instruments used by the female working population in France.[3] Fewer still have emphasized the ubiquitous presence of women working in *almost every* sort of craft. Let us first examine the craftwork of women and children in small urban ateliers, in family workshops, or on their own, who were not linked to large-scale manufacturing. This is the milieu from which large-scale manufacturing evolved.

SMALL URBAN CRAFTS

The fact is that almost everywhere products were made, women and girls were busy in ateliers. They cleaned the floor, tended the fire, fetched raw materials, sorted the stock, and packaged the goods, all unskilled tasks. But they were also integrated into the skilled manufacture of articles, either in completely female workshops or in concert with male workers of all ages. From fashioning artificial pearls with fish scales to polishing knives and pots, from spinning cotton to working in shipyards, from plating silver to weaving linen, women labored in virtually every specialty. It was the most ordinary thing to encounter them in ateliers and byways, working in their own family trades or in some completely different occupation.[4]

On any street one could see women sitting outside to catch the light, spinning, embroidering, making lace, or knitting gloves, stockings, or (by the late seventeenth century) mittens. In the few places where they sold their goods separately to small merchants, they might possibly have the independence of deciding which merchant to do business with, and which trade to follow.[5]

In cities, tanning drew women into the putrid, smoky basements where various processes transformed raw hides into leather. Outside, on riverbanks, women stretched the hides. The tanning vats contained bones that women brought to the workshop from butchers' discards and livestock yards. Before artificial substances were readily available, much material for industry came from street scavengers. These scavenging women and men carried all sorts of animal parts, from hide to hoof, off of the streets where dead creatures lay abandoned. They picked up wood, coal, rags, grease, paper, glass, and any other usable object to be turned into part of a saleable item.[6]

Some women were exclusively in charge of growing *verdigris*, the green patina adhering to copper, that was used in drugs, dyes, and printing. Others joined the numerous gangs that swarmed across abandoned buildings, scraping saltpeter from ruins. Women also participated in the ultimate unskilled work of carrying things. Firewood, coal, raw fish, and textile goods were among their loads; they served as laborers in building sites—carrying wood, metal, and stone in barrows that we associate with bricklayers. Some females were water carriers, supplying street workers and apartment dwellers.[7]

While male guilds monopolized cooking, forming sausages, baking, and pastry making, their female relatives sold the goods in shops and kept the books. The many people too poor to buy a whole meal at once were serviced by female venders, who sold flowers and food in small quantities—eggs, fruit, butter, and breadstuffs. Small-scale peddlers, these *regrettières* (and some male *regrettiers*) might also be hucksters of used clothing. They had to buy licenses from the ranks of women who were retiring or survivors of the dead, since towns limited the number of regrettières.

Not all women depended on small trade, however; some were wholesale merchants with legitimate stalls in the huge central markets, like the great food market in Paris and the Halle des Toiles in Rouen. Women ran substantial businesses in the Nord.[8] Fish markets existed in most towns, run by the proverbial "fishwives." Women also staffed the butcher shops, but here they were only in command of the sales counter and the account books, as wives or widows of guild masters.[9]

It is important to note whether workers, female and male, were bona fide members of a guild, or whether they worked in so-called free trades that were not incorporated into legal associations. While most guilds excluded women from the mastership, in some towns women with full masters' rights formed all-female and mixed-sex guilds. In Rouen guild mistresses formed 10 percent of the guild population, counting some seven thousand persons in a city of ninety thousand. (This number did not include widows working in male guilds through the permission of their late husbands.) The guild members had privileges in taxation, financial investments, and technical monopolies that helped to buffer economic downturns. Those without guild membership were considered unskilled, having learned whatever trade they plied without official training and tests. The majority of working women fell into this second category and were paid as unskilled workers. In most trades the gender division of labor kept women in tasks considered unskilled; but even when they did the exact same work as men, producing the same quality, a woman's pay was generally half that of a man's.[10] Important to industry for their labor, nonguild women also allowed it flexibility, as they could both switch from one trade to another and sustain layoffs during the dead seasons.

The quality of women's output, even without guild certification, was often equal to that of the masters. Women were as likely as men to possess "the mindful hand" that Lissa Roberts and her colleagues described, in which workers put their craft experience and their sharing of knowledge within the group to good use.[11] Although the guild statutes had lengthy provisions banning nonguild workers from their professions, the continual reiteration of these warnings testified to their ineffectiveness. To save money, guild masters often hired as daily laborers women without qualifications or regular training. They might work alongside the master's wife and daughters, whose involvement was legal. Nonguild women were also used as "scab" labor when entrepreneurs wanted to challenge the traditional, agreed-upon work practices of male workers—the "custom"—or to lower their wages.

Police records are filled with accounts of women illegally engaged in the widest range of licit and illicit manufacture. Often their temporary illegal workshops were set up by guild masters hoping to lower production costs by funding "off-street" ventures. Working in tenement rooms as *chambrelans* (individuals working in their own rooms), women, children, and men made parts of the products sold by guilds. In Lyon, Paris, and other areas, such illegal manufacture formed a thriving black market economy that was a surprisingly significant part of commerce.[12] However, following the time-honored truth that everything in the early modern period had exceptions, some guilds actually had statutes legalizing rural workshops with nonguild workers processing cloth or females collecting hair for wig manufacture.

Although they labored in a wide range of trades, typically the women and children producing goods were involved in textile manufacture. In urban and rural areas, they spun, carded, and wove cotton, linen, silk, and wool. They used natural resources to help: streams provided beds for fulling woolens; rivers were used to wash *coupons* (large rectangles) of cloth tethered to poles in the water; riverbeds and the seashore were the site of cloth stretched out to bleach in the sun. In Paris, Rouen, Montpellier, Marseille, Le Havre, and other cities, all-female guilds of *lingères* (linen workers) and seamstresses, as well as mixed-sex guilds of spinners, sometimes dominated the manufacture and sale of linen goods, thread, and new and used women's garments.[13] Given the strong connections of urban work with large-scale manufacturing, it is hard to make a definite distinction between women in urban handicraft and large industrial centers.

RURAL INDUSTRY

In the countryside thousands of girls and women were eager to find employment. Entrepreneurs and officials alike were dedicated to putting these women to work by introducing the new tools of textile manufacture into the suburbs and rural areas around cities. Whether they were full-time craft workers or part-time farmers, rural workers were less costly than urban labor. Entrepreneurs appreciated the opportunity to expand manufacturing beyond city confines and guild restrictions. Intendants were eager to alleviate rural poverty and fix agrarian labor on the land. These impulses combined to stimulate dozens of requests for government subsidies to implant textile machines in rural areas increasingly over the eighteenth century.

The product needed most by cloth manufacturers was more thread so they would no longer have to depend on the traditional ratio of six spinners that were required to supply one weaver. Since this was the trying-out time of various devices, entrepreneurs placed hand-spinning wheels, as well as the newly invented spinning jennies, with farm wives and daughters. As the women learned to manipulate the jennies, government officials hoped that the thread they produced would be as fine, sturdy, and controlled as hand-spun products. Continued surveillance of the machines was part of the mechanizing program. An intendant from Picardy demonstrated this when urging his inspector, "Be attentive, also, to the particular quality of spinning apparatus, whether it is effective or faulty. If the former, we would wish to generalize its use in less fortunate places; if the latter, one of the clever inspectors general of manufacture, like M. [John] Holker, may be able to adjust the machines for better functioning."[14]

The campaign to instruct spinners in new methods sometimes ran into resistance as crowds of workers blamed the mechanical innovations for their unemployment, especially during the economic crisis of 1788. A curé in Falaise, Normandy, pleaded for leniency at this time, commenting: "Last November 11, many men and women surrounded the houses of several manufacturers of cotton, seized their machines, broke and burned them. . . . In their excess, these craft workers fortunately respected the life of the citizens; they wanted only the machines and not people. It is hunger that made them act so."[15] Hundreds of machines were destroyed in workers' uprisings in the late century. But in other regions and earlier times, deep need impelled workers to take on the employment that entrepreneurs offered.

The countryside was also home to industry that made heavy use of wood, coal, and water. These were the paper, glass, metallurgical, and mining manufactures, each a community unto itself. Isolated in areas that offered the right natural resources, these industries developed dynasties of specialized workers that excluded outsiders. The women and children in these families were integrated into the industrial tasks on a regular basis. In papermaking, they were as numerous as the male workers. The women first sorted the rags that comprised the raw material of paper, tore the rags into fragments, and removed knots and caked dirt. At a later stage in its preparation, they stirred the emulsion of rags and water continuously to prevent lumps from forming. When the pulp was set into sheets, they hung them up to dry. Finally at the end of the process, they took the finished paper down, rid the sheets of blemishes, and sorted, folded, and wrapped them into reams.[16]

Little of this was considered skilled work, although it would have been disastrous for a novice to perform these tasks. Nevertheless, entrepreneurs tacitly recognized that experienced female workers were needed to sort the paper and to remove blemishes with a sharp knife, and they chose mature, competent women for the task. Younger women learned unskilled work within their families; the daughters gradually gained from their mothers' training and added to the family wage. Little as it was, the women's pay was important to the family livelihood, and the male workers protested when the boss tried to reduce it or to withhold traditional payment in kind. A serious dispute arose when the women were afraid they would no longer be able to "dip their bread into the soup," and the patron had to reinstate the benefit.[17]

The glassmakers had a similar situation. Necessarily placed close to supplies of wood or coal in the countryside, they also formed close-knit family groups that did not welcome outsiders or share the mores of nearby villages. While the male glassmaker might take his two assistants from outside the family, he reserved the training in the art of blowing glass for his sons. The wives and daughters were also present in the workshop, though, assisting the master. As Denis Woronoff commented, "They could even become 'attiseuses,' helpers who had the principal task of maintaining the furnace at the required temperature. The success of manufacturing depended above all on the proper execution of this task."[18] At work next to the master glassmakers, the women were a regular presence in the workshop, and they were thoroughly familiar with the practices of glassmaking.

Even in metal works and mines, women acted as auxiliary workers, carrying wood and coal for the forge, working the bellows, sewing bags for salt, and providing food. The often-quoted proverb that a menstruating woman would "curdle" the molten metal was a testimony not to their absence, but to their presence. For mining, "windlass women" turned the apparatus lowering a basket to raise coal; in the north of France, children pulled carts along underground tunnels. At the mouth of mines as well, women gathered to break up coal into smaller chunks, smashing it by foot or by rocks, and piling it onto wagons. They pushed loaded sledges and carried barrows of coal or made briquettes that they stacked up for distribution, as late as the mid-nineteenth century.[19]

Many countrysides became part of urban-rural fabriques, as regions of cottagers began working for urban manufactures. By 1770, inspector of manufactures Antoine-François Brisson reported a successful establishment of some six thousand spinners in the Lyonnais. A worker named Le Brumet, who set up a school for apprentices, boasted of having trained and placed five hundred spinners in his first year, and twice that in his second. In 1776, Gabriel Prévost and J.-G. Richard declared that their new establishment in the town of Sens combined cotton preparation and spinning. There, cleaning ("battage, épluchage, and savonnage"—beating, picking, and soaping) and spinning occupied 426 persons; 39 men aged twenty-five to forty years, 250 *femmes* and *filles* (women and girls) aged fifteen to fifty years, and 137 children aged nine to fifteen years. Weaving a range of cloth types busied 137 men, eighteen to sixty in age. The team was completed by fifteen dyers, one designer, one engraver, and another 132 women and girls spinning in the city. The total workforce of this successful operation numbered 716, of which more than half were female. Officials were gratified that it became a center for training spinners who, in turn, could teach the craft to women in other enterprises.[20]

As Serge Chassagne pointed out, "In the Vivarais, in 1773, women made up three-quarters of the textile workers. In Amiens, in 1778, eighty-eight percent of married women had a job in the industry." William Reddy estimated that the cotton industry that was founded only in 1700 expanded by 1780 to some three hundred thousand cottagers.[21] In Paris, at least one quarter of workers in the textile and clothing trades consisted of women, some of whom were in the prestigious seamstress guild.[22] Even if reports exaggerated the precise numbers, it is clear that women played an important role in these industries.

THE URBAN-RURAL FABRIQUE

Jean-Baptiste Colbert, Louis XIV's minister of finances from 1665 to 1683, provided important stimuli for French manufacture and trade. In addition to promoting royal manufactures in glass and tapestry, establishing regulatory standards to raise the quality of textile production, and establishing a guild for seamstresses in Paris, he supported other improvements in domestic manufacture. Realizing the benefit that women and children in rural handicraft added to the economy, he brought expert female lace makers, embroiderers, and weavers from Ireland and England to start schools for cottagers.[23] Girls also benefitted from training as apprentices in the seamstresses' guild in Paris, the linen workers' guilds in Rouen, and elsewhere.[24] In Puy-en-Velay, the communities requested *béates*, pious lay women, to come and teach girls reading and lace-making. These efforts paved the way for the later government initiatives to help increase and refine women's work, especially in cottage industry. Despite the inferior place that women held in the law codes—married women did not have adult status—the royal administration appreciated their role in helping support the family and in increasing manufactures, in the city and countryside.[25]

This important structure of the handicraft era has received much attention from modern scholars. Evident in the seventeenth century and earlier, the "putting-out system," also known as "cottage industry," has been called "proto-industry."[26] Since Franklin Mendels originated the concept in 1972, calling proto-industry "the first phase of industrialization," historians have challenged and elaborated upon the idea. Guillaume Daudin helpfully defines proto-industry and proto-industrialization as having three elements: (1) markets outside the region of production, indicating a step away from artisanal village work; (2) peasant participation, even if the product is finished by skilled urban workers; (3) commercialized agriculture, freeing a part of the workforce for rural industry.[27] These three criteria were seldom met simultaneously in France. Commercial agriculture was not yet developed, regional traits and customs had their own "shape," and industry characteristics caused a wide variety of manufacturing structures to appear. Despite these differences, the French system, with its fabriques, or massed industry, was one form of proto-industry. The urban-rural fabriques that this chapter highlights used the handicraft labor of the putting-out system to increase French production for a world market.

The French designation of "fabriques" needs to be understood in this context. In the eighteenth century, the fabrique was, in its urban-rural variant, a production complex situated in an urban center usually with guilds that received goods made by workers in the surrounding countryside. Urban merchants supplied the cottage workers with raw materials, and then brought the semi-manufactured goods to the town in a production pattern later called the *Verlagssystem*. Skilled city workers then finished these products, and powerful merchants, who dominated the workers, distributed the goods in widespread overseas market networks. The fabrique was an economic unit that linked "unskilled" rural workers, sophisticated master *ouvriers* (workers), and merchants. Inevitably, there were also nonguild workers in the towns who also supplied the guilds with semi-finished goods.

The term "fabrique" is a "false friend" for English speakers. In this era, it applies only to handwork or preindustrial manufacture. The eighteenth-century fabrique was not a modern factory even when some manufactures came to be enclosed in dedicated buildings because until the very end of the century it did not use steam power. However, historians like Jan de Vries considered the shift of manufacture from an entirely urban process to one that pulled in the countryside through the putting-out system to be an important step toward economic development and industrialization in the Netherlands and elsewhere.[28]

The urban-rural fabrique also has to be understood in the context of the burgeoning textile production and the response to the inflexibility of guilds. A few statistics show the importance of fabric production. Manufactured goods as a whole accounted for 48 percent of French production in the late eighteenth century. Of this percentage, textiles represented some 44 percent of total industrial output, excluding construction. And of this number, according to Daudin, the majority of cloth was made in the countryside by nonguild workers.[29] While not all fabriques produced textiles, a great many of them did, and their development was maintained by the expanding textile markets.

Crucial to the fabrique, the putting-out system was usually a family enterprise, where, in the case of textiles, women and children carded or spun thread that the men (and sometimes women) wove. In areas like the Pays de Caux in Normandy, however, women's production of thread brought in so much of the family support that men undertook household duties to let their wives spin. Elsewhere the men lent a hand in spinning or the women wove. Some households took up craftwork and abandoned farming entirely.[30] The advantage of the putting-out system to workers was that it permitted flexible daily and seasonal schedules, so that household care and farm chores could be done. But the advantages to entrepreneurs—lower wages, reduced overhead costs, and not having to supervise the work—also brought disadvantages. Uneven results in terms of quality and quantity were endemic in cottage industry.

In the first half of the eighteenth century, merchants made do with the problems of cottage industry, and sometimes they were rewarded with cloth of surprisingly good quality. Women's skill in manipulating spinning wheels and primitive spindles made for exceptionally fine thread and woven goods that set a high standard. Today we are astonished by the superlative quality of their handiwork; it clearly outperformed machine-made cloth stuff in amazing refinement. However, handwork had a limited output, and quantity was becoming what entrepreneurs prized. By mid-century, the market for consumer goods was widening and merchants wanted to take advantage of this "consumer revolution." Increased competition from Europe and overseas brought additional pressures. Responding to the new realities, royal administrators enacted more liberal policies, encouraging nonguild rural artisans to compete against the monopolistic guilds. In 1759, the restrictions prohibiting the import and manufacture of India prints (*toiles peintes*) were rescinded. No doubt ratifying existing practice, in 1762 the government ruled that nonguild workers in the countryside could legally contract to make and sell their goods without intermediary merchants. In the 1760s and later, liberal government administrators followed their predecessors of the seventeenth century and invited inventors to apply for subventions to found businesses. The 1775 award of honorary nobility to Philippe de Lasalle for his ingenious improvements on the silk brocade loom was part of this movement, as were the numerous subsidies given to other Lyonnais weaver-inventors.

The reforming minister Anne-Robert-Jacques Turgot sought to suppress the guilds in 1776. The political power of guilds thwarted this step toward liberalizing manufacturing, but most of the restored guilds technically permitted women to enter, even if their entry was seldom actually achieved.[31] After much dispute in economic policies, in 1779 textiles entered a new system: Director General of Finance Jacques Necker offered a choice for entrepreneurs either to conform to the industrial regulations, or to let the weaving take any form that might appeal to consumers. Far from disappearing, rural manufacturing gained new life as entrepreneurs sought the cheaper labor of the countryside and less rigid requirements for textiles became the norm. The widening freedom of manufacturing stimulated rural production, as a consumer revolution served to demand cloth that was cheaper or more varied, even if less well constructed—and for the wealthy, cloth more finely spun and woven.

The consumer appetite for new goods stimulated the economies of all the European nations, especially France's great rival across the English Channel. England's thriving cottage industry has been extensively studied in relation to her industrialization, which was earlier than that in France. In England, as in France, the role of women and children at work was significant. As Jane Humphries has found, industries were even designed with processes and components specifically suited for child labor.[32] Children were tasked not only with fetching raw materials or sweeping floors, but with actually using machines. As in France, inventors took pride in creating devices that were easy enough for a ten-year-old to use. The British also subscribed to the idea that it was beneficial for children to work, that it kept them out of trouble, and that it allowed them to "earn their bread." Maxine Berg and Pat Hudson are among those scholars who revealed the large role that women and children took in the British economy.[33] The English example held true for manufacturers all over the world.

THE URBAN CENTER IN THE FABRIQUE

Because the urban center with its home workshops scattered throughout the city was a key component of the second variant of the fabrique, it is worth examining in more detail. With some forty thousand employees, the huge silk works of Lyon is a good example. This type of manufacturing grew up naturally as male masters formed home workshops to weave the cloth. Their ateliers were too small to accommodate the many tasks needed to prepare the silk thread for weaving, so it was common for the female workers to take the silk and work it up at home. In this way some women established trades in their own workshops, gaining personal independence, but little advantage in pay. The twenty-seven thousand or so skilled female auxiliary workers were indispensable to the silk industry, and their low salaries supported many a master weaver's business. Even amid the ill-paid female silk workers, a few categories of women garnered prestige and high pay: the *remettreuse,* who attached the heddles to the warp thread on the loom, and the *liseuse,* who "read" the colored pattern and prepared the bundle of strings (*semple*) as the programming device for brocade fabric.[34] It is worth emphasizing that the quality of female silk workers' output met the highest standards of the industry. These women were labeled "unskilled" because (with the exception of the decorative braid makers) they were not permitted to become members of silk guilds—hence they could be paid less, despite their evident expertise.

ENCLOSED INDUSTRY

The shape and pace of some production changed as businessmen received capital to install new technology and to establish centers where work could be overseen, still without modern steam power. Thus was born the concentrated large-scale industrial institution that Denis Woronoff and others have called the urban *proto-*

fabrique.[35] In its strictest form, the proto-fabrique was a group of large buildings, in which all the processes of the industry were undertaken, whether or not they were in towns. The proud entrepreneurs sometimes erected sizeable, much-decorated structures surrounded by elaborate grounds on the edge of towns. Among the huge enterprises could be counted the royal manufacture Poupart de Neuflize at Sedan, with a building seven stories high, and the ironworks of Buffon, with numerous workshops clustered around a stream. Handsome principal buildings, separate workers' quarters, and facilities for every technique made these enclosures into virtual company towns. As Paul Delsalle commented of one large-scale manufacture, "It is a factory on the outskirts of the city, a closed world."[36] A genuine innovation in manufacturing, the concentration of workers within walls grew out of entrepreneurs' wish to exert discipline over their workers and to maximize the use of raw materials. Enclosed manufacture *preceded* the use of steam engines in textile-making that imposed its own discipline on indoor work. And enclosed manufacture also focused attention on the potential of employing hundreds of female workers.

While armories were early sites of rationalized discipline among large numbers of workers, manufacturing enterprises also adopted such new designs. In 1665, the Van Robais woolen mill excelled as a notable example of large, co-ordinated manufacture. As the century wore on, consumer demand and the imperative of competition with England, Holland, Switzerland, Germany, and Spain focused attention on increasing French production. Especially needed for the large textile industry, thread was high on the list of crucial products. The government developed a concerted interest in its production, and inspectors of manufacture were pressed to find new sources of thread on their tours of inspection. As intendant Jacques Marie Jérôme Michau de Montaran wrote to Olivier Jean Vaugelade, inspector of manufacture at Poitiers: "The Council asks that you pay special attention to the state of spinning in your region, since the manufactures [of textiles] are so dependent on it. We have heard various conflicting reports about the quality of spun thread to be found throughout the countryside and we wish you to ascertain whether thread spun under guild regulations in the towns is of better quality and more abundant per spinner than that produced in the rural areas. Do not fail to discover the proportion of spinners to weavers and other trained workers."[37]

This sort of government focus suggests the importance of textiles, the product that comprised over half the output in preindustrial Europe. It stands to reason that many innovations in technology and business practice sprang from the desire to improve textiles, and that the history of large-scale industry was so involved with making cloth. These motives stimulated entrepreneurs to seek funds for industrial complexes, both from private capital and state subvention. Anyone, male or female, was eligible to petition the royal Bureau de Commerce for privileges and subsidies. Industrialists throughout France (and some were women) wanted their firms to be qualified as privileged or royal manufacturers, with the advantages of some tax relief, their workers exempted from military conscription, and their technology freed from industrial regulations and guild control. Along with financial subventions for the use of new machines, the lucky entrepreneurs received monopolies for fifteen years and protection from the establishment of competing firms in their vicinity. Important industrialists like the Van Robais even managed to win the right to forbid others, within fifteen leagues, to use the same novel machinery the Van Robais had bought.[38]

The French government was as keen on establishing industry as were the entrepreneurs. Officials concerned with the economic vitality of France took the initiative of funding industrial espionage in England (as well as in the Netherlands, Switzerland, and elsewhere) and luring skilled workers to bring their new techniques across the channel.[39] Domestic inventors also received encouragement. Through its corps of inspectors of manufacture and intendants, Versailles paid close attention to the capacity of the French workforce and its success in adopting new technology. At times, for instance, the inspectors reported that spinning was at such a slow pace—with hand distaffs—that significant progress could be achieved just by distributing small spinning wheels. The government itself donated spinning wheels to poor spinners, sending some fifteen hundred to the area of Limousin between 1760 and 1775.[40]

Since entrepreneurs used their inventions and their subsidies as the basis of new manufactures, much rode on the advice of the inspectors of manufacture, members of the Académie Royale des Sciences, and especially the Bureau de Commerce and the controller general, who made the decisions. So often were the new devices intended for female operators that a number of women workers traveled to Paris or elsewhere as demonstrators.[41] To win approval, the machines had to contribute a new technique *and* offer an economic advantage to the prospective locale. In most cases, the declared benefit was to increase employment, underscoring anew the issue of women's work. Intendants and inspectors of manufacture were continually attuned to the project of increasing female employment. Even after a machine had been approved and subsidized, officials continued to note whether or not rural women and girls thought they could work well on it. Inspectors of manufacture were dispatched to evaluate how the new machines actually ran *in situ* and if they benefitted the local economy.[42]

THE FABRIQUE AS ENCLOSED MANUFACTURE

While mechanical innovation intensified in the last half of the eighteenth century, the pattern of large-scale manufacturing—the fabriques, for example—was already in place. Alongside a flourishing cottage industry, it was the combination of new machines and big industrial centers after the 1760s that expanded French commercial output and drew in a vast female workforce. As we saw, a first step toward enclosed industry had been taken by Josse Van Robais in 1665, when he developed a woolens manufacture at Abbeville under the sponsorship of minister Jean-Baptiste Colbert. By 1708, as many as three thousand men and women worked there. Placing workers into adjacent buildings and workshops to supervise the shop floor and produce the finest possible goods, Van Robais vowed to put "all the workers gathered together under the same key" ("tous les ouvriers rassemblés sous une même clé").[43] He was following a trend that placed the technology used for finishing into an urban shop of skilled masters, but he initiated a system of integrating all the processes of textile production. Each mechanical function had its own room, and the textiles were easily transferred to the next process. By specializing work in various rooms and keeping different processes close together, entrepreneurs controlled quality and saved time. Teaching new techniques, like the change from small hand spinning wheels to large "Dutch/English" foot-controlled wheels, was also more efficient under such close supervision.[44]

The roster of male and female workers in the Van Robais works signaled an equation that was typical of a fabrique. By 1767 there were some 560 skilled male workers compared to the 200 skilled women, and 700–800 "unskilled" female spinners, a two-to-one proportion of female to male workers.

Documents give a clear view of how the sex-segregated tasks were apportioned. The 560 skilled men were weavers with a regular or small shuttle; they also washed, carded, oiled, teased, fulled, and felted the wool. Some brushed, cut off stray ends, and folded the woven cloth. They supervised the other men's work, and two were appointed to oversee the female spinners. The skilled women cleaned, pressed, processed, and straightened the woolen fabric. All the craft laborers, both male and female, were paid by the piece, or by the number of turns of their machine, by day, week, or month. This makes it extremely difficult to compare their earnings with workers in other places, since we seldom know how many pieces or "turns" they made. Overseers received a weekly or yearly salary, and the women in this class, four *maîtresses à gage*, earned 400 livres per year, a median salary for this category of employment. The Van Robais woolen manufacture was unusual in having women occupy as much as 36 percent of the *skilled* workforce.[45] However, even the Van Robais could not do without the hundreds of hand spinners in the surrounding area.

For other examples of enclosed manufacture, we must turn to cotton. As a new industry, the printers of calicoes or toiles peintes (we call them "India prints" today) set up concentrated manufacture from the beginning. Already an object of smuggling and illegal manufacture, toiles peintes began to flourish in France after the prohibition against making and importing the printed cloth was lifted in 1759. Pierre Caspard estimated that 100,000–150,000 men and women were employed in the European calico industry in the eighteenth century, and up to 200,000 at its peak in 1830.

Women's tasks in calico making ranged from washing and bleaching cotton fabric to filling in the designs with brushes as "*pinceleuses*," and further to skilled work as assistant printers. From age fifteen, some of the female calico paint-ers began an apprenticeship to become assistant printers, performing the same tasks as boys, who alone could rise to the status of full-fledged printers. The boys used heavier printing blocks and earned one and a half times what the assistant printer women and girls received. However, even those women who remained calico painters could, with time and experience, "rise to the 'first tables' to which the most difficult and the best-paid tasks were entrusted." Despite the general discrimination against women, entrepreneurs recognized that training and ex-perience promoted skill.[46]

As in the Van Robais woolen works in Abbeville, the Oberkampf calico print house in Jouy-en-Josas placed each function in a separate room and situated the rooms next to each other to facilitate a smooth flow of operation. Every room had its own male or female overseer who checked to see if the work was done properly. Following Van Robais's practice, Oberkampf's workers had to remain within the factory walls, eating meals served by the boss's daughter or a hired matron, and sometimes sleeping on pallets near the machines. By these means, the entrepreneurs hoped to keep the "trade mystery" and secrets of their tools and techniques from being stolen. In addition, they could make full use of the economy of scale, buying quantities of material at bargain prices. They were also in a position to monopolize the most skillful workers, to determine the length of apprenticeship, and to set salaries.[47]

With their strict control of the manufacturing process, such entrepreneurs were able to shift the workers or fire them as the firm experimented with mechanical and chemical innovations. From hand-sized blocks, they began printing with larger blocks, and then with rollers, using new dyes, mordents, and bleaches. Finally, when they incorporated the steam engine into the process at the end of the century, child workers no longer had to pull the cloth along to the next process. Although the use of factory buildings imposed a limit on the size of calico firms—few exceeding eight hundred to a thousand workers—they were truly large groupings for their time, when the average town workshop usually had no more than twenty workers.

In shipyards, too, especially that of the Compagnie des Indes, women workers did a variety of tasks that included making rope and sail cloth. This and other military arsenals were enclosed and closely monitored to prevent theft of materials and designs. Over time, the development of new technologies accustomed the workers, female and male, to using complicated, novel machines.[48]

CONDITIONS OF WORK: SOCIABILITY, THE WORKDAY, AND CRAFT DISCIPLINE

From the point of view of the workers, the change from village handicraft to enclosed industry must have been jarring. In villages, work in craft industry in the form of veillés, or nighttime "work parties," was far freer than tasks conducted under the sight of overseers. In one example, a curé from Montigny described a local village woman's house where "the girls get together to spin and the boys then come by to kid and laugh with them."[49] A different reality held sway for women in one Jouy print shop, where the overseer banned singing or talking by the women under his supervision. It is no wonder that families in Normandy tried to avoid sending children into enclosed factories.[50]

We know that women in crafts prized their freedom to move around and talk as they worked. Some embroiderers resisted using the round frame because they would have to remain seated instead of carrying around their cloth and thread. The same complaint retarded use of the spinning wheel, as many spinners preferred to spin with distaffs while they walked. Can we imagine, then, how the workers in the Van Robais manufacture or Oberkampf's wooden barracks felt when they were shut up near their machines in the factory building for the entire day? The Van Robais workers "went about their monotonous tasks to the sound of a drum."[51] It is hard to know whether their half-hour for lunch and an hour for dinner, served right where they worked, were welcome breaks to socialize or quiet periods in which to recover.

The fifteen-hour workday probably was not unusual, since it followed the rhythm of farming and of cottage industry. Rising early to get to work at five o'clock must have been a normal way to take advantage of daylight, and even night work by the light of candles was part of farm and village life. However, at the Vidalon-le-Haut paper mill, work began at four o'clock so that the women could accomplish their thirteen-hour workday. The half-hour allotted to give their children breakfast and the hour for the other meals were not included in their pay.

Discipline was far more rigorous and constant in the large industries than in home workshops. Instead of having work assessed every so often when merchants came around to collect the products, the output of workers in concentrated manufactures was examined and priced every day. With an overseer circulating through a room of sixteen tables, at the Oberkampf works correction would be swift. The women sorting rags into categories at the Vidalon paper works were arranged in rows, so that the male overseer could watch them more easily. In spinning works, entrepreneurs promoted a process called "English spinning," or "*tarif anglaise,*" that kept female workers under tight scrutiny, paying them for exactly the amount of thread they produced, and keeping them from adulterating the thread with coarse filaments, water, or oil to hide any theft. Since women of all ages continued to work as long as they could, these conditions might have been a daily experience through their entire working lives.

It is true that women in cottage industry, especially spinners, embroiderers, and lace-makers, also suffered from poor lighting as they extended work into the night. But large-scale concentrated industries were no better in saving workers' health, and perhaps they were worse. In tanneries the heat and dust caused bleeding from nose and mouth. In textile works, damp air was conducive to tuberculosis; in glass workshops and foundries, heat and dust were occupational hazards. An inspector of manufactures reported that after some years of enclosure, woolen cloth weavers became "pale and ashen, with swollen or ulcerated legs." Spinners suffered from abraded and swollen hands. Women who unwound silk thread lost feeling in their ulcerated hands from having to dip cocoons into boiling water. And Lyon's drawgirls "destroyed" their backs after pulling down cords attached to sixty pounds of weight on the looms day after day.

There might be economic as well as physical hardships in regions where there were monopolies. In Normandy, for instance, independent spinners might possibly be able to play one weaver against another to get a better price for their thread.[52] The lace makers of Puy-en-Velay sometimes had the same chance. By contrast, whether laid off by a large firm or dismissed by merchants who controlled the area, regions with a single industry left labor with few alternatives. During an economic downturn as early as 1716, Van Robais's workers complained that they had been left without work and "in a sort of servitude."[53]

Despite these obstacles, women workers persisted, and even gained more skilled work by century's end. In papermaking, the employers sometimes threatened to use female workers instead of recalcitrant males. In shipbuilding arsenals, women took over rope making and other complex tasks. Haim Burstin tells us of women who managed networks of artisans in the faubourg Saint-Marcel in Paris. And during the Revolutionary and Napoleonic wars, the shortage of men caused women to undertake male jobs in weaponry, metallurgy, and a host of other trades.[54]

AN ERA OF MACHINES

While large-scale manufacturing centers have been documented as early as the sixteenth century, they did not become prevalent until the eighteenth century. The founding of concentrated industries gained momentum by the 1760s as increasing numbers of entrepreneurs received the privileges of royal manufacturers. A proposal to use new machinery or to teach a new process, with workers imported from England or Holland, was frequently given as the rationale for the privilege. At the same time, as we have seen, new laws gave craft workers throughout France more flexibility in their products and business arrangements.

These changes emerged in response to international trade and the increasing requirements of the government as a consumer. Competition with other countries put ever-greater pressure on the desire to produce thread faster and more cheaply, for faster and cheaper thread production. French hand-spinning could turn out extremely fine thread, but as the English-born industrialist John Holker claimed, after he became inspector general in 1755, woman-powered spinning machines (spinning jennies) in France saved two-thirds the cost. As an infant industry, cotton was poised to adopt these spinning jennies brought from England. Holker installed them as clusters in Rouen, Sens, and Bourges; Oberkampf set them up in his buildings in Jouy-en-Josas, as a vertically integrated industry.[55]

Numerous other machines were invented to mix various kinds of raw wool together, to finish the surface of textiles, and to card and comb raw cotton more efficiently. A few examples give a flavor of the activity. The woolen works of Elbeuf and Louviers tried out a French wool-carding machine as well as an Arkwright device for spinning. Linen works and cotton mills also saw attempts to harness new machines to waterpower. Printing on silk, cotton, and woolen cloth improved. The Académie Royale des Sciences, the Bureau de Commerce, and the controller general were kept busy deciding which new machines merited royal support. Entrepreneurs continually introduced new devices into their works to improve products and reduce expenses, especially the cost of spinning. Constant refinements were needed because, as David Landes has pointed out, in "the early years . . . rudimentary machines [were] awkward and jerky in their movements." Writing of the cotton industry, both Maxine Berg and Serge Chassagne called the period between 1785 and 1815 "the era of manufactures."[56] However, it might well be called the era of introducing women to modern machines.

CONCLUSION

As we add up the number of women in large-scale, privileged industries, and rural concentrations, it becomes clear that they were a large constituent of the labor force and some of the primary users of the newly invented machines. This was the cutting-edge technology for which the entrepreneurs had sought freedom from regulatory and guild control. The new devices were invented by men, but many of them were to be used by a workforce composed of women and children. Indeed, inventors emphasized that their machines were easy to use in order to justify their claims to be creating tools for female employment.

Clearly, nobody considered the women of early modern France to be "technophobic." Quite to the contrary, the French government as well as the businessmen counted on the female workers, without whom manufacturing would come to an end. Entrepreneurs relied on their female staff to be employees throughout the women's lives, whether in unskilled, low-paid work or skilled, well-compensated tasks. Women had long prepared raw materials and produced thread on spinning wheels; in the age of large, concentrated industries, they were among the first to use the new machines of the coming industrial age. Their facility with these inventions and the discipline of working were precursors of the early Industrial Revolution.

While eighteenth-century industrialists presented themselves as harbingers of a new age, they rested on a long tradition that valued work among the common people. The belief that government had a responsibility to discipline and foster industry stemmed from Colbert's mercantilist ideal of a population energetically producing goods for export. Females and child workers were included in this scenario. Women's work was a long-standing social expectation in Old Regime France, when men were enjoined never to marry a woman who could not earn her share of the family wage. But female employment could then be valued as a private resource, as the saying went, earning the woman's means "to feed her children."

With the nineteenth-century era of new machines, their work became a formal commodity, not just a means of helping the family economy or avoiding prostitution, but an objective aspect of national prosperity. *Ouvrières* (women workers) were placed within a new, seemingly independent, public context, working outside the home and in contact with men unrelated to them, at a time when the social ideal for an honest woman was to remain chaste and at home. Repelled by the implications of this change in status, nineteenth-century writers denigrated the woman worker, calling her "*L'Ouvrière! Mot impie, sordide*" ("Working woman! Impious, sordid word . . .").[57] In the transitional era of first machines, however, women workers were a significant part of the kingdom's resource. Their participation in large-scale, massed industry, with its new technology, marked an essential step in the process of French industrialization.

NOTES

1. As Paul Delsalle commented, "Le monde ouvrier des XVIe–XVIIe–XVIIIe siècles est en grande partie, féminin, surtout dans les secteurs textiles." *La France industrielle aux XVIe–XVIIe–XVIIIe siècles* (Paris: Ophrys, 1993), 155.

2. Jan de Vries and A. M. van der Woude, *The First Modern Economy: Success, Failure, and Perseverance of the Dutch Economy, 1500–1815* (Cambridge: Cambridge Univ. Press, 1997).

3. But see Deborah Valenze, *The First Industrial Woman* (Oxford: Oxford Univ. Press, 1995), for English women's experience with early industrial machines.

4. See Geraldine Sheridan, *Louder Than Words: Ways of Seeing Women Workers in Eighteenth-Century France* (Lubbock: Texas Tech Univ. Press, 2009), for an excellent survey of women's work shown in Diderot's *Encyclopédie* and the *Descriptions des arts et métiers*, published by the Académie Royale des Sciences.

5. Natalie Zemon Davis signaled the omnipresence of females in the crafts, citing the many nicknames related to their commerce. "Women in the Crafts in Sixteenth-Century Lyon," in *Women and Work in Preindustrial Europe*, ed. Barbara A. Hanawalt (Bloomington: Univ. of Indiana Press, 1986), 167–197.

6. André Guillerme, *La naissance de l'industrie a Paris entre sueurs et vapeurs, 1780–1830* (Seyssel: Champ Vallon, 2007). See chapter 2 for saltpeter, chapter 3 for gelatin and dye from bones, and chapter 4 on collecting. Saltpeter collection became a significant business.

7. Reed Benamou, "Women and the Verdigris Industry in Montpellier," in *European Women and*

Preindustrial Craft, ed. Daryl M. Hafter (Bloomington: Indiana Univ. Press, 1995), 3–15. See also Guillerme, *La naissance,* chapter 4.

8. Rene Marion, "*Les Dames de la Halle:* Community and Authority in Early Modern Paris" (Ph.D. diss., Johns Hopkins University, 1994), has detailed views of the Paris market and its significance in provisioning the city. Bonnie G. Smith was the first to explore women's role in this segment of commerce, in *Ladies of the Leisure Class: The Bourgeoises of Northern France in the Nineteenth Century* (Princeton: Princeton Univ. Press, 1981), especially chapters 1–3.

9. Sydney Watts, *Meat Matters: Butchers, Politics, and Market Culture in Eighteenth-Century Paris* (Rochester: Univ. of Rochester Press, 2006).

10. See Deborah Simonton's statement that the attribution of skill was determined according to gender, irrespective of the actual dexterity of the worker. *A History of European Women's Work, 1700 to the Present* (London: Routledge, 1998), 76–83.

11. See Lissa Roberts, Simon Schaffer, and Peter Dear, eds., *The Mindful Hand: Inquiry and Invention from the Late Renaissance to Early Industrialisation* (Amsterdam: Koninklijke Nederlandse Akademie van Wetenschappen, 2007).

12. Daryl M. Hafter, "Women in the Underground Business of Eighteenth-Century Lyon," *Enterprise and Society* 2 (March 2001): 11–40; Liliane Hillaire-Pérez, "Le vol de déchets dans l'industrie en France et en Angleterre au XVIIIᵉ siècle," *Actes du colloque international de Dijon* (Dijon: EUD, 1998).

13. Clare Haru Crowston, *Fabricating Women: The Seamstresses of Old Regime France, 1675–1781* (Durham: Duke Univ. Press, 2001); Daryl M. Hafter, *Women at Work in Preindustrial France* (University Park: Pennsylvania State Univ. Press, 2007).

14. Archives Nationales (henceforth AN), series F 12 650 [1780–1781?].

15. AN F 12 678, No. 73. Letter from Godechal, Curé of St. Gervais, Dean of Paris Church in Falaise, 5 December 1788. Jeff Horn suggests that fear of machine-breaking riots was a significant factor in retarding French industrialization. Jeff Horn, *The Path Not Taken: French Industrialization in the Age of Revolution, 1750–1830* (Cambridge, Mass.: MIT Press, 2006), 46–47, passim.

16. Leonard N. Rosenband, *Papermaking in Eighteenth-Century France: Management, Labor, and Revolution at the Montgolfier Mill, 1761–1805* (Baltimore: Johns Hopkins Univ. Press, 2000), chapter 2, "Making Paper." See also Leonard N. Rosenband, "Hiring and Firing at the Montgolfier Paper Mill," in *The Workplace before the Factory: Artisans and Proletarians, 1500–1800,* ed. Thomas Max Safley and Leonard N. Rosenband (Ithaca: Cornell Univ. Press, 1993), 227.

17. Conversation with Leonard Rosenband. See also Rosenband, *Papermaking in Eighteenth-Century France,* 89, 105.

18. Denis Woronoff, *Histoire de l'industrie en France du XVᵉ siècle à nos jours* (Paris: Éditions du Seuil, 1994), 138.

19. Sheridan, *Louder Than Words,* 24–27, 35–41. See also Rolande Trempé, *Les mineurs de Carmaux, 1848–1914* (Paris: Les éditions ouvrières, 1971), 1:132–141.

20. Serge Chassagne, *Le coton et ses patrons: France, 1760–1840* (Paris: Éditions de l'école des hautes études en sciences sociales, 1991), 70.

21. For examples of widespread implanting of spinning in the countryside, see Chassagne, *Le coton et ses patrons,* 39–73, especially page 70. See also William M. Reddy, *The Rise of Market Culture: The Textile Trade and French Society, 1750–1900* (Cambridge: Cambridge Univ. Press, 1984), 24.

22. Crowston, *Fabricating Women.*

23. For a thoughtful review of Colbert's legacy, see Philippe Minard, *La fortune du colbertisme: État et industrie dans la France des Lumières* (Paris: Fayard, 1998), 15–26.

24. Clare Haru Crowston, "An Industrious Revolution in Late Seventeenth-Century Paris: New Vocational Training for Adolescent Girls and the Creation of Female Labor Markets," *Secret Gardens, Satanic Mills: Placing Girls in Modern European History*, ed. M. J. Maynes, Birgitte Soland, and Christina Benninghaus (Bloomington: Indiana Univ. Press, 2005). David Hopkin describes the function of the *béate* in *Voices of the People in Nineteenth-Century France* (Cambridge: Cambridge Univ. Press, 2012), 214–231.

25. However, widows and adult unmarried women (*filles majeures*) might have more independence in the law. Widows, for example, could carry on their late husband's trade in many guilds. See Janine M. Lanza, *From Wives to Widows in Early Modern Paris: Gender, Economy, and Law* (Aldershot, Eng.: Ashgate, 2007).

26. Among the many publications on the role of proto-industry, see Franklin F. Mendels, "Proto-Industrialisation: The First Phase of the Industrialisation Process," *Journal of Economic History* 33, no. 1 (1972): 241–261. On proto-industrialization and export, see Didier Terrier, *Les deux ages de la proto-industrie: Les tisserands du Cambrésis et du Saint-Quentinois, 1730–1880* (Paris: Éditions de l'école des hautes études en sciences sociales, 1996), 29.

27. Guillaume Daudin, *Commerce et prosperité: La France au XVIIIe siècle* (Paris: Presses de l'université de Paris-Sorbonne, 2005), 52.

28. See Jan de Vries's discussion in *The First Modern Economy* of how workers lost their independence to merchants.

29. See page 39 of Daudin, *Commerce et prosperité*, for his discussion of statistics, and pages 36–38 and 52–53 for rural versus urban output.

30. Gay L. Gullickson, *The Spinners and Weavers of Auffay: Rural Industry and the Sexual Division of Labor in a French Village, 1750–1850* (Cambridge: Cambridge Univ. Press, 1986); Tessie Liu, *The Weaver's Knot: The Contradictions of Class Struggle and Family Solidarity in Western France, 1750–1914* (Ithaca: Cornell Univ. Press, 1994).

31. As Steven L. Kaplan discovered, most male guilds resisted the entrance of women. See Steven L. Kaplan, *La fin des corporations* (Paris: Fayard, 2001), 216–218, 229–230, passim.

32. Jane Humphries, *Childhood and Child Labour in the British Industrial Revolution* (Cambridge: Cambridge Univ. Press, 2010).

33. Maxine Berg, *The Age of Manufactures: Industry, Innovation and Work in Britain 1700–1820* (London: Routledge, 1994); Pat Hudson and W. R. Lee, "Women's Work and the Family Economy in Historical Perspective," in *Women's Work and the Family Economy*, ed. Pat Hudson and W. R. Lee (Manchester: Manchester Univ. Press, 1990), 2–47.

34. Hafter, *Women at Work*, 133, passim. The classic work on Lyon's Grande Fabrique is Maurice Garden, *Lyon et les Lyonnais au XVIIIe siècle* (Paris: Les belles lettres, [1970]).

35. Woronoff, *Histoire de l'industrie en France du XVe siècle à nos jours*, 93. See also D. C. Coleman, "Proto-Industrialization: A Concept Too Many," *Economic History Review*, 2nd Ser., 36 (1983): 443.

36. See the discussion by Delsalle on the ambiguous classification of proto-fabrique and proto-industrialization, as well as distinctions between *atelier, boutique, fabrique, usine,* and *manufacture* in *La France industrielle*, 118–125. Quotation is from page 123.

37. AN F 12 650 [1780–1781?].

38. For the classic exposition of industrial privileges, see Germain Martin, *La grande industrie en France sous le règne de Louis XV* (1900, Paris; reprint, Genève: Mégariotis Reprints, 1970).

39. John R. Harris, *Industrial Espionage and Technology Transfer: Britain and France in the Eighteenth Century* (Aldershot, Eng.: Ashgate, 1998), 420. See also Paola Bertucci, "Enlightened Secrets: Silk, Intelligent Travel, and Industrial Espionage in Eighteenth-Century France," *Technology and Culture* 54, no. 4 (October 2013): 820–852.

40. Minard, *La fortune du colbertisme*, 232.

41. For instance, in 1775 a *maîtresse fileuse* named Colombe Thomas demonstrated a jenny with thirty spindles to Trudaine, Turgot, and Malesherbes. See Chassagne, *Le coton et ses patrons*, 70.

42. Minard, *La fortune du colbertisme*, 224–228. Liliane Hilaire-Pérez estimated that two-thirds of the entrepreneurs promoting inventions were located outside Paris. Liliane Hilaire-Pérez, *L'Invention technique au siècle des Lumières* (Paris: Albin Michel, 2000), 58.

43. Cited in James Farr, *The Work of France: Labor and Culture in Early Modern Times, 1350–1800* (Lanham: Rowman and Littlefield, 2008), 107–108. Philippe Minard commented that "the obsession of surveillance" flowered toward the end of the eighteenth century (*La fortune du colbertisme*, 166).

44. For an extensive discussion of the cotton printing industry, including illustrations, see Serge Chassagne, *Oberkampf: Un entrepreneur capitaliste au siècle des Lumières* (Paris: Éditions Aubier Montaigne, 1980), 231–236. On the originality of this type of industrialization, see Serge Chassagne, "La diffusion rurale de l'industrie cottinière en France," *Revue du Nord* 240 (1979): 97–114.

45. Martin, *La grande industrie*, 276; Daudin, *Commerce et prospérité*, 53–55, 97–102.

46. Pierre Caspard, "The Calico Painters of Estavayer: Employers' Strategies toward the Market for Women's Labor," in *European Women*, ed. Daryl M. Hafter, 109–112. Citation from page 112. For a comparative perspective with Swiss calico printing, see pages 112–136. See also Chassagne, *Oberkampf*, passim.

47. Chassagne, *Oberkampf*, 231–236. Rope-making, especially the firm at Rochefort, was another example of a successful enclosed industry. Daudin, *Commerce et prospérité*, 47.

48. Martine Acerra and Jean Meyer, *La grande époque de la marine à voile* (Ouest-France: Ouest-France Université, 1987), 55–61.

49. Liana Vardi cited this comment in *The Land and the Loom: Peasants and Profit in Northern France, 1680–1800* (Durham: Duke Univ. Press, 1993), 139.

50. Gullickson, *Spinners and Weavers*, 137. See also Alain Dewerpe and Yves Gaulupeau, *La fabrique des prolétaires: Les ouvriers de la manufacture d'Oberkampf à Jouy-en-Josas, 1760–1815* ([Paris]: Presses de l'École Normale Supérieure, 1990), 153–193.

51. James R. Farr writes that by 1728 the Van Robais firm had thirty-five hundred male workers and four hundred female workers under this discipline. Farr, *The Work of France*, 108.

52. Reddy emphasized that some spinners there could do without the intermediary courtiers, and bring their thread to market themselves. See Reddy, *The Rise of Market Culture*, 24–26.

53. Émile Levasseur, *Histoire des classes ouvrières et de l'industrie en France avant 1789*, 2nd ed. (Paris: Arthur Rousseau, 1901), 2:767. An inquest of 1767 revealed that wages were stagnant, even as the price of necessities and of the cloth the workers made rose.

54. Haim Burstin, *Une révolution à l'oeuvre: Le faubourg Saint-Marcel (1789–1794)* (Paris: Champ Vallon, 2005).

55. For technical innovation in cotton, see Chassagne, *Le coton*, especially chapter 3, "La force de

l'innovation," and Charles Ballot, *L'Introduction du machinisme dans l'industrie française* (Lille-Paris: Rieder, 1923).

56. David S. Landes, *The Unbound Prometheus: Technological Change and Industrial Development in Western Europe from 1750 to the Present* (Cambridge: Cambridge Univ. Press, 1972). For characterization of the period, see Berg, *The Age of Manufactures, 1700–1820*; Chassagne, *Le coton*, chapter 4, "Le temps des mécaniques (1785–1815)."

57. Jules Simon, *L'Ouvrière*, 3rd ed. (Paris: Librarie Hachette et Cie, 1864), iv.

WOMEN IN THE PARIS MANUFACTURING TRADES AT THE END OF THE LONG EIGHTEENTH CENTURY
Continuity and Change
Judith A. DeGroat

L 'Ouvrière! Mot impie, sordide ("Working woman! Impious, sordid word"). So in 1860 did Jules Simon quote Jules Michelet, his contemporary considered expert on all things feminine.[1] Simon's citation, in the preface to his study of the woman worker, has come to reflect for many scholars the attitude of mid-nineteenth-century French society to the condition of working women as a consequence of industrialization: exploited economically and sexually as a pool of unskilled labor, a threat to the male breadwinner and to the survival of the working-class family.[2] This portrait developed in the two decades of the July Monarchy (1830–1848), during a period when economists, politicians, social reformers, and working-class radicals debated the "social question" of how to deal with an industrializing society and the consequences of paid female labor. However, as the essays in this collection demonstrate, women's manufacturing labor, if not the cultural meanings later assigned to it, emerged long before the 1830s; the impact of changing means of production and economic law that began in the mid-eighteenth century reshaped the structure of work in an economic revolution that incorporated increasing numbers of women into the wage economy. Certainly much had changed through the transformations wrought by the Revolution of 1789 and the subsequent restorations and revolutions. Yet the continuity in Parisian women's roles in handicraft manufacturing from the mid-eighteenth to the mid-nineteenth centuries is striking: women worked in diverse areas employing a range of skills. Simultaneously, working women were responsible for the domestic labor and consumer activities needed to maintain the household. While France's economy and society had seen several transformations in important ways by the mid-nineteenth century, perhaps the most significant to the experience of women workers was the change in the cultural understanding of women's labor, as reflected in the picture painted by Simon in the middle of the Second Empire.

The first half of the nineteenth century is an important, if uncommon, point from which to assess women's labor at the end of a century of significant economic, political, and cultural transition. Historians have long established the centrality of manufacturing work to the lives of women in early modern Europe and to the societies in which they lived. The Revolution of 1789 brought significant legal transformations as well as social and economic upheaval to the lives of working women. Most scholars pick up the story of the impact of industrialization only in the second half of the nineteenth century, with a particular emphasis on the Third Republic (1870–1940). The intervening period has been identified as the time when women fell into a pool of sweated labor that served to undermine the remnants of artisanal production, while political economists and socialist reformers, among others, identified female labor as a threat to the well-being of the working-class family.[3] A closer look at the lives of manufacturing women during the July Monarchy reveals both important continuities with the period before the Revolution of 1789 and a transformation in the image and the work of women as the long eighteenth century came to an end with the Revolution of 1848.

This essay examines the lives of women in the Parisian manufacturing trades in the 1830s and 1840s. These women were a diverse and complex group from across the urban economy that included former guild mistresses and casual workers, highly as well as less skilled labor. Working to maintain their households was a concurrent responsibility, one that belied an emerging notion of separate spheres that located femininity solely within the home. This aspect of female labor, defined here as domestic labor and which included consumer activity, engaged women on the margins of a growing retail economy. Such enterprise increased the importance of female wage-earning even as those activities became socially suspect. The interconnections of the activities of Parisian women and the resulting redefinition of women's labor merit study. An examination of women's work from the perspective of the end of the long eighteenth century offers the opportunity for important insights into French culture and society as well as an understanding of why the Revolution of 1848 was a turning point for women's labor and the lives of women in Paris manufacturing.

HISTORIOGRAPHY

Historians of women have long been concerned about how the record of feminine enterprise did not necessarily follow standard chronological divisions. In

1976, Joan Kelly began her pathbreaking essay on women in the Renaissance with the statement: "One of the tasks of women's history is to call into question accepted schemes of periodization."[4] Kelly and others queried: What would history look like if examined from perspectives that used moments significant to women rather than wars and treaties as chronological boundaries? We might define the nineteenth century not by the Congress of Vienna (1814–1815) and the outbreak of the Great War (1914), but rather by the institution of the Napoleonic Code (1804), which redefined the legal status of women, and the reforms that gave women access to careers in teaching (1880s). Studies such as those of Rachel Fuchs and Jo Burr Margadant, for example, respectively offer new ways of understanding the importance of gender to the law and the role of women in shaping the ideal of republicanism. Whitney Walton at the same time has given us a riveting portrait of bourgeois women who rewrote the masculine vision of the republic in the mid-nineteenth century. Such rethinking of historical periodization has proved difficult and yet has been rewarding. No less instructive have been the debates among scholars over the origins and meanings of the distinction between public and private spheres that emerged in the discourse and laws of the Revolutionary era.[5]

Debate over the consequences of industrialization has offered another way of rethinking women's and gender history. It has produced many important studies, forcing a readjustment of our approaches to history. Laura Lee Downs, for example, identifies the importance of the development of women's history in the first wave of the feminist movement, when scholars such as Ivy Pinchbeck sought the origins of contemporary gendered distinctions in the workplace. Of equal importance are the studies of gender and labor that appeared in the 1990s, such as that by Kathleen Canning on women in German industrialization, and the essay collections edited by Ava Baron, Laura Frader, and Sonya Rose.[6] All of these scholars agree that women worked in agriculture, handicraft manufacturing, and service to provide livings for themselves and their families. Gender, the understanding of femininity framed by class and, as more recently argued, ethnicity or race, determined the value given their labor and what actual tasks they were permitted to do.

In the English case, industrialization has long been studied in the 1750–1850 time frame. In France, with the rupture (as it was viewed by many) of the Revolution, a different periodization has emerged. Scholars have long attempted to fit the French case into the English, just as the eighteenth- and nineteenth-century French government and politicians worked to replicate or at least compete with

British manufacturing success. The characterization of French "backwardness" blamed on the continued production in smaller family-owned firms led scholars to search for developments that replicated the English case: the movement of women and girls into factory settings and the transformation of production methods to ones that displaced handicraft with sweated homework. As a result, for the most part, studies of French women's manufacturing labor in the eighteenth and nineteenth centuries have remained separate undertakings, as scholars of the former have explored handicraft production, while those of the post-Revolutionary era have focused on the development of the factory. Thus, it is worth exploring what the history of women's work looks like from the perspective of the end of the long eighteenth century (1750–1850).

Economic historians such as Jan de Vries and Jeff Horn have, however, overturned the primacy of the "English Road" to industrialization. De Vries's use of the term "industrious revolution" underscores the significant transformations in the eighteenth century of both production and consumption that came well before industrial mechanization. Horn, in particular, has demonstrated both the continuity from the Old Regime and the transformations wrought by the Revolutionary and Napoleonic period in France's own productive path to industrialization.[7] So, too, France emerged after 1815 with legislation that both restored and restricted women's capacity to act in the workplace. Thus, our understanding of women's manufacturing labor benefits from attention to the influence of both continuity and change.

Daryl Hafter's recent work raises an important question about the role of continuity that is suggestive for the early nineteenth century. As she demonstrates, the transformation of the organization of production along with the elimination of guild privileges during the 1789 Revolution shifted the roles of women in the manufactures of Rouen and Lyon, albeit in different ways. A decline in opportunity, due both to changes in markets and production methods and to loss of skills—or the refusal to recognize women's work abilities and knowledge—hit guildswomen hard. Revolutionary legislation that restricted the ability of guildswomen to contest illegal competition and preserve their guild privileges had an equal impact. It narrowed their options and allowed the labor market to be flooded by women outside of the guild structure. Hafter shows that the pool of women available to replace guildswomen expanded in the later eighteenth century, which calls attention both to the significance of women's labor outside of the guild structure and to continuity of work processes beyond the Revolutionary period.[8]

Identifying women's unpaid household labor as "consumer" activities reflects my effort to understand the changing gendered constructions of working-class domesticity in the first half of the nineteenth century. Working women of the Old Regime did not make such a distinction; for many of them, domestic labor included work for home use (or consumption) and work for sale as wage or product. Certainly, for the women employed at work for wages, especially in the developing *fabriques,* a separation did occur that caused families to weigh the value of each member's labor. However, the use of the term "reproductive labor" emerged from early nineteenth-century political economy to describe the opposite of masculine "productive" labor, which was defined as that which created "exchange" value. In this formulation, reproductive activity took place outside of the market and created a less valuable, and less valued, product gendered feminine. Marxist feminists in the 1970s, following Marx's conclusions, underscored that this "use" value, the exhausting work of managing a family's food, lodgings, and other basic necessities on a varying budget (that was often outside of the housewife's control), was the factor that allowed industrial capitalism to reproduce its labor force almost free of charge. While this view acknowledged the wage labor of girls and, importantly, the major contribution of women's domestic labor to the development of industrial capitalism, it missed the active engagement of working-class women in the public urban marketplace in early industrialization. While contemporary feminist economics correctly rejects the distinction between productive and reproductive work, calling attention to women's actions as consumers both reflects the distinction that was clear in nineteenth-century thinking and, as importantly, underscores the extent of commodity exchange in which working women engaged. Recent studies of consumerism have focused on elite and popular consumption in the early modern period, and the development of a bourgeois-led domestic consumption in the later nineteenth century.[9] I wish to extend that focus to include the labor of manufacturing women in the mid-nineteenth-century household, which included using their wages for the purchase of child care, cooked foods, and laundry as part of the market exchange of Paris. This labor was recognized and valued as such in the eighteenth century.

SOURCES

One important reason for the absence of studies on Paris manufacturing in the first half of the nineteenth century is the state of primary sources, as compared to both earlier and later periods. The extensive guild and judicial records of the Old Regime, and in some cases the Revolutionary period, have allowed scholars to trace the evolution of particular trades and document the changes experienced by women into the nineteenth century. Likewise, there was an increase in information gathering on work, poverty, health, and criminality in the early years of the Third Republic (1871–1914). Newspapers, parliamentary debates, and the minutes of trade union and political party meetings joined memoirs produced by an increasingly literate working class to provide an alternative perspective, the voices of the people, for this later period. Few of these sources are available for the July Monarchy. Moreover, the challenge of finding working women's voices in archives and libraries for both the eighteenth and later nineteenth century is almost as difficult as is their analysis.

Yet even while some archival materials are available for the study of women's labor in the early nineteenth century, most historians have drawn predominantly on printed material. Printed tracts by the emerging advocates of political economy and by utopian socialists and their working-class followers struggled to define the meaning and role of labor for both women and men in the new century. The government, together with purportedly independent institutions, such as the Paris Chamber of Commerce, began to collect and present statistical data on the economic and social life of the city. Newspapers flourished. Bourgeois and working-class women contributed to this debate in pamphlets and in female-oriented (and even female-owned) journals.

Archival sources have been less frequently used to study women's labor in this period, largely because so many were destroyed or damaged in the fire that burned the Hotel de Ville during the Commune in 1871. But information concerning working women as economic and political actors can be found in the reports of various ministries and courts, including those of Commerce and Industry, Police, and Justice. The records of women arrested between 1830 and 1848 contain much useful information both in terms of interrogation of arrested women and the testimony, favorable or not, of their neighbors and employers.[10] Archival sources are no less mediated than printed text, yet there one finds more voices that responded to and resisted the transformations in the lives of working women. Through these sources an understanding of women's working lives in the 1830s and 1840s takes shape.

THE IMPACT OF "INDUSTRIALIZATION" IN PARIS

Paris at mid-century was a city in transition. The center of political administration as well as a vibrant hub of handicraft manufacturing, the capital attracted migrants from all over France and Europe. The city's population reached almost a million people by the time of the Revolution of 1848, and observers identified the majority of them as migrants. Working people found employment in a range of manufacturing and service trades that supplied both the urban and export markets. Working-class living conditions were difficult—overcrowded housing, overtaxed sanitation systems, high food prices, low wages, and economic downturns that further lowered wages or, worse, led to unemployment. Although the formal guild structure had been abolished during the Revolution, a hierarchical system of apprenticeship and advancement—one based on concepts of skill that excluded women from the most well-paying work—organized much handicraft manufacturing in the capital. Simultaneously, the subcontracting that fueled industrial capitalism destabilized this labor hierarchy. It did so by employing women and men deemed less skilled and by paying them less per piece than those artisans who had previously done the same work for higher wages, artisans who had often owned their own tools and even been masters of their own workshops. The "unskilled" workers not only earned far less than did their predecessors, their wages faced continual downward pressure. Journeymen and masters displaced by these changes responded, as did those at the mercy of subcontractors, who were willing to depress wages for work defined as unskilled. They did so through work actions, which were illegal, and through political activism, considered treasonous. Work coalitions, strikes, and membership in republican societies led to arrest and imprisonment. Participation in utopian socialist reading groups was less severely sanctioned, but those involved were often targeted by police spies. The working people of Paris retained their reputation for revolutionary activity.

The state of Parisian manufacturing during the July Monarchy had its origins in the eighteenth century. During the Old Regime, Parisian women prepared spindles for weaving, gilded furniture, polished glass and ceramics, and worked in the book, wallpaper, upholstery, and garment trades.[11] Following the Revolution, women continued to find employment across most of the capital's manufacturing trades. A sexual division of labor emerged that accorded women employment in finishing work, for example, as polishers of metal goods. Women made up a significant part of the workforce in the furniture and precious metals trades, and constituted more than a quarter of those in the printing, paper, and chemical trades. Female wood gilders and porcelain painters worked alongside male workers in furniture and ceramics production. According to the data collected by the Paris Chamber of Commerce in the wake of the 1848 Revolution, the largest concentration of women in 1848 labored in the luxury trades, textiles, and, most of all, garment production. Almost sixty thousand worked in the latter group, just under half of all the women in Parisian manufacturing.[12] The garment trades were made up of a diverse group of workers: from custom to piece workers, from shoe binders to hat makers, and from fur cutters to dressmakers—a category that included *lingères* (fine linen seamstresses) and *couturières* (seamstresses). The majority of women working in the trades were employed in workshops rather than in their own homes. Women's wages were generally less than half those of men, although in a few industries, such as upholstery making, women earned close to the 3 francs-per-day average of men in manufacturing work. Married women made up a large part of the female workforce both in workshop and home production. While needlework, broadly defined—from upholstery and bookbinding to fine linen sewing—employed the largest number of women engaged in handicraft work, public conception of female labor increasingly equated it with the work of the seamstress toiling in her home—or more specifically, in her garret room. Certainly the division of labor, in particular the sexual and gendered division of labor, intensified throughout the nineteenth century in the Paris trades. At the same time, the presence of women throughout those trades remained remarkably the same.[13]

One set of changes over the past century and particularly through the Revolutionary era concerned the legal status of female labor. In the eighteenth century, certain classes of working and businesswomen could sue to protect their right to work and own businesses. The institution of the Napoleonic Code undermined that option, as did certain social and cultural shifts. They showed the emerging notion of separate spheres and the growing assumption that the purpose of female labor was to care for home and family. As Joshua Cole notes, "The Civil Code's exclusion of women from active participation in the political and economic life of the nation found its theoretical counterpart in the writings of those political economists" of the period.[14] Thus, while a widow or an unmarried woman could control her property both before and after the Revolution, the ability of working women to bring lawsuits was significantly weakened in the later period by the strong perceptions that they should not, and that nineteenth-century working women did not have the ultimate right to their own earnings.[15]

Legal experts, employers, and working-class men debated the place and role of women in the trades, and to what sort of regulation they should be subject. They did so without consulting the women themselves. One dispute concerned the *patente,* or employers' tax, which tailors argued couturières (seamstresses) should be forced to pay, as a means to challenge the downward pressure they exerted on male wages; the commercial courts agreed in 1834.[16] Later in the July Regime a vigorous argument broke out in the Chamber of Peers as well as in the bourgeois and working-class press over whether or not female labor should be subject to the restrictions of the *livret* (worker's passport) reinstituted under Napoleon. Some working men argued that such a requirement would make women more vulnerable to sexual exploitation by unscrupulous employers. A number of reformers, both noble and bourgeois, agreed. Most employers and political economists, however, insisted that the livret was the only way to control an unruly workforce, be it female or male.[17] Women's voices were not heard in such debates. This stands in contrast to the silk and woolen workers or the seamstresses of the Old Regime, who brought lawsuits to defend their rights. Subjected to an enlarged sphere of masculine authority, working women in the 1830s and 1840s were supposed to retreat quietly to their homes and occupy themselves solely with their domestic responsibilities, even as manufacturing continued to demand their labor.

WAGE LABOR, DOMESTIC LABOR, AND CONSUMPTION

In the early nineteenth century, bourgeois women contended with the cultural forces that defined their duties as exclusively domestic, located primarily in the home. Consequently, these women were concerned with the comfort that their personal attention would bring to their families in a setting they established by extensive material consumption.[18] Working-class women also faced a growing consensus that they should abandon waged labor in order to attend to their families—even as those very families became increasingly dependent on the cash earned by that labor for the basic necessities of shelter and food. Productive labor for working women thus included provision for and management of the household as well as wage earning. The complexity of domestic labor in tiny one- or two-room apartments on a small and uncertain budget was considerable, as the obligations included feeding and caring for family members, cleaning, and negotiating payments for lodging, bread, fuel, and light. The need for cash was a constant source of anxiety, as the literature on visits to pawnshops underscores.[19] The space and time constraints experienced by women in the manufacturing trades in early nineteenth-century Paris meant that their unpaid domestic labor took place in the broader marketplace of the city. This labor included purchasing inexpensive meals at one-dish restaurants, as well as child care, second-hand clothes, and laundry services. As the work of Arlette Farge and others have shown, laboring women of eighteenth-century Paris faced the same challenges of feeding and housing their families. In the first half of the nineteenth century, however, many of what I choose to call consumer activities—activities that later in the century would become associated more directly with women's access to restaurants and department stores. Even consumer cooperatives, as Helen Chenut has shown so well, were being redefined as household tasks to be undertaken by working women whose sole concern was now supposed to be the home and family.[20] By the time of the July Monarchy, the reality that working women lacked time to keep up the household themselves and that they relied on a market in consumer goods and services to do so flew in the face of what was defined as women's proper sphere.

Domestic responsibilities required careful management of household budgets in order to meet the expenses of food, rent, and clothing. In the eighteenth and early nineteenth centuries, both working- and middle-class women had charge of household budgets. Yet, while this practice declined for the bourgeoisie in the later decades of the nineteenth century, poor women continued to manage their family finances. During the period both men and women contributed their wages to this end, but female control of the budget could create tension, especially in a cash economy. Sometimes men were unwilling to hand over some or all of their pay; in the latter cases, contemporaries noted that "women were obliged to stand sentinel at the boss's door on pay days in order to obtain some money to feed themselves and their children."[21] While such observations were part of the bourgeois lore of the shiftless or perhaps exploited working class, official records illustrate the tensions and even violence within families that stemmed from women's apportioning of family funds. The laundress Maire LePlatre, for example, gave her partner 1 franc each day for his meals and received a beating from him one day when she refused to give him more.[22] Even when budget decisions did not end in violence, women often were forced to engage in extraordinary measures in order to find resources to meet their families' needs. While the primary fear of middle-class reformers and political economists was that working-class women would resort to prostitution to meet their financial obligations, and certainly many did, many women simply took whatever work they could find. During the financial crisis of the Revolution of 1848, Jeanne Goursault, a seamstress, wrote poignantly to the municipal government of Paris: "Without work for three months, my husband with a chest ailment, responsible for an infirmed mother of seventy-two, behind two terms at the pawn shop, our goods will be sold. I am not asking for charity, I ask, I plead for work that will at least keep us from dying of hunger."[23]

Working women thus combined domestic activities with wage-earning, engaging in the consumer market in addition to the labor market throughout the Parisian economy. This balancing act increasingly challenged economic and social understandings of femininity. When women in the trades defended the very wage work that enabled them to feed themselves and their families, the resulting clashes with authority were shaped by conflict over gender norms as much as by class interests. In the process, the voices of working women became increasingly difficult to discern, as the following examples suggest.

CONFLICTING VERSIONS OF THE "WORKING WOMAN"

Like those in earlier centuries, working-class women in the early and middle nineteenth century developed numerous strategies to provide for themselves and their families.[24] They did so, however, in an environment in which the very concept of a woman's place in the economy and society was changing. In the decades before the 1848 Revolution, working-class women became the center of a discourse equating them with social and moral disorder, one that shaped and was shaped by the upheaval generated by transformations in contemporary economic and social organization. In addition, as part of the emerging "social question" on the condition and place of the working class in a "liberal" society, female wage labor and domestic responsibilities came under intense scrutiny.[25] In particular, working women's presence in the city's streets associated them with prostitutes.[26] The study of prostitution by the municipal health official A. J. B. Parent-Duchâtelet, published in 1836, articulated the immediate link between prostitution and women's presence in the streets and the workshops of the city. Yet he also argued that an even greater danger existed in the isolated and hidden, rather than public, expression of female sexuality. Thus, he led calls for strict enforcement of existing state regulation of prostitution and greater attention to be paid to single women living on their own who, in his view, were or would soon become prostitutes. Women who worked—in a shop or in their home—exceeded the bounds of respectability. For Parent-Duchâtelet, women engaged in wage earning in unregulated domestic environments posed the greatest threat to social order.[27] While scholars have rightly debated his figures and his assessments of the moral character of women, Parent-Duchâtelet presented contemporaries with a compelling description of their own fears of social change.

While Parent-Duchâtelet focused his anxiety on the clandestine, other commentators found greater danger in women's public activities, particularly the practice of wage labor. The political economist Honoré Frégier, among others, described the social danger he saw in the capital's mixed workshops. These brought men and women together in a promiscuity that destroyed working-class morality and the family. Frégier believed that women were the foundation of what he called the "dangerous classes," claiming that two-thirds of the female workers in the city were among the most corrupt workers in society due to "their base inclination, their immorality and their excesses." He argued that disorder began from the moment a child entered any shop employing children of the opposite sex. He also found that groups of women working together created an unhealthy atmosphere, one that corrupted the innocence of young female apprentices. Others joined Frégier in calling for home apprenticeship, where the mistress would engage in maternal instruction in the sanctity of the domestic sphere. For this group, laissez-faire (albeit supported by state regulation), representative not revolutionary government, and a Rousseauean view of motherhood would answer the social questions raised by industrialization. These reformers, along with the political economists who influenced them, did not call for women's exclusion from the workforce; on the contrary, they understood the importance of female labor to the French economy and only wished to regulate it, not only through legislation but also by reimagining the woman worker.[28]

Working-class men and socialist reformers, in contrast, described working women as leading lives of virtue and chastity. The demoralization of women workers, in this view, came not from an unruly, almost primitive working class but rather from an exploitative economic system created by a grasping bourgeoisie. Working women represented working men's claim of respectability; workers were not degraded children in need of supervision but adult males with a right to an elevated position in the social order. Changing relations of production eroded efforts toward this goal. Fearing women's economic competition, working-class men joined middle-class reformers in relegating working women to the role of wife and mother within the home under the authority of husband and father. In this role the working woman would resemble her bourgeois sister, whose own image was that of angel of the home. These contradictory images—the sexually vulnerable female worker and the chaste working-class wife and mother—echoed those presented by bourgeois men and reflected tensions in the images that made them suitable for use by all but the subject herself: the working woman.[29]

A major source in shaping the struggle over women's work came from women's own political activism, as recorded in police records and the *Gazette des tribunaux*. The *Gazette* was the paper of record for the royal courts, commercial as well as criminal, covering the topics in family law as well as concerning political insurrection. The *Gazette* daily ran a column called *Chroniques* that presented in short paragraph form features from the streets and courts. These very often depicted the working-class as naive, vicious, and always quaint in speech and appearance. For the bourgeois reader, these chronicles confirmed class assumptions, including those which held women's wage labor to be a source of trouble for the working-class family and for social order. One article from 1838 did acknowledge the connection between female wage labor and survival, yet the account of an elderly woman left without a family to support her represented such labor as only a desperate last measure. The impoverished chair mender la mère Lecaillé, on trial for theft, defended herself, according to the *Gazette's* report, by her lack of employment. She stated, "I work to eat."[30] The *Gazette* presented her desperation as the debasement of a woman struggling to survive outside of the domestic sphere.[31]

Early in the July Monarchy, the *Gazette,* together with the police, described the participation of women in labor protests as very dangerous because such activities were not part of, and indeed were outside of, the female sphere. In September 1831, women from the female-dominated shawl cutting trade launched a protest in Montmartre over the introduction into a neighborhood workshop of cutting machines that threatened to eliminate female work. Gathering outside of the shop on the rue de Cadran, a group of two hundred women threatened to destroy this menace to their trade. The shawl cutters were soon joined by workers from other shops and angry residents of the community, who protested the consequences of the current economic crisis: unemployment and high bread prices. The protests continued over six days and resulted in dozens of arrests, including that of nine shawl cutters.[32] Over the course of the week, the police reports shifted in how they presented the protest. After the second day, the prefect of police dropped any mention of the shawl cutters or any other female participants. An article in the *Gazette* did the same, and then on 8 September the paper related a particularly interesting event: "One noticed among the group a woman whose gestures were no less animated than [her] speech; as it was recognized that the dress, shawl and hat of this person feebly hid a man and not a woman, that order was given to arrest him."[33] In its coverage of the trial of the nine women shawl cutters arrested for insurrection, dubbed a "revolt in skirts," the *Gazette* literally constructed gender. It described the women as "young and pretty," while showing them to be shy and incoherent in the public setting of the court, and in doing so dismissed the possibility, and perhaps the threat, of working women's activism: "None of [the women charged] presented to us those male and marked traits, that strong voice of a hussy, finally, that collection of gestures, organs, features and movement that seem to us must be the defining sort of the rebellious woman."[34] These accounts erased women's voices even as they rewrote women's activities in the discourse of contemporary laboring womanhood. They reflected further the changing conception of the female person in the public sphere.

WORKING WOMEN SPEAK AND ACT

In contrast to their representation by authorities, reformers, and working-class men, working women clearly articulated their own understandings of the inter-sections between their paid and domestic labors, and made claim to the right to do both. The actions of the shawl cutters suggest that working women moved to defend work that combined wage and domestic labor, even as these actions were dismissed as unsuited to their sex. In a clear statement of these values, female fur cutters in the hat trade petitioned the revolutionary government in 1848 to address the decline in wages and increase in unemployment that threatened thousands of "hard-working mothers of families." Employed in workshops that were beginning to replace their labor with that of cutting machines, these women demanded protection of the trade which "gave them the means to live, to nourish their children and to provide trades [*états*] for their daughters."[35] The fur cutters did not separate work, home, and family into distinct spheres; such distinctions had no meaning for them. Throughout the first half of the nineteenth century, women in the manufacturing trades participated in and instigated actions to defend their right to earn a wage and care for their families. During the Revolu-tion of 1848, working women also made political demands as female citizens (*citoyennes*) who had a stake in the social republic.[36]

Yet the significance of the discourse of separate spheres also appears to have been clear to working women of the period. Anne Vieilhomme was a homeworker in the hat trade. She was arrested in the wake of the April 1834 insurrection that spread from Lyon to Paris and ended in the massacre of the rue Transnonain. When questioned by the police, Vieilhomme maintained her noninvolvement in the revolt with testimony of her domestic virtues; except in the conduct of her work when either she, her husband, or both transported com-missions and picked up materials throughout the city, she was occupied with the care of her family. Her neighbors supported her with a letter to the authorities that stated Vieilhomme had never left home during the insurrection, which in fact contradicted her testimony that she only went out that day to fetch her son home to safety. Later, individual testimony elaborated the story. Jacques Rousseau related that the entire neighborhood was shocked at Vieilhomme's arrest because she is known to be hard-working, concerned only with her home and her son. "She hardly goes out except to transport her work." Although her innocence is far from clear, with the help of her neighbors' testimony Anne Vieilhomme located herself within the private sphere and was freed.[37]

While women workers understood the importance of the home as the prescribed female social space, they simultaneously asserted their right to move outside of it when their work required that they be in the streets. Augustine Jazet was a piercer in the boot making trade; she prepared soles and uppers for joining by piercing them with holes. Working in her home made Jazet part of the growing sweated trades created by the increasing division of labor that fragmented handicraft production. Yet Jazet's work activities challenged the notion of the social isolation of sweated labor, that it was confined to the private sphere of the home. In order to make ends meet, Jazet worked for two different concerns, one of which was near her home in the Saint-Martin des Champs quarter, at the eastern edge of the city. She also carried the boot pieces that she pierced in her home back and forth to a shop in the center of Paris. Jazet asserted that this familiarity with the city streets had served her well when she joined the outbreak of revolution in February 1848, making shot, loading weapons, and even firing one from a position on the barricades. She made this assertion while under arrest for similar activities during the June Days (23–26 June 1848), charges she denied with a sly reference to her republican credentials established in February.[38]

During the Revolution of 1848, women workers joined the fight to overthrow the monarchy, demanded and won inclusion in the national workshop system through the *ateliers des femmes* (women's workshops), and joined the defense of the social republic in the battle of June. Women's demands for employment, such as those made by Jeanne Goursault, contributed to the pressure that forced the government to open the national workshops to women, as they had to men. Thousands of women, not all of them seamstresses by training, demanded places in the workshops to sew shirts for the National Guard, even though they would be paid less than the going piece rate for such work. Some women requested that they be allowed to take the work home rather than be required to report to, and remain in, the workshops each day. Their reasons reflected the domestic obligations that many working-class women paired with that of wage earning. The *femme* Guérard explained that she preferred "work in my home if that is possible, given that my daughter is still too young to be able to take part in workshops of that sort." Another woman wrote for several of her neighbors "who wish to obtain work in their homes, one of them is close to giving birth, the other is quite old and always ill." She also requested homework for "a poor young woman who supports her brother and aged mother by her labor, which does not allow her to leave home and go to the workshops."[39] Participation in a public work program thus combined waged and domestic activities.

When women acted publicly in ways that did not conform to contemporary notions of the female role as a fundamentally domestic one, the consequences could be more serious. When the atelier des femmes closed, many women sought other means to support themselves and their families. Street vending was an available option that women such as Hélène Bertonnier—who began to sell news-papers—employed. Marie Chauvin, a forty-five-year-old porcelain burnisher, lost her position in a workshop. After the ateliers had closed, she began to sell cocoa in the streets, where she was arrested in June. Only the testimony of her former employer of eight years secured her release. Both Bertonnier and Chauvin were arrested for participation in the June insurrection only on the basis of their presence in the streets.[40] Other female vendors were arrested for allegedly sell-ing poisoned brandy to the National Guard, although the military tribunal later dropped the charges against the ten women brought before it. Three of the ten women gave "vendor" as their occupation; the rest were unemployed manufac-turing workers trying to survive. All had registered with municipal authorities for permits to sell their wares, which, according to the shoemaker Henriette Collaen, they did "in order to be able to live." Collaen stated that her brandy was safe because she "drank it in front of those who arrested me."[41] The others testified that they, too, safely drank the liquor; however, the Widow Hoss testified that she had been forced to drink it. She also claimed that she heard "that a man who sold drink had poisoned four or five guardsmen." Yet only women were arrested for this crime.[42] All of the women were later released after weeks of interrogation and long after the Guardsmen had "recovered." The combination of productive and consumer labor was a dangerous mix in the midst of a revolution.

CONCLUSION

These few examples suggest the complexity of the negotiations in which working women engaged as they wove together productive and consumer roles in the transitional economy of early and mid-nineteenth-century Paris. Whether as ven-dors or as part of the manufacturing economy, women's work took them outside of their homes. The capital's economy employed women throughout its urban workforce. The expansion of industrial capitalism in the first half of the nineteenth century enjoined many working-class women to continue, for wages, the labor in handicraft manufacturing begun by women in the eighteenth century. Even the supposed sanctuary offered by home (or domestic) production took women outside of the confines of the private sphere. The discourse of laissez-faire insisted that workers reject sloth and subject themselves to the demands of the market, even as those who advocated for and were the beneficiaries of the policies of political economy received state support. Women thus moved between manufacturing, street selling, and, in some cases, prostitution to meet these demands and, more importantly, their material needs and those of their families.

At the same time, women workers understood that their activities—wage labor and action in the streets—contravened the bourgeois discourse of true womanhood, and that the cost of contravention could be high. Women employed the language of domesticity as they sought to explain their presence in the streets. Anne Vieilhomme asserted that she only left her home to tend to her family's affairs; her neighbors supported her. Bertonnier and Chauvin defended their presence on the barricades of revolution by evoking the nurturing care of a mother. Those involved in street selling had a more difficult task. They could and did defend their presence in the streets as necessary in meeting the needs of their families, as did Augustine Jazet. Yet, as we have seen, selling goods in the street was very close to selling oneself in the domestic discourse of the era. All women's economic activity could be equated with prostitution and often was. Women's very presence in the street then became suspect, the possibility of which these women seemed quite aware. Again, the hysterical assumption of poisoning by female street vendors left the accused with little to defend themselves; they could only drink their wares, the source of their wage earning. Women employed in the Parisian manufacturing economy all worked to eat and so that their families could eat. And thus they engaged in both productive and consumer activities that blurred distinctions increasingly important to order in French society.

At the end of the long eighteenth century, then, women's manufacturing labor had come under the control of industrial capitalism and its attendant ideology of separate spheres. The transition from an artisan economy—with a limited but significant role for women—which had begun with the development of subcontracted labor before the 1789 Revolution, had reached the point where women's labor was considered a threat to society. Defeat in the 1848 Revolution consolidated the image of the woman worker that the economist Jules Simon would later present in the 1860s: downtrodden, exploited economically and sexually, a threat to the family. It was a concept deemed sordid, impious. The active producer-consumer disappeared beneath the passive duties of a housewife concerned with her home and her family. Certainly much had changed since the introduction of cottage industry in the early modern period, including new and renewed legal limitations on women's economic rights and greater cultural limitations on the exercise of those rights that remained. At the same time, working women continued to assert those rights and to act on behalf of their need to engage in both waged and unwaged labor for themselves and their families. The shift in perspective, employing the framework of the long eighteenth century, allows us to see these transitions more clearly and to make sense of what followed.

NOTES

1. Jules Simon, *L'Ouvrière,* 3rd ed. (Paris: Librarie Hachette et Cie, 1864), iv.

2. See, for example, Joan Wallach Scott, "'L'Ouvrière! Mot impie, sordide . . .': Women Workers in the Discourse of French Political Economy, 1840–1860," in *Gender and the Politics of History* (New York: Columbia Univ. Press, 1992).

3. See, for example, Judith G. Coffin's fine study of the Paris garment trades that moves from two chapters on women's work in the eighteenth century and the introduction of the sewing machine (1830–1870) to a lengthy study of women's work in the Third Republic. Judith G. Coffin, *The Politics of Women's Work: The Paris Garment Trades, 1750–1915* (Princeton: Princeton Univ. Press, 1996).

4. Joan Kelly-Gadol, "Did Women Have a Renaissance?" in *Becoming Visible: Women in European History,* 2nd ed., ed. Renate Bridenthal, Claudia Koontz, and Susan Mosher Stuard (Boston: Houghton Mifflin, 1987), 10.

5. Rachel Ginnis Fuchs, *Contested Paternity: Constructing Families in Modern France* (Baltimore: Johns Hopkins Univ. Press, 2008); Jo Burr Margadant, *Madame la Professeur: Women Educators in the Third Republic* (Princeton: Princeton Univ. Press, 1990); Whitney Walton, *Eve's Proud Descendants: Four Women Writers and Republican Politics in Nineteenth-Century France* (Stanford: Stanford Univ. Press, 2000); Joan Landes, *Visualizing the Nation: Gender, Representation, and Revolution in Eighteenth-Century France* (Ithaca: Cornell Univ. Press, 2001); Suzanne Desan, *The Family on Trial in Revolutionary France* (Berkeley: Univ. of California Press, 2004).

6. A good summary of the varying perspectives of Downs and Scott appears in Laura Lee Downs, *Writing Gender History* (London: Hodder Arnold, 2004). Kathleen Canning, *Languages of Labor and Gender: Female Factory Work in Germany, 1850–1914* (Ithaca: Cornell Univ. Press, 1996); Ava Baron, ed., *Work Engendered: Toward a New History of American Labor* (Ithaca: Cornell Univ. Press, 1991); Laura Frader and Sonya Rose, eds., *Gender and Class in Modern Europe* (Ithaca: Cornell Univ. Press, 1996).

7. Jan de Vries, "The Industrial Revolution and the Industrious Revolution," *Journal of Economic History* 54, no. 2 (1994): 249–270; Jeff Horn, *The Path Not Taken: French Industrialization in the Age*

of Revolution, 1750–1830 (Cambridge, Mass.: MIT Press, 2006).

8. Daryl M. Hafter, *Women at Work in Preindustrial France* (University Park: Pennsylvania State Univ. Press, 2007). Clare Haru Crowston had similar findings in her study of Parisian seamstresses, *Fabricating Women: The Seamstresses of Old Regime France, 1675–1791* (Durham: Duke Univ. Press, 2001).

9. Victoria De Grazia and Ellen Furlough, eds., *The Sex of Things: Gender and Consumption in Historical Perspective* (Berkeley: Univ. of California Press, 1997); Daniel Roche, *Histoire des choses banales* (Paris: Librarie Arthème Fayard, 1996).

10. Bankruptcy records are a rich source for economic history in this period, as demonstrated by Charles Crouch, whose studies focus on what he identifies as the lower middle class. Charles P. Crouch, "The Petit Bourgeois of Paris During the Bourbon Restoration, 1814–1830: A Prosopographical Inquiry into the Political and Economic Integration of the Parisian Lower Middle Class" (Ph.D. diss., University of Illinois, 1991), and Charles P. Crouch, "'Femmes separées, veuves, femmes célibataires, épouses': Gender, Civil State and Social Strata in Paris, 1830–1848," *Consortium on Revolutionary Europe, 1750–1850: Selected Papers* (Tallahassee: Institute on Napoleon and the French Revolution, Florida State University, 1998), 608–619.

11. Angela Groppi, "Le travail des femmes à Paris à l'époque de la Révolution française," *Bulletin d'histoire économique et sociale de la Révolution française* (1979): 27–46; Dominique Godineau, *Citoyennes tricoteuses: Les femmes du peuple à Paris pendant la Révolution française* (Paris: Alinea, 1988). For the garment trades, see Crowston, *Fabricating Women*.

12. Of course, such statistical sources were criticized for bias from the date of their publication. For the Paris Chambre of Commerce report of 1851, see Armand Audiganne, *Les populations ouvrières et les industries de la France*, 2 vols. (1854; reprint, New York: Burt Franklin, 1970), 1:305–306; Hilda Rigaudias-Weiss, *Les enquêtes ouvrières en France entre 1830 et 1848* (Paris: Presses universitaires de France, 1966), 210–211; Joan W. Scott, "Statistical Representations of Work: The Politics of the Chamber of Commerce's *Statistique de l'industrie à Paris, 1847–1848*," in *Work in France*, ed. Steven L. Kaplan and Cynthia J. Koepp (Ithaca: Cornell Univ. Press, 1986), 335–363.

13. See the figures in the Chamber of Commerce study. For an examination of the Paris economy in the post-1848 period, see Claire Lemercier, "Looking for 'Industrial Confraternity': Small-Scale Industries and Institutions in Nineteenth-Century Paris," *Enterprise and Society* 10, no. 2 (2009): 304–334.

14. Joshua Cole, *The Power of Large Numbers: Population, Politics, and Gender in Nineteenth-Century France* (Ithaca: Cornell Univ. Press, 2000), 120.

15. [François Etienne] Mollot, *Le contrat de louage d'ouvrage et de l'industrie expliqué aux ouvriers*, 2nd ed. (Paris: Louis Colas, 1847).

16. "Les couturières, sont-elles sujettes à la patente?" *La gazette des tribunaux*, no. 2801 (19 August 1834).

17. *Notice sur la législation relative aux livrets d'ouvriers: Session des Conseils général de l'agriculture, des manufactures et du commerce, 1841–42* (Paris: Imprimerie royale, 1842); "Projet de loi sur le livret," *L'Atelier* 6 (March 1845); Mollot, *Le contrat*, 29–30.

18. The first and still definitive study of this phenomenon is Bonnie G. Smith, *Ladies of the Leisure Class: The Bourgeoises of Northern France in the Nineteenth Century* (Princeton: Princeton Univ. Press, 1981).

19. The subject of pawning goods in nineteenth-century cities deserves more attention. See

Cheryle Lynne Danieri, "Credit Where Credit Is Due: The Mont-de-Piété of Paris, 1777–1851" (Ph.D. diss., University of California–Irvine, 1987); Yannick Marec, "Au carrefour de l'economique et du sociale: Le Mont-de-Piété de Rouen, 1778–1923," *Le Mouvement Social* 116 (1981): 67–94.

20. Arlette Farge, *La vie fragile: Violence, pouvoirs et solidarités à Paris au XVIIIᵉ siècle* (Paris: Hachette, 1986); Helen Harden Chenut, *The Fabric of Gender: Working-Class Culture in Third Republic France* (University Park: Pennsylvania State Univ. Press, 2005).

21. Anonymous, *De la condition des ouvriers de Paris de 1789 jusqu'en 1841, avec quelques idées sur la possibilité de l'améliorer* (Paris: J-B Gros, 1841), 135.

22. Archives Nationales (hereafter AN), CC 792, Déposition de la femme Leplatre, Paris, 14 September 1841.

23. Archives de la Seine (hereafter AS), VD6 619, n. 7, Jeanne Pierre Goursault au M. le Maire, n.d. [1848].

24. Olwen Hufton, *The Poor of Eighteenth-Century France, 1750–1789* (Oxford: Clarendon Press, 1974); Olwen Hufton, "Women and the Family Economy in Eighteenth-Century France," *French Historical Studies* 9, no. 1 (spring 1975): 1–22.

25. For a discussion of the changing constructions of gender and the social question in this period, see Victoria E. Thompson, *The Virtuous Marketplace: Women and Men, Money and Politics in Paris, 1830–1870* (Baltimore: Johns Hopkins Univ. Press, 2000). See also Cole, *The Power of Large Numbers*; Coffin, *The Politics of Women's Work*; and Scott, "'L'Ouvrière! Mot impie. . . .'"

26. More work needs to be done on prostitution in this period, following the path-breaking studies of Alain Corbin and Jill Harsin, although Victoria Thompson's work has expanded the discussion in the theoretical framework of gender. Alain Corbin, *Les filles de noces: Misère sexuelle et la prostitution (19ᵉ et 20ᵉ siècles)* (Paris: Aubier Montaigne, 1978); Jill Harsin, *Policing Prostitution in Nineteenth-Century Paris* (Princeton: Princeton Univ. Press, 1985); Thompson, *The Virtuous Marketplace*.

27. A.J.B. Parent-Duchâtelet, *De la prostitution dans la ville de Paris*, 2 vols. (Paris: J. B. Ballière, 1836).

28. Honoré Frégier, *Des classes dangereuses de la société dans les grandes villes et les moyens de les rendre meilleures* (Paris: J. B. Ballière), 1:154–159. See also Mollot, *Le contrat de louage d'ouvrage*, and Cèsar Fichet, *Mémoire sur l'apprentissage et sur l'éducation industriel* (Paris: Imprimerie Galban, 1847).

29. For a more detailed discussion of these various positions on women's labor in the July Monarchy, see Judith A. DeGroat, "Virtue, Vice, and Revolution: Representations of Parisian Needlewomen in the Mid-Nineteenth Century," in *Famine and Fashion: Needlewomen in the Nineteenth Century*, ed. Elizabeth Harris (Aldershot, Eng.: Ashgate, 2005), 201–214.

30. *Gazette des tribunaux*, no. 3895 (5 and 6 March 1838).

31. Victoria Thompson's work on the grisette underscores the common characterization of female wage labor being the work only of women who were not married. Thompson, *The Virtuous Marketplace*, 52–85.

32. AN F/7 3885; *Bulletin de Paris*, 5–10 (September 1831).

33. *Gazette des tribunaux*, no. 184 (8 September 1831).

34. Ibid., no. 1923 (12 October 1831).

35. AN F/12 4898. Les coupeuses de poil de lapin au gouvernement provisoire, 13 March 1848.

36. The following discussion draws on Judith A. DeGroat, "Working-Class Women and Republicanism in the French Revolution of 1848," *History of European Ideas* 38, no. 3 (September 2012): 399–407.

.

37. AN CC 602, no. 114. Interrogatoire de la femme Vieilhomme, Paris, 21 April 1834; Notes des voisins, Paris, 23–24 April 1834.

38. France, Service historique de l'armée de terre, Series Justice militaire (hereafter JM), 12261, Procès verbal, Augustine Jazet, femme LeBlanc, 42, piqueuse de bottines, Porte Saint Martin, 24 July 1848.

39. AS V.D6 619, no. 7; Femme Guérad au M. le maire, Paris, n.d. [1848]; AS V.D6 22, no. 2, Paris, n.d. [1848].

40. JM 12140, Interrogatoire de Marie Louise Chauvin, Femme de Chauvin, menusier, Paris, 5 July 1848; Ricard, Peintre-doreur sur porcelain, Paris, 4 July 1848.

41. JM 2042, Interrogatoire de Henriette Collaen, cordonnier, Paris, 28 June 1848.

42. JM 7745, Interrogatoire de Veuve Hoss, née Caroline Kauffman, cantiniére, Paris, 6 July 1848. For another account of a woman selling brandy who was forced to drink it, see *La République,* nos. 122–126 (1 July 1848).

AFTERWORD

Bonnie G. Smith

THE history of women's work lives offers many a surprise for students, teachers, and the general public, as we have seen in this volume. The average person often believes that women only entered the workforce in the West since the second wave of the women's movement began late in the 1970s; in the rest of the world, only "globalization" began women's "oppression" on the assembly lines run by multinational corporations. Before that, the common wisdom goes, they led "traditional" lives caring for children and serving as responsible wives. Even the women's movement itself was seen as composed mostly of nonworking women, erasing the incredible contributions to the drive for equality and opportunity that characterized the activism of women working in the fields, artisanal workshops, factories, places of commerce, or at home. That noble women supervised any number of occupations on their lands and in family enterprises or that small children had a series of regular and exigent tasks, such as tending geese, fetching water, and pulling carts in coal mines, often remains unknown. The lives of girls of most classes prepared them for assiduous labor, while their brothers often did much less work. Despite being a workly society, we often face ignorance when it comes to understanding women's hard-working past.

THE "PAST" OF WOMEN AND WORK

Some four decades ago, when setting out on my first large research assignment—a doctoral dissertation on wealthy women from manufacturing families in northern France—there was not the slightest thought that they might have had a vibrant work life. The idea in those Marxist and reformist days was that women of the "leisure class" were idle and even parasitic. They were the worst example of bourgeois or middle-class leeches on workers and peasants, who supported their useless way of life. Misogyny came into play in this evaluation. Whereas the workers' housing, parks, and other amenities provided by factory owners were analyzed in rich detail and often judged to be beneficial, similar creations by their wives were dismissed as self-interested and useless make-work. Their activities were often seen as hypocritical. When I wrote an article on middle-class women's charitable efforts, a reviewer disbelieved the evidence, stating bluntly: "What wealthy woman ever cared a whit for working women." Scholarship then, as always, reflected the anti-women values of the time.

Archives, family papers, genealogies, and other sources tell a different story for French women and, one knows from wide-ranging and careful research, for all women. French women of the so-called leisure class—those of the Nord, for example—who were reputedly idling their lives away were in fact active participants in building and directing what would become the large family textile enterprises in the northern region that I studied. In the eighteenth century, for example, a woman named Madame Barrois kept all business accounts and dealt with some 150 workers. Ensuring that they had the materials they needed and maintaining high productivity were just two of her many tasks. In the days when firms often put wool and flax out into the countryside to be spun, Madame Barrois oversaw most of the operations while her husband traveled to make sales of the spun thread.

Aristocratic women are increasingly understood to have shouldered responsibilities of real consequence for their families. The scientist and philosophe Emilie du Châtelet (1706–1749), whose husband served in the French army and whose official duties kept him from home, traveled great distances to pursue legal matters concerning family estates. Even though aristocratic families had majordomos, there were still tasks that could best be handled by the heads of families themselves—whether husband or wife. Du Châtelet is an interesting case because she (like other noble women) did intellectual work, receiving learned visitors and sparking intellectual debate and conversation, while she fulfilled the legal and financial tasks of the family. She herself wrote books and was the principal French translator of Newton. Such unpaid labor was labor nonetheless, as students and scholars today know all too well.

Work life is almost always shaped and even determined by gender. Such is the finding of labor historians, and to date it seems to apply to all parts of the globe and all historic epochs. Some clichés about the gendered division of labor are falling, however, in the face of new research and archeological discoveries. For example, in prehistory it is now accepted that women were not just the gathers and men exclusively the hunters, but that both men and women hunted. A second cliché is that work was always organized in a "family economy," and that this work revolved around the occupation of the male head of the family.

The problem was in the absolute nature of these assumptions. To be sure, many families did structure their work together, and allocate tasks according to gender. However, in a sign of the maturity of the field, women's history now validates the presence of exceptions to the traditional patterns. Thus, while research has brought to our attention the prosperous eighteenth-century Barrois family, and has described the families of more modest artisans, both with gendered divisions of labor, that is not the whole story. As this volume shows, many women developed skills unlike those of their relations, and professions in which they became expert. Even if they contributed monetary support to their families, they found themselves in a category somewhat separate from those in domestic production.

Moreover, while the family economy system assumed that the profession of the male head dominated work, and downplayed the enterprise of the female members, a new perspective discovered the crucial and skilled contribution of the women. Women's labor was as essential as that of men in the family. Artisans such as the glazier Jacques Ménétra took wives from artisanal families, drawing as partners those with crucially needed experience in keeping books and tending the shop. It was also the case that women in artisanal families were generally better educated than their male counterparts, who served apprenticeships that gave them craft skills, not literate ones. In contrast, women in artisanal families were more instructed in reading, writing, and arithmetic—all of these necessary for managing a firm, no matter how small. These skills also made them adept at deploying family funds. In the Motte textile family, it was Madame Motte who launched one of the first major cotton factories in the French department of the Nord by financing and supervising it. Yet, as the essays in this book show, such a family economy, while dominant, was not the only type of arrangement. There was variety in women's roles as breadwinners, and past society noted with accuracy women's independent work. Indeed, great care was taken to describe women's work and calculate women's property beyond the family economy by tax collectors and government assessors. The diversity of women's effort and skill emerges with greater precision in the wide-ranging scholarship on work life in these essays.

NEW DIRECTIONS

The depth and variety of women's work shown in recent scholarship of the early modern and even into the modern period constitute a new paradigm to understand the richness of women's identities in the past. This new perspective adds accuracy to our understanding of history itself. It may take many years, however, before the studies at hand fully overturn such truisms as that of the overwhelmingly male family economy, the exclusive male dominion of artisanal work and other labor, and the idleness of aristocratic women. The diversity of women's labor, the intricacies of their work with men, and the negotiations with authorities on behalf of property and privilege are now on the path to being fully documented. These essays work to integrate women's experiences as economic actors into wider considerations of legal, family, labor, and gender history. In the process, they model a contemporary approach to women's history in which women are de-isolated, in which attention to their role in the family is concomitant with the ways in which other frameworks similarly contributed to their work lives. We should take this integration further (and in many cases we already are), by considering women's labor history in even wider contexts. This requires continuing the process of nuancing and extending our definition of work and integrating women's experiences into the newly emerging fields in French history.

Global Work in Early Modern French History

French families extended their operations abroad during this active time in global trade. Bordeaux merchants went to the west coast of Africa as part of their enterprises, partnering with local women from merchant families. Like women in France, these merchants were part of new Afro-European units and they advanced the family fortunes, even when the family was based in Europe. Investigations should bring these women onto the same historical canvas as women working in the metropole. It was on the basis of their connections with influential local women that men such as the Bordelais could conduct businesses profitably. Women slaves became pivotal to the agricultural work in the colonies, often tending gardens that were virtual horticultural wonderlands of great interest to plant hunters and botanists alike. Their field and domestic labor fed the hunger for tobacco, sugar, coffee, cocoa, and other raw materials then exploding in France. These exotic goods spawned new jobs for women in the metropole, such as painting snuff boxes, servicing cafés, and creating desserts. Free women in non-European territories were often the main teachers of languages and foreign cultural ways to soldiers, adventurers, and businessmen in Asia, Africa, and the Americas. They continued to serve as translators, guides, and general housekeepers to French men based abroad. Some returned with their partners to Europe. In the seventeenth century, Marie de l'Incarnation in French North

America compiled dictionaries of Native American words and did other intellectual work on the global stage.[1]

The global perspective generates a wealth of new insights for those studying French women's work lives. One hopes that all of these findings will be more solidly integrated into what we know about French women's work in the metropole. For example, in the seventeenth and eighteenth centuries new products from regions beyond Europe were changing the patterns of everyday life. Small merchants in the French countryside and the cities alike sold sugar, tea, and other commodities produced outside of continental France in the seventeenth and eighteenth centuries. Their business capacities were being shaped by the explosion in global commerce, as were their intellectual skills. What were women's contributions to the expansion of marketing and consumer knowledge? Innovations coming from Europe's insertion into the global web were part of women's work experience. How such global innovations and changes in taste transpired and women's roles in producing them should be on our agenda.

One late seventeenth-century shopkeeper in the French countryside had in her stocks ginger, cloves, and tea. It is not too much to wonder how the practices of this shopkeeper changed with the importation of such new products, especially as the speed of importation and the complexity of the types of goods imported advanced. What skills and changing habits of mind existed to make the transition? Adaptability—not rigid adherence to tradition—must have been a skill of urban market women dealing with a widening variety of foodstuffs, imported fabrics, and other goods across the entire century. Historians have done little to chart the assimilation of such products into the mentality of these small merchants. Cooks and other household workers would similarly have had to adapt to using commodities from around the world. The care of lacquer ware, cottons, and novel types of wood demanded experimentation and adaption.

The early eighteenth-century servant whose clothing included a cotton dress made from fashionable imported fabric—whether the dress was inherited from her mistress, assigned her to wear while at work, or created from her own funds—possibly found her workaday world in flux. Women heads of household and ordinary cooks came to deal with new products in the conduct of their tasks, and their agendas multiplied as well. We may speculate on how they integrated such products as sugar into the well-worn patterns of cooking in a subsistence economy. Cotton clothing, as another example, could be and was laundered more frequently. Standards for cleanliness changed. Work life on the Continent came under pressure from the greater sensitivity to smells brought about not only by new products, but also by reports from the colonies concerning the superior cleanliness of South Asians and Native Americans. One wonders about the mind set of workers and their cultural landscape as they pondered and used a wider range of goods, not only at work but in their everyday lives. They invented new uses and dealt with different demands on their skilled labor.

Women also migrated in the early modern period, working as prostitutes, missionaries, teachers, shopkeepers, and artisans. Some of this migration came because of oppression, such as that of Huguenot families who had to give up their ties to France to work not only in England and the Netherlands, but in such distant places as North America or South Africa. Other families and individuals migrated to work in the New World colonies, handling furs and then determining their use, especially as the "Little Ice Age" made furs such an important consumer item.

Spiritual and Intellectual Work

It is surprising that although men's intellectual lives receive so much attention, women's receive comparatively little in the context of their study and achievement by historians. Women serving in nunneries helped fortify the doctrinal beliefs of the French monarchy and its religious establishment. Young adolescent girls from middle- or upper-class families attended convents or boarded there to learn a range of feminine skills and behaviors. Nuns also instilled basic religious principles, a process criticized by Jean-Jacques Rousseau, who believed that learning complex doctrine, such as that prescribing the Eucharist, was far beyond the comprehension of the young and only made them hostile to honest religious feelings. In nunneries, women did every kind of work, depending on the social status they had before leaving the secular life. From the labors of the meanest domestic to the loftier work of music and study, nuns were also major providers of charity and medical assistance. The category of spiritual labor still needs exploring, however, as spirituality and work can seem to contradict one another in the evolution of Western thinking. We additionally wonder how spiritual labor changed during the intellectual turbulence of the eighteenth century. Although there are many studies of women writers and individual artists, much remains to be done in considering writing and intellectual thought as part of women's work lives. We are fortunate in having as models the study by Natalie Zemon Davis on Marie de l'Incarnation and the German-born Maria Sybilla Marian, and Cynthia M. Truant's essay on artists' wide-ranging activities.

Technology

Women's history has generally helped expand understandings of technology and women's relationships to it, as Daryl M. Hafter's essay in this volume shows. An old-fashioned definition equated technology only with machines. In this understanding machines are seen as complicated—too complex for women's capabilities. However, even that standard definition, based on the idea of a heroic inventor, does not preclude such women as the wife of Cyrus McCormack, Nettie Fowler McCormack, said to be the actual inventor of the reaper, because women often could not take out patents in their own names or because they stayed home inventing while their husbands took care of the legal work. Or perhaps because it was not "seemly" for women to be inventors, men have gotten credit with inventing such machines as the reaper. Beyond that, invention in some domestic fields—let us say of food—has not generally counted as a technology: the inventions of a wide variety of profit-making cheeses, for example, are usually omitted from the history books.

Over the past decades, our understanding of technology has developed, becoming more nuanced and complex. For instance, it has come to include the idea of practices, such as laundering, spinning, weaving, and other housekeeping activities. The use of new sewing techniques on recently popularized cloth such as cotton, or the production of new crops such as maize and tomatoes, are included in technology. As Nina Gelbart shows in *The King's Midwife,* nursing or healing is seen as a technology, too; cloth models of the female reproductive system and the growth of the fetus used to teach country women the practices and knowledge about childbirth constitute a technology. Women were pivotal to the development of the knowledge-based society that emerged with the expansion of Europe in other ways. They participated in the running of schools, and they taught some of the crucial subjects in those schools, such as handwriting or languages, as James B. Collins showed in the case of Breton towns in his essay in this volume. Communication became increasingly important, leading educated women to serve as scribes for the illiterate, documenters of new plant imports through their drawings, and recorders of scientific discoveries. They ran bookstores, cafés, inns, and printing establishments that also served the commercial and industrious revolutions.

Those who have expanded definitions of technology are not only historians of women but also historians of non-Western societies who focus on techniques and special knowledge beyond the workings of steam- and water-powered machines.

Women painters served as another type of technician. Italian painter Rosalba Carriera brought her use of pastels and her techniques for miniature painting to Paris in 1721, where they were enthusiastically adopted by rococo artists. Shut out from the training in large-scale nude and history paintings, women came to excel at the techniques of portraiture. Elisabeth Vigée-LeBrun and several other notable women painters saw the body as a site of technology to be exploited by the painter. Their success was notable at a time when revolutionary ideologies of individualism and the transparent visage came to characterize the age. Though less celebrated, the everyday artists described by Cynthia Truant were as innovative in their knowledge of the new technologies of decoration and creation. Painting on the new "china" or decorating the imitation oriental "fans" required that women know or participate in inventing techniques for executing these imitations in ways that would satisfy demanding consumers, for whom authentic foreign goods were still the hallmark of quality.

Representations of Women and Work

The field of critical history, in part emerging from the post-modern definition of gender, often avoids investigating women's actual jobs and their varied position in the workforce. Instead, it probes the work of the binary male-female and also looks for the ascription of gendered meaning to words and processes. It then interrogates normative narratives from the past by investigating the play of meaning and the effects of verbal and other representational acts. For example, Joan Scott's article from the 1980s "'L'Ouvrière! Mot impie, sordide . . .'" ("Working woman! Impious, sordid word . . .") describes the ways in which the ignominy attached to the mere term "woman worker" produced not only the stereotype of the gendered, ill-paid, and degraded woman worker, but resulted in her virtual disappearance from statistical and other compilations that might have normalized and even validated the woman worker's activities. As Daryl Hafter remarks in her investigation of large industrial establishments, representations of gender were used to produce categories of skill and thus pay. Although work itself may have been neutral in many regards, the gendering of work by assuming that women's work was unskilled because women were naturally unskilled and men's work was skilled because men were inherently skilled was at once untrue and harmful, facilitating discrimination in the workforce. As Judith A. DeGroat shows in her essay, the hierarchical nature of gendered representations shaped conditions for laboring women and men.

Representations of the working woman's body were also powerful expressions in the gendering of labor. Historians ponder the meanings of depictions of servant women in the seventeenth and eighteenth centuries, for example, with their frank and open gazes, in comparison to depictions of working women, such as laundresses, in the nineteenth century. The latter are worn and flagging, hair straggling and faces deformed by toil. Depictions of market women in the French Revolution similarly portray dishonor and bloodthirstiness, marrying working women to their politics as negative signs. Nina Kushner and Daryl Hafter, in their introduction, point to depictions of the servant woman sitting with her broom. We have other images of women serving food, great numbers of them painting artistic objects, and many pictures of them reading and serving as scribes during this period. These open new vistas on the interpretation of women's work.

Finally, the sum of scholarship in this book points to women's role in what is now being called the "industrious revolution"—that is, the increasingly active work lives of people in many parts of the world that preceded the better-known Industrial Revolution of the late eighteenth century. In the industrious revolution, productive life accelerated in intensity and became more diverse. People worked longer and more strenuous hours to bring income to their families. Some of this income went to boosting the family's ability to consume, which signaled the transformation of economies from bare subsistence to a more abundant social order. In order to procure the new commodities the globe had to offer Europeans or the more abundant mixed textiles Europeans themselves were inventing, many may have seen the need for harder work and greater innovation.

Women's contribution to this industriousness was immense. As is clear from this volume, women "drove the revolution in consumption," in the words of James Collins. Some thirty years ago, one standard interpretation of work life in the eighteenth century was that women were being pushed out of production. This may have been so in some cases, but the studies at hand suggest that for every opportunity that might have closed down for women, new ones appeared and allowed them to participate in the productive revolution in French society that occurred from the end of the seventeenth century. We know that across Europe women contributed to the diversity of products by creating the recipes that used colonial products such as sugar, by fashioning the styles for garments made from foreign fabrics, and by designing new trifles for bodily adornment. Even the traditional farm woman could contribute to industriousness as she grew more vegetables (and a greater variety of them) to sell to the growing number of town and city dwellers who craved them.

Emotions, Values, and Working Lives

The history of emotions and values in the context of work begins to unfold in these essays. Nina Kushner claims that "kept women, like aristocrats, were obsessed with things"; for working women this obsession may have indicated the need for financial security. Objects could also translate back into funds in tough times. Veena Oldenburg's study of courtesans in Lucknow shows a group similarly engaged in ensuring material security. They amassed wealth beyond that of many working women, and they invested it in buildings and other tangible assets. These courtesans had a good sense of humor about their exploits and achievements, so secure did they seem. We surmise other emotions and values from the early modern French working women at hand: a commitment to social roles and family survival, for example, and to their rights as working women. More interestingly, the implications of the industrious revolution suggest an emotional flexibility that allowed women to take advantage of new opportunities and exigencies in the new market conditions. They entered novel enterprises, sold an array of products to varieties of customers, and increasingly stood guard over family finances—meager or substantial. Ambition continued to be a distinct value among artisanal wives, who skirted the restrictions on their activities to promote family businesses, kept careful account of the cash, and pursued those who cheated or robbed them. As Jacob D. Melish shows, working women could also be stubborn, tyrannical, usurious, argumentative, and enraged—all of these emotions and values about which we would like to know more, perhaps in more explicit studies of working women's emotions. Understanding the emotional culture and emotional roles in families adds depth and advances the "old" social history of working women.

The study of the lives, roles, and cultures of working women in early modern France has a major contribution to make to our understanding of the cultural, social, and economic history of the times. We see industriousness and innovation, allowing us better to comprehend the full range of activities that comprised the industrious revolution. Women workers contributed to early modern globalization with their spiritual, intellectual, commercial, and consumer activities. Through these activities they created the diversity so characteristic of this great unfolding of economic life. Their diversity spanned classes and status groups, and virtually no group of women was excluded from it. The material in this volume thus raises working women to new heights of visibility. Simultaneously, it provides us with material to critique the standard histories of such phenomena as the industrious revolution, as scholarship in need of revision. Finally, it silences the invocation of "woman" as only one unchanging type of person within a static gender system. If all of this constitutes a new paradigm of women and work, its contours still remain unclear. For the moment, we might take delight in the richness of these archive stories and the energy and inventiveness of the women these stories portray.

NOTE

1. See Natalie Zemon Davis, *Women on the Margins: Three Seventeenth-Century Lives* (Cambridge, Mass.: Harvard Univ. Press, 1997).

CONTRIBUTORS

RAFE BLAUFARB holds the Ben Weider Eminent Scholar Chair in the Department of History at Florida State University and is director of the Institute on Napoleon and the French Revolution. He received his Ph.D. from the University of Michigan. Professor Blaufarb has written many monographs, including *The Politics of Fiscal Privilege in Provence, 1530s–1830s* (Washington, D.C.: Catholic Univ. Press, 2012). Currently he is writing a book on the transformation of the idea of property during the French Revolution.

JAMES B. COLLINS is professor of history at Georgetown University. He received his Ph.D. from Columbia University. The author of many monographs and syntheses of French history, including *The State in Early Modern France,* 2nd ed. (Cambridge: Cambridge Univ. Press, 2009), Professor Collins is currently working on a book about Republicanism and the state in late medieval and early modern France.

JUDITH A. DEGROAT is associate professor of history at St. Lawrence University. She received her Ph.D. from the University of Rochester and is the author most recently of "Working-Class Women and Republicanism in the French Revolution of 1848," *History of European Ideas,* vol. 38 (September 2012). Currently, Professor DeGroat is completing a study of gender and socialism in the life of Pauline Roland (1805–1852).

DARYL M. HAFTER is professor emerita of history at Eastern Michigan University. She earned her doctorate at Yale University. Professor Hafter is author of *Women at Work in Preindustrial France* (University Park: Pennsylvania State Univ. Press, 2007) and numerous articles on women, technology, and work. Her current research focuses on the role of technology in the consumer products of eighteenth-century France, and women as merchants in eighteenth-century Normandy.

NINA KUSHNER is associate professor of history at Clark University. She received her Ph.D. from Columbia University and is the author of *Erotic Exchanges: The World of Elite Prostitution in Eighteenth-Century Paris* (Ithaca: Cornell Univ. Press, 2013). Her current work examines the ramifications of adultery and the formation of sexual culture in Old Regime France.

NANCY LOCKLIN is associate professor of history at Maryville College. She earned her Ph.D. in history from Emory University. She is the author, most recently, of ""'Til death parts us': Women's Domestic Partnerships in Eighteenth-Century Brittany," which was published in the winter 2011 issue of the *Journal of Women's History*. Her current projects involve the social and emotional ties expressed in notarized contracts and the interplay of such affective expressions with jurists and the law.

JANE MCLEOD is associate professor of history at Brock University. She received her Ph.D. from York University and is the author of *Licensing Loyalty: Printers, Patrons, and the State in Early Modern France* (University Park: Pennsylvania State Univ. Press, 2011). Her interest in state-media relations continues in her current project: "Printers Confront the French Revolution: Profits, Principles, and Perils."

JACOB D. MELISH is assistant professor of history at the University of Northern Colorado. He received his Ph.D. from the University of Michigan. Professor Melish is the author most recently of "Women and the Courts in the Control of Violence between Men: Evidence from a Parisian Neighborhood under Louis XIV," published in *French Historical Studies* in 2010. He is currently writing a book concerning gender relations and working women in early modern Paris.

JENNIFER L. PALMER is assistant professor of history at the University of Georgia. She received her Ph.D. from the University of Michigan. Most recently she has published articles in *Gender and History* and *French Historical Studies*. She also has contributed several chapters on race and family in the Atlantic world to edited volumes. Her current research focuses on how intimate relationships shaped French ideas about slavery, colonialism, and race in the eighteenth century.

BONNIE G. SMITH is Board of Governors Professor of History at Rutgers University. She received her Ph.D. from the University of Rochester. Professor Smith focuses on women's, European, and world history. She is the author of numerous books on women within the broad field of French and global history, most recently coauthoring *Crossroads and Cultures: A History of the World's People*. She is currently working on a history of empires and a book on women in world history.

CYNTHIA M. TRUANT is associate professor of history at the University of California at San Diego. She received her Ph.D. from the University of Chicago and is the author most recently of "Corporations et Métiers des Femmes," in the *Dictionnaire des femmes des Lumières* (Paris: Honoré Champion, 2013). Currently, Professor Truant is working on a book on women's paid labor, focusing on the Parisian guilds from 1650 to 1789.

INDEX